HOLMAN
New
Testament
Commentary

HOLMAN
New Testament Commentary

Mark

GENERAL EDITOR

Max Anders

AUTHOR

Rodney L. Cooper

HOLMAN
REFERENCE

Nashville, Tennessee

Holman New Testament Commentary
© 2000 Broadman & Holman Publishers
Nashville, Tennessee
All rights reserved

ISBN 0–8054–0202–0

Mark / Rod Cooper
     p.   cm. — (Holman New Testament commentary)
Includes bibliographical references.
ISBN 0–8054–0202–0 (alk. paper)
     1. Bible. N.T. Mark—Commentaries.   2. Bible. N.T. Mark—
Commentaries. I. Title.   II. Title: Mark.   III. Series
226.6'07—dc21   98–39365
                                                                        CIP

2 3 4 5 6   02 01
D

$\mathscr{W}$riting this commentary on the book of Mark was not only inspirational but transformational as well. I want to thank three key people who were my "team" in finishing well.

Thanks Cheryl Smith, without your word smithing and research I would not have been able to complete the task.

Thanks to my mom, Avanell Cooper, whose love and encouragement are always an inspiration.

And thanks to Nancy, my dear wife, who modeled servanthood to me and for me during this project. I love you.

— March 2000 —

Contents

Contents

Editorial Preface

Today's church hungers for Bible teaching, and Bible teachers hunger for resources to guide them in teaching God's Word. The Holman New Testament Commentary provides the church with the food to feed the spiritually hungry in an easily digestible format. The result: new spiritual vitality that the church can readily use.

Bible teaching should result in new interest in the Scriptures, expanded Bible knowledge, discovery of specific scriptural principles, relevant applications, and exciting living. The unique format of the Holman New Testament Commentary includes sections to achieve these results for every New Testament book.

Opening quotations from some of the church's best writers lead to an introductory illustration and discussion that draw individuals and study groups into the Word of God. "In a Nutshell" summarizes the content and teaching of the chapter. Verse-by-verse commentary answers the church's questions rather than raising issues scholars usually admit they cannot adequately solve. Bible principles and specific contemporary applications encourage students to move from Bible to contemporary times. A specific modern illustration then ties application vividly to present life. A brief prayer aids the student to commit his or her daily life to the principles and applications found in the Bible chapter being studied. For those still hungry for more, "Deeper Discoveries" take the student into a more personal, deeper study of the words, phrases, and themes of God's Word. Finally, a teaching outline provides transitional statements and conclusions along with an outline to assist the teacher in group Bible studies.

It is the editors' prayer that this new resource for local church Bible teaching will enrich the ministry of group, as well as individual, Bible study, and that it will lead God's people to truly be people of the Book, living out what God calls us to be.

Contributors

Vol. 1 Matthew

Stuart Weber

Pastor

Good Shepherd Community Church

Boring, Oregon

Vol. 2 Mark

Rod Cooper

Professor

Denver Theological Seminary

Denver, Colorado

Vol. 3 Luke

Trent C. Butler

Editor, Bibles

Broadman & Holman Publishers

Nashville, Tennessee

Vol. 4 John

Kenneth Gangel

Distinguished Professor Emeritus

Dallas Seminary

Dallas, Texas

Vol. 5 Acts

Kenneth Gangel

Distinguished Professor Emeritus

Dallas Seminary

Dallas, Texas

Vol. 6 Romans

Kenneth Boa   &   William Kruidenier

President   Freelance Writer

Reflections Ministry

Atlanta, Georgia

Vol. 7 1 & 2 Corinthians

Richard Pratt

Professor of Old Testament

Reformed Theological Seminary

Maitland, Florida

Vol. 8 Galatians, Ephesians, Philippians, Colossians

Max Anders

Senior Pastor

Castleview Baptist Church

Indianapolis, Indiana

Vol. 9 1 & 2 Thessalonians, 1 & 2 Timothy, Titus, Philemon

Knute Larson

Senior Pastor

The Chapel

Akron, Ohio

Vol. 10 Hebrews, James

Thomas Lea

Dean, School of Theology

Southwestern Baptist Theological Seminary

Fort Worth, Texas

Vol. 11 1 & 2 Peter, 1, 2, 3 John, Jude

David Walls   &   Max Anders

Pastor

Church of the Open Door

Elyria, Ohio

Vol. 12 Revelation

Kendell Easley

Professor of New Testament

Mid-America Baptist Theological Seminary

Memphis, Tennessee

Holman New Testament Commentary

Twelve volumes designed for Bible study and teaching to enrich the local church and God's people.

Series Editor	Max Anders
Managing Editors	Trent C. Butler & Steve Bond
Project Editor	Lloyd W. Mullens
Marketing Manager	Greg Webster
Product Manager	David Shepherd

Introduction to

Mark

LETTER PROFILE

- Written for Gentile readers, especially Romans.
- Mark presents Jesus as the ultimate servant.
- Mark emphasizes what Jesus did rather than what he said. The word *immediately* is used over forty times to show Christ as a servant of "action."
- Eighteen miracles (over half of Christ's thirty-five recorded miracles) are in the Book of Mark.
- Mark is the earliest and shortest of the Gospels.
- Some consider that Mark recorded the recollections of the apostle Peter about Jesus' life.
- Chapters 1–8 center on Christ's ministry to the multitudes; chapters 8–10 deal with his ministry primarily to the disciples.
- Chapters 11–16 focus on Jesus' rejection by the Jewish rulers and his sacrifice of his life for the multitudes.
- Mark devotes almost as many chapters to the last week of Christ's life (six chapters) as he does to the prior three years of ministry (eight chapters).
- Key verse to summarize Mark's message is 10:45.

AUTHOR PROFILE

- Tradition holds that Mark is the author of this Gospel.
- Jewish; born in Jerusalem, probably from a well-to-do family. His mother, Mary, had a large house that was a meeting place for believers and they had servants (Acts 12:12–16).
- He was Barnabas's cousin, and he went on the first missionary journey with Paul and Barnabas.
- Mark deserted Paul and Barnabas on their first missionary journey. Restored by Barnabas's not going with Paul on the second missionary journey.

- Very close to the apostle Peter, who may have been the one who led Mark to Christ.
- Fully restored to service because Paul, nearing the end of his life, said Mark was useful for service and asked Mark to come see him.

Mark 1

Sent to Serve

"In the master there is a servant,

in the servant a master."

Cicero

Mark 1

IN A NUTSHELL

This is what Mark is saying to the Gentiles, especially those who are Romans, in chapter 1: According to prophecy, John the Baptist got people ready for the Messiah's ministry by preaching a message of repentance and forgiveness. Jesus appeared and was baptized by John at which time he received "the commission and blessing" from his father to start his ministry. Jesus then confronted his greatest enemy—Satan—and defeated him. After passing the "wilderness test," Jesus began his ministry of "servanthood."

Sent to Serve

I. INTRODUCTION

Lights, Camera, Action!

"*L*ights, camera, action!" These are the words I heard when I saw a scene being filmed for the movie *Jingle Bells,* a light action comedy starring Arnold Schwartzenegger. I was walking through this mega-mall called "Mall of America" in Minneapolis, Minnesota, when I saw a crowd of people standing at the railing shrieking and yelling, "Hi, Arnold." I walked over to the railing and sure enough, this mountain of muscle, "Mr. Action" himself, was below waving up at us. They put some makeup on him, combed back his hair, and then the producer yelled, "Lights, camera, action!" Off Arnold went to save the day.

These are words we have all heard at one time or another. But what is their significance? Why use this ritual to start a scene of a movie or television show? I asked one of my friends who is a video producer why they uttered these three key words. When he told me, it made sense.

Before one frame of film can be shot, hours and hours of preparation are required to make sure the scene is perfectly set. They would like to get the scene on the first take. The two things that are crucial for filming the scene are the lights and the cameras. The cameras are important because too much light could wash out the key features of the actor or overshadow a key prop that needs to be displayed. Too little light and one would not be able to see the slight movements or facial expressions of an actor that could be crucial to the scene. Also, the cameras are important because they need to be in certain positions and at certain angles to catch the flow of the action. There may be as many as six or seven cameras for one scene.

The director is the person who coordinates the position of the cameras and tells the camera operator when to come in for a close-up or when to back away. Each camera has to be ready to do its job on command. If the camera people are not ready, then the scene must be taped over. Therefore, once the preparations are made and everything is set, the director says, "Lights, camera, action," as a check-off of final preparation to start the scene. The director is basically saying, "Get ready—this is for real."

Mark, in essence, is uttering, "Lights, camera, action!" In chapter 1 of his Gospel, Mark sets the stage by positioning the *lights* of Old Testament prophecies from Isaiah and Malachi and the messenger who will fulfill this prophecy—John the Baptist. John heralds the message of the coming Messiah as well as prepares the people through the act of baptism for the upcoming entrance of the Messiah. He is not that light, but he positions the lights in such a way that when Jesus appears everyone will know he is the main player in this drama.

The *cameras* are in position to start the filming through the baptism of Jesus, his blessing from the Father, and his temptation and defeat of Satan in the wilderness. From every angle we are seeing that this is not just another person to be baptized; this is the One who will baptize with the Holy Spirit.

The *action* begins when Jesus starts his ministry of service in the synagogues of Galilee preaching the "good news" and performing a series of miracles: casting out demons, healing Peter's mother-in-law, and healing a leper. The stage has been set, the cameras are rolling, and the drama has begun with incredible action.

As Christians, we often forget that God is just as concerned about the "lights and the positioning of the camera" in our own lives as the actions that follow. God is a God not only of action but of preparation. The Lord painstakingly sets up events in our lives and prepares us personally for what lies ahead so that when "action" is necessary the groundwork has been laid. You may feel that there is not much "action" in your life right now or that God is not at work.

Do not fret. Remember, God is "preparing the way" and preparing you so that when it comes time for action you will be ready. Remember, God may not always come when you want him, but he is always right on time. Lights, camera, action!

II. COMMENTARY

Sent to Serve

> **MAIN IDEA:** *After Jesus is presented by John the Baptist and empowered by the Spirit, he begins his ministry, preaching the good news. Then he calls his disciples and performs various miracles.*

A The Prologue (1:1)

> **SUPPORTING IDEA:** *Jesus is the unique servant of God.*

1:1. Mark wastes no time in telling us the theme of his book. It is the good news of Jesus Christ, the Son of God. Since Mark is writing to a Roman audience, he has no need, like Matthew or Luke, to establish Christ's lineage to prove his credentials as the Son of God to his readers. There are two reasons the Romans did not need such information. First, the Romans had the same attitude as those who are from Missouri—"show me." They were not so much interested in qualifications as they were in actions.

Second, since Jesus is being portrayed as a "servant" or "slave," there would be no need to show his genealogy since, from a Roman's standpoint, slaves do not have genealogies.

Finally, Mark makes it clear about Jesus' uniqueness. Jesus is a personal name; it was common among the Jews, being the same as "Joshua" and meaning "the salvation of Jehovah." **Christ** is an official title; it is the Greek equivalent of the term "Messiah." It declares the "anointed one" who is coming to save us from our sins. **Son of God** expresses the divine nature of our Lord. Mark wanted to make it clear that this was no ordinary servant or just a good man—this was the Son of God, who had come to take away our sins.

B John the Baptist Prepares the Way for the Sacrificial Servant (1:2–8)

SUPPORTING IDEA: *John the Baptist fulfills the Old Testament prophecies as the messenger to prepare the people for the ministry of the sacrificial servant.*

1:2–3. Mark quoted from two Old Testament prophets to show that Christ's coming had been foretold long ago. In fact, it had been at least three hundred years since a word had come from God. The two prophets that Mark quoted from were Isaiah (40:3) and Malachi (3:1). Mark combined the sayings of these two prophets but named only Isaiah probably because Isaiah emphasized the servanthood and salvation of the Messiah whereas Malachi highlighted the judgment of the Messiah. In both cases, a messenger was sent to prepare the way for Christ's coming.

The figure of speech, **prepare the way for the Lord, make straight paths for him**, refers to the custom of sending an officer before a monarch who was to make a royal journey. This person was to level and smooth out any ruts in the road so the monarch's journey would be smoother. The **messenger** being sent to **prepare the way** was John the Baptist.

1:4. The appearance of John the Baptist in the wilderness was the most important event in the life of Israel for more than three hundred years. It had been that long since Israel had heard a "word from God." The **desert region** in which John started his ministry of **baptism** is estimated by scholars to be between Judea and the Dead Sea. This area is known for its stark surroundings and rugged terrain. In the Old Testament, it is sometimes called *Jeshimmon*, which means "the devastation." John was no city dweller; he was a man of the wilderness, and he performed his ministry in the wilderness to make a point.

The wilderness in Israel's history symbolized rebellion and disobedience. The nation of Israel, after the deliverance of God and the Exodus from Egypt, disobeyed God by not going into the promised land. As a result they wandered in the wilderness for forty years before they actually entered the promised land as God's people. By coming to the wilderness to be baptized, the people were admitting their wandering from God and their rebellion toward God and their desire for a fresh start.

Also, John's preaching of a **baptism of repentance for the forgiveness of sins** was highly unusual for a Jew. Jews believed that only Gentile converts to Judaism needed to be baptized. The baptism of Gentiles was a ritual washing from all the defilement of their past. The Jews were being asked to do something they had never done before. To call all Israel to be baptized meant that in some way all of Israel was defiled and needed cleansing. In Matthew 3:9 John criticized the people for presuming to be righteous and secure with God just because they were children of Abraham, the father of the Jewish race. He warned, in Matthew 3:7–12, that they would be purged and rejected if they did not bear fruits of repentance.

The baptism by John was a baptism of **repentance**. Repentance means a turning away from something and turning in a new direction. Israel was being asked to turn away from its disobedience and rebellion and to start anew by turning toward the coming Messiah. By doing so they would be for-given—released—from their sins and would experience the grace of God through the Messiah.

1:5. This verse says that **The whole Judean countryside and all of the people of Jerusalem went out to him.** It is estimated that as many as three hundred thousand people came out to be baptized by John. **Confessing their sins** demonstrates their acknowledgment of disobedience and rebellion toward God. The location of the baptism was the Jordan River, which was several miles outside Jerusalem.

1:6. The reference to John's clothing and diet emphasizes that he was not *mainstream.* John's dress and lifestyle were a protest against the godlessness and self-serving materialism of his day. You would not see John staying at the Jerusalem Hilton—nor would he be welcome. To go out to be baptized by this man meant a break with the institutions and culture of Jerusalem. His clothing and food were those of a wilderness nomad. John wore clothing made of **camel's hair, with a leather belt around his waist.** His camel-hair robe was the kind worn by the very poor, and his belt was nothing but a leather thong.

His clothing also, especially the leather belt, was reminiscent of another man of the wilderness who was also a prophet preparing the way—Elijah (2 Kgs. 1:8). The explicit identification of John with Elijah is referenced by Mark later in 9:9–13. Not only did John dress like Elijah, but he also under-stood his ministry to be one of reform and preparation, just as Elijah's was. A popular belief of the time was that Elijah would return from heaven to prepare the way for the Messiah (Mal. 4:5–6). John reminded the people of Elijah because of his dress and behavior.

His food was **locusts and wild honey.** There are two possible meanings for these words. The **locusts** could be the actual insect or also a kind of bean or nut that was the food of the poorest of the poor. The **honey** could actually be from the honeycomb of bees or a kind of sweet sap that distills from the bark of certain trees. John's diet was very simple and "down to earth."

1:7. John made it clear that he was the servant of the coming Servant. John's task was to prepare the way and then get out of the way. John appeared as a powerful figure, but he made it clear that he would pale in comparison to the Messiah when he appeared. He showed his insignificance compared to the Messiah by saying, **the thongs of whose sandals I am not worthy to stoop down and untie.** Sandals were made of leather soles fastened to the foot by straps passing through the toes. The roads in those days were not paved. In dry weather they were dust and in wet weather they became rivers of mud. To remove the sandals and wash the feet was the job of a slave. John was saying that he was not even worthy of the office of slave when compared to the One coming after him.

1:8. John made it clear that his ministry was only preparatory, symbolic, and temporary. His baptism was **with water.** John was administering an external rite that symbolized moral cleansing and a desire to break away from the sin that had separated people from God. The one to follow him would **baptize you with the Holy Spirit.** John was pointing out that the Messiah's baptism would bring about lasting change. The Messiah's baptism would be internal, changing a person from the inside out. Jesus' baptism would secure purity of heart and life, deliver his followers from the guilt and power of sin, and bring them into fellowship with God.

Ⓒ The Presentation and Preparation of the Sacrificial Servant (1:9–11)

SUPPORTING IDEA: *The sacrificial servant obediently submits to John's baptism and is affirmed by his father in preparation for the ministry of service.*

1:9. In verses 1–8 John had been preparing the people for the coming of the sacrificial servant. He had declared that the coming Messiah would be "mightier" than himself—one whose sandal thong he was not worthy to untie. Yet, with such a great declaration Mark showed Jesus entering public life as a servant, without great fanfare. Mark tells us that Jesus came **from Nazareth in Galilee.** The people being baptized for the most part were from Jerusalem, the center of the religious life of Israel. One would think the Messiah would come from there. Yet, Mark, in keeping with his theme of the sacrificial servant, has Jesus coming from a remote village of no reputation in Galilee. Jesus was **baptized by John** not because he needed to repent of sin but to identify himself with sinful humanity (2 Cor. 5:21) and to give approval to John's ministry.

1:10–11. After Jesus was baptized, three key events happened in quick succession. The first two appear together where Jesus **saw heaven being torn open** and **the Spirit descending on him like a dove.** Mark seems to suggest that only Jesus saw the heavens open and the Spirit descend. The descent of the Spirit was **like a dove.** The dove is usually a symbol of gentleness, possibly contrasting the ministry of Jesus as a gentle servant who brought healing and restoration with the ministry of John, who proclaimed judgment. Whatever else the descent of the Spirit on Jesus meant, it clearly indicated his anointing and empowerment for ministry. Jesus himself proclaimed this anointing in the synagogue in Nazareth (Luke 4:18) when he said, "The Spirit of the Lord is on me."

The third event happened shortly after the Spirit descended. Mark says the Father spoke to his Son by saying, **You are my Son, whom I love; with you I am well pleased.** The Father's response joins the concept of the messianic king of the coronation psalm (2:7) and that of the Lord's Servant of the prophet Isaiah (42:1). The main emphasis is on the unique sonship of Jesus. Mark opened his Gospel (1:1) by confessing that Jesus was the Son of God. Here, the Father himself proclaimed Jesus as his Son and expressed his approval. This event in a remote place in the Judean wilderness has cosmic significance. Here is the blessed Trinity—Father, Son, and Holy Spirit.

Ⓓ The Testing of the Sacrificial Servant (1:12–13)

SUPPORTING IDEA: *The sacrificial servant is tested by his greatest enemy, Satan, in his final preparation for fulfilling his mission.*

1:12. After his baptism Jesus **at once** went into the wilderness. Mark says the Spirit **sent him out** into the wilderness. The other Gospel writers used the term *led,* but Mark used the word *sent* in keeping with his servant theme. Servants are not led—they are "driven" or "commanded to go." The humbling of Jesus at the baptism by his identification with the failure and sin of humankind is continued by his subjection to the onslaughts of Satan.

1:13. Mark does not present the testing of Jesus in detail as the other Gospel writers do, but as one major clash. Mark's account of the testing is brief, recording no victory over Satan. This seems to indicate that Jesus' entire ministry would be a continuous encounter with Satan—not limited to this one experience in the desert. In fact, Mark uses the term Satan (adversary) as opposed to Devil (accuser), which is used by the other Gospel writers. Mark is getting ready to write about the mighty works of the sacrificial servant, but in the process Jesus will continually be striving with his "adversary"—Satan.

The **forty days** are symbolic. They recall the experiences of Moses (Exod. 24:18) and Elijah (1 Kgs. 19:8,15) in the desert. Both were delivers of Israel from bondage. They also remind us of the forty years of wandering by the nation of Israel in the wilderness. Only Mark mentions the **wild animals**. This demonstrates the fierceness of Jesus' wilderness experience and God's protection from lions and other dangerous animals. Mark is the only Gospel writer who mentions that **angels attended him**. It seems that these angels sustained Jesus in the midst of his testing. There is no indication by Mark that these angels withdrew after the testing.

E The Ministry of the Sacrificial Servant Begins (1:14–15)

> **SUPPORTING IDEA:** *The sacrificial servant begins his ministry with the preaching of the good news.*

1:14. Jesus now began his public ministry in the province of Galilee. Palestine had three major provinces. Galilee was the northernmost province. It contained beautiful lakes, forests, and mountains. Most of Jesus' ministry was conducted in this province. Jesus embarked on what is called his early Galilean ministry (1:14–3:12).

The beginning of Jesus' ministry is related to the imprisonment of John the Baptist. Mark does not give us the events that took place after the temptation of Jesus and the imprisonment of John. The other Gospel writers fill in those details. Mark concentrated on the work of the servant, so he pointed out that John's work of preparation had ended by his imprisonment and the ministry of Jesus was now to begin.

Jesus began his ministry of service by **proclaiming the good news of God**. The good news is both from God and about God. This good news is the gospel that brings forgiveness, restoration, and new life. Men and women have been longing to hear such a message. Now they not only hear it but actually encounter the One who is able to deliver it.

1:15. The phrase **the time has come** shows the exact timing of God. Jesus was saying that the critical moment in history had arrived. God was about to act decisively by bringing redemption and restoration to his people through his servant, Jesus.

Jesus' message was that **the kingdom of God is near**. The kingdom of God was central to Jesus' teaching. The kingdom of God was simply the rule of Messiah on earth. This had been promised in the Old Testament (e.g., Exod. 15:18; Ps. 29:10; Isa. 43:15), and the Jewish people had longed for it. The kingdom "is near" because Jesus, the ruler of that kingdom, has now arrived. Yet, the only way into that kingdom is to **repent and believe.** John had already been preaching for the people to **repent,** but Jesus added the word **believe.** Only through "repentance" from their sinfulness and "belief" in the **good news** (i.e., the gospel of Jesus Christ) would they enter the kingdom. Jesus was presenting an urgency about the nearness of God's kingdom and the need to act decisively.

ⓕ The Calling of the Servant's First Disciples (1:16–20)

SUPPORTING IDEA: *The sacrificial servant begins his ministry by forming a team to help him preach the good news of the kingdom.*

1:16–18. Jesus' task was to gather around him a community whom he could teach so they might be sharers of this good news. Jesus, after his resurrection, would commission his disciples to carry the gospel "unto all the world." He began the preparation of his disciples to carry out that commission.

Jesus was walking by the Sea of Galilee. The Sea of Galilee is a beautiful fresh-water lake. Fed by the waters of the upper Jordan River, it is seven hundred feet below sea level, fourteen miles long, and six miles wide. It was also called the Lake of Gennesaret (Luke 5:1) and the Sea of Tiberias (John 6:1; 21:1). In Old Testament times, this lake was known as the Sea of Kinnereth (Num. 34:11). Most of Jesus' teaching and miracles were performed in this area.

A lot of fishing took place at this lake. Josephus, a famous historian of the Jews, recorded that up to 330 fishing boats sailed this lake. Among those who fished this lake for a livelihood were Simon and his brother, Andrew. Jesus called Simon and Andrew to **Come, follow me.** Mark says nothing of a previous encounter of these two disciples with Jesus. These men may have been followers of John. Perhaps they were encouraged by John to follow Jesus. Also, they may have been in the crowd when Jesus was preaching.

Jesus declared that he would make them **fishers of men.** This phrase was a metaphor used by the Old Testament prophets for the gathering of people for judgment (Jer. 16:14–16; Amos 4:2). Jesus was calling Simon and Andrew to the urgent task of rescuing people from the impending judgment implied by the coming of the kingdom in the person and work of Jesus. This urgency demanded a response. The phrase **at once** indicates that urgency. Leaving their nets showed their willingness to make a total commitment as disciples of Christ.

1:19–20. Jesus extended the same call to James and John, who were known as the sons of Zebedee. The price of discipleship is further illustrated in their actions. They not only left their livelihood; they also broke family ties and tradition by leaving their father.

G The Sacrificial Servant Begins His Ministry of Service (1:21–28)

SUPPORTING IDEA: *The sacrificial servant begins his ministry of service by preaching with authority and proving this authority by casting out a demon.*

1:21. Jesus and his team entered a small city called Capernaum, located on the northwest shore of the Sea of Galilee. This city was probably the home of Peter, Andrew, James, and John, his new disciples. Capernaum became a major site for Jesus' healing and preaching ministry—a kind of base of operations for his Galilean ministry. The Sabbath was set aside as a day of worship and rest. The people would gather at the synagogue for prayer and exposition from the Old Testament Scriptures. Jesus entered the synagogue and **began to teach.** A Jewish custom permitted visiting teachers, like Jesus, to preach by invitation of the leaders of the synagogue.

1:22. The people were **amazed** at Jesus' teachings. His teachings were different because he taught as **one who had authority, not as the teachers of the law.** The scribes were professionally trained scholars who applied and interpreted the law. The difference between Jesus' teaching and the scribes was that the scribes never gave an independent opinion. They always quoted other experts such as "rabbi such and such" to back up their interpretations of the law. Jesus did not quote any source. He was the ultimate authority in and of himself. Jesus taught with authority that came straight from God.

1:23–24. The synagogue service was interrupted by the cries of a man **who was possessed by an evil spirit.** Immediately Jesus was opposed by Satan. This was a key event because Jesus had the opportunity to show his authority over the power of Satan. The term "evil spirit" means that this man's personality had been damaged to the point that the core of his being was under the control of a demon.

The question **What do you want with us, Jesus of Nazareth?** shows that there was more than one demon in the man. There must have been several demons possessing this man and causing him to cry out. The demons also clearly recognized the authority and mission of Jesus. The demons seemed to know that Jesus' preaching brought judgment. If one did not respond to Jesus' preaching, then judgment would occur.

The use of Jesus' name by the demons and his title **the Holy One of God** is believed to be an attempt by the demons to gain control over Jesus. It was widely believed that by uttering one's name, an individual could gain power or control over that person. The demons seemed to hope to do this with Jesus.

1:25–26. Those who could cast out demons, called exorcists, would usually identify themselves by name to some deity or power and then pronounce some authoritative phrase to cast out the demon. Jesus needed no magical formula to exorcise the demon. He was the ultimate authority. He ordered the demon to **be quiet**. At this authoritative word of power, the evil spirit convulsed the man, then left him with a **shriek**.

1:27–28. The people were **amazed** once again. In fact, they said, **What is this? A new teaching—and with authority!** They had never experienced such power and authority. Jesus' authoritative teaching was backed up by authoritative action. Jesus' authority was inherent within himself. As usual, Jesus' teaching not only generated great discussion but caused his fame to **spread quickly over the whole region of Galilee.**

The Servant Continues His Ministry through Healing Miracles (1:29–45)

> **SUPPORTING IDEA:** *The sacrificial servant backs up his words with works and in the process solidifies the faith of his disciples. He also draws crowds to hear the good news of the gospel.*

1:29–31. According to Jewish custom, the main Sabbath meal came immediately after the worship service in the synagogue—at the sixth hour, or around 12 o'clock noon. The Jewish day began at 6 A.M. and the hours were counted from there. It appears that Simon (Peter) and Andrew's house was close to the synagogue. This miracle was private, and not public, possibly to begin to solidify the faith of these early disciples in the claims of their leader. The "team" found Peter's mother-in-law **in bed with a fever**. Simon and Andrew told Jesus about her condition. This was a personal need, and they felt comfortable in going to Jesus with their needs.

In Jesus' time many people considered fever an illness in itself and not a symptom of a disease. According to Leviticus 26:16 and Deuteronomy 28:22, a fever could be interpreted as a punishment sent by God to those who violated his covenant. According to custom, only God could intervene in such cases. And he did! The recovery of Peter's mother-in-law was so complete that **she began to wait on them.** Jesus showed his compassion and love in the way he healed her. Notice that **he went to her, took her hand and helped her up.** Then the fever left her. He could have just spoken the words, but Jesus reached out and touched her. Jesus came to enter into our pain—not just observe it.

1:32–34. The people waited until **that evening after sunset** because Jewish law did not allow the carrying of any burden through a town on the Sabbath. That would have been considered work, so it was forbidden on that day. A new day began after 6:00 P.M. The people probably knew it was safe to come out and not break the law when the sun had set and the stars were out.

The whole town gathered at the door, and Jesus healed many people of their diseases and cast out demons. Everyone in Capernaum knew Jesus was in town. The exorcism of verse 26 and the healings of verse 31 were not isolated cases. Jesus also continued to **not let the demons speak because they knew who he was.** Jesus wanted to show by word and deed what kind of Messiah he was before he declared himself openly as the Messiah. He would declare who he was—not the demons.

1:35–37. The events up to this point had been rapid, coming one after the other. They also would have been emotionally and spiritually exhausting. The humanity of Jesus is evident in these words: **Jesus got up and went off to a solitary place, where he prayed.** Even Jesus needed to recharge his batteries by withdrawing from the crowds and talking with his Father. This was a time of renewal and preparation for Jesus. Two other times in Mark's Gospel we see Jesus getting away to pray (6:46; 14:32–41). Each time he was preparing for a crisis.

While Jesus was concerned about focusing on God's mission for him, the disciples seemed to be caught up in the increasing popularity of Jesus. Perhaps they felt they should seize the day: **Simon and his companions went to look for him; and when they found him, they exclaimed, "Everyone is looking for you!"**

1:38–39. Jesus' desire to go **to the nearby villages** showed his desire not to be seen as just a popular miracle worker. He reiterated his purpose by saying, **so I can preach there also. That is why I have come.** Jesus' primary mission was to preach the good news. The miracles of healing and casting out of demons was secondary—a means to the end of presenting the gospel and getting people to respond to that good news. Jesus continued a pattern of presenting the gospel by going into their **synagogues and driving out demons.** The synagogue was the primary place where the Scriptures were interpreted. What better place to proclaim the good news to the people and their leaders? The preaching of the word preceded the demonstration of miracles, showing that the miracles backed up the authority of the Messiah's proclamations.

1:40. The account of the healing of the leper seems to connect 1:21–29 and 2:1–3:6 as two distinct units in Mark's Gospel. The word **leprosy** was used in biblical times to designate a wide variety of skin diseases. In Leviticus 13 seven forms of this skin disease are described. According to ceremonial law, a person with leprosy was to wear distinct clothing to signify he had the disease as well as to shout "unclean, unclean" as he approached others. A person with leprosy was not allowed to touch others for fear he would defile them and make them unclean. A person with leprosy was considered a walking corpse.

Instead of the leper keeping his distance from Jesus, as the law directed, he came directly to Jesus, fell on his knees, and cried out for Jesus to make him clean. This man was full of faith. He did not doubt Jesus' *ability* to heal him, but he was not sure of Jesus' *desire* to heal him. But he was willing to take the risk.

1:41–42. The phrase **filled with compassion** is probably better translated as "being angered." Jesus was probably angry because he recognized this foul disease as the work of Satan. Jesus' anger was not focused on the man and his desire for healing but on Satan, whose work he came to destroy.

Jesus expressed his compassion for the leper by touching him. Most people would have healed the man first and then touched him. But not Jesus. He knew this man had not felt human touch in a long time, so he reached out to touch him first. By touching the man, Jesus revealed his attitude toward ceremonial law. By touching the leper, he himself would be made ceremonially unclean. Jesus placed love and compassion above ritual and regulation.

1:43–44. Jesus then **sent him away.** This phrase is also used of driving out demons. Jesus also gave the man **a strong warning.** Jesus did not want to gain the reputation of being just a miracle worker. This would hinder his ability to spread the good news and fulfill his mission. Instead, he instructed the cleansed leper to show himself to the priest to be pronounced ceremonially clean (Lev. 14:2–31). The phrase **as a testimony to them** means a testimony to the priest and the people of the reality of the man's cure. If leprosy was like being a walking corpse, then the cleansing of leprosy would be the equivalent of raising a person from the dead. The religious authorities would ascribe such healing to God, thus admitting that Jesus was truly God.

1:45. The leper disobeyed Jesus by proclaiming his healing to everyone. Because he ignored Jesus' warning, Jesus **could no longer enter a town openly but stayed outside in lonely places.** Jesus had to curtail his public ministry and stay in isolated places. But even in his isolation, people still found him.

> **MAIN IDEA REVIEW:** *Through the preparation and presentation of John the Baptist; blessing of the Father, and empowerment of the Spirit for the work of service; Jesus begins his ministry of sacrifice and service by preaching the good news of salvation, which is spread through his team and verified through his miracles.*

III. CONCLUSION

Service Is His Business

There is a service station by our house. There is a saying under the sign that reads, "Service is our business." The sign implies that whatever your needs might be concerning the care of your car, do not worry, do not even lift a finger. The service station will take care of it. Mark is essentially saying the same about Jesus in chapter 1. Service is Jesus' business. Whether confronting a fever, demons, or the crippling curse of leprosy, Jesus displayed the power and love of God for lost and hurting people. Jesus was willing to do whatever it took to meet our needs. Jesus came to meet our needs, but especially our primary need to hear the good news for salvation.

Many years ago the Prince of Wales visited India. A formidable barrier had been set up to keep back the masses of people who wanted to catch a glimpse of royalty. When the prince arrived, he shook hands with some of the dignitaries who were presented to him. Then, looking over their heads to the crowds beyond, he said, "Take down those barriers." They were quickly removed and all of the people, regardless of social rank, had free access to the heir to the British throne. Some time later when the prince came to that district again, ten thousand outcasts waited under a banner inscribed with the words, "The Prince of the Outcasts." What the Prince of Wales did in that moment sounds very much like what Jesus would have done in the same situation. He was a king to be sure but a king who demonstrated his power through service to his people. The entire Gospel of Mark captures the servant heart of Jesus, and chapter 1 starts us on our way.

PRINCIPLES

- Believers can trust in the perfect timing of God. He may not always come when you want him, but he is always right on time.
- Believers can trust in God's Word. He is faithful to do what he has promised.
- Believers must consistently repent and confess sin so that God can work in and through them.
- Believers can trust God to protect, preserve, and provide for them during the "desert times" of their lives.

APPLICATIONS

- Trust in the fact that God keeps his word and submit your fears to him.
- Select a special place you can go to daily for quality time with the Lord.
- Recognize that God is at work on your behalf, whether or not you see anything happening. Thank him for what he is doing and look expectantly for him to work.
- Recognize that there is no wasted experience for a believer. Rejoice that God will use all your experiences to prepare you to be more effective for him.

IV. LIFE APPLICATION

Special to God

I was hot, tired, sweaty, and most of all—angry. I had what my friends affectionately call a "stupid attack."

I had just finished playing a round of golf. It was one of those rounds where you leave the course knowing that the only thing about your game that has improved is your prayer life. After stuffing my golf bag in the trunk of the car and changing shoes, I was ready to go home. I was sitting in my little sports car, which means there was not a lot of room.

I carry a little bag where I keep all of my valuables like money, car keys, and wedding ring. I emptied the pouch into my hand—and then it happened. My hands were sweaty from playing golf. Instead of wiping off my hands, I tried to put on my wedding ring. It slipped out of my sweaty hands and dropped through a narrow opening next to the emergency brake of the car. I looked through the crack in the floor and could see the ring barely hanging on a small bolt.

I tried to reach the ring with a penknife, but it was just out of reach. My frustration was mounting. I was already late for dinner—and this is where the "stupid attack" happened. I thought if I drove home slowly enough, the ring would stay on the bolt. When I got home, I could get the proper tools to retrieve it. I began my journey home, stopping every few feet to make sure the ring was still there.

After about the fourth stop, I looked and—you guessed it—no ring. I got out of my car and retraced my steps for the several hundred feet I had gone. I got down on my hands and knees and crawled over the area as if I was looking for a contact lens—but no ring. I drove home frustrated and angry, repeatedly reminding myself I could have called my wife to bring the tools I needed. But nooooo!

It was dinner time when I got home, but I couldn't eat. Instead I stayed out in the garage and tore apart the emergency brake assembly, hoping I would find the ring. Alas, no ring. I was depressed for weeks.

Why the mad search for this ring? It was only, at most, a fifty-dollar gold band. But it was valuable because of what it represented. It was my father-in-law's wedding band. He couldn't wear it because of an accident that had caused his finger to swell. The doctor had been forced to cut the ring off. There was not enough gold in the ring, after cutting it off, for the ring to fit his finger. After my father-in-law and his wife talked, they offered the ring to me. They wanted me to wear it as a continual reminder of their love and support of our marriage. Every time I put it on, it reminded me not only of the bond between my wife and me, but also of her family's commitment for us . . . for me.

That ring was special. It was irreplaceable—a one-of-a-kind item. Maybe something similar has happened to you. You know the disappointment and ache that comes from losing something that is precious and valuable to you. You know what it is like to search for it and long for its return. So does God.

God was like Hallmark greeting cards: He cared enough to send the very best. He cared enough to put aside his kingly status and become a sacrificial servant to bring us back to himself. We are one of a kind. We are valuable to God, and he proved it by serving us and then sacrificing himself for us through his Son, Jesus.

The next time someone tries to put a bargain-basement price tag on your worth, remember what Jesus did: "For even the Son of Man did not come to be served, but to serve, and to give his life as a ransom for many" (Mark 10:45). A ransom for me. Now in return, live in a way that shows your gratitude for his sacrifice for you.

V. PRAYER

Father, thank you for sending the very best. Thank you for Jesus. Grant that I may live and love like Jesus. Help me first of all to ask what I can give rather than what I can get. May I "improve my serve." May I impart the same sense of value to those around me as you imparted to me through your sacrifice for my sin. Thank you, Lord. Amen.

VI. DEEPER DISCOVERIES

A. Repentance (1:4)

Someone once said that you cannot keep walking down a wrong road and hope that it will eventually turn out right. That is a good picture of repentance. Repentance is realizing that you are on the wrong road and then turning around so you are going the right way. You can know you are on the wrong road and still not turn around. You can even be sorry that you are on the wrong road. But until you turn around and head the right way, you have not repented.

The Bible uses two words for repentance: *niham* and *shub. Niham* is most frequently used of God in the Old Testament. It signifies a contemplated change in God's dealings with humanity. The word *shub* carries the meaning "to turn back, away from, or toward." It is confessing that you are on the wrong road, turning away from your current direction and turning toward the right way (Matt. 3:6).

Commentator William Barclay notes that confession must be made to three different people. First, men and women must confess to themselves. We all want to justify ourselves, to rationalize our sinful behavior. Sometimes we rationalize it, based on physical characteristics that we have no control over: "I'm Irish; I can't help it if I get angry." At other times, we justify ourselves by comparing ourselves to others: "At least I don't drink as much as he does" or "at least I don't smoke like she does." The sin of "at least" may be one of the biggest pointers to sin in our lives!

Luke recounted a wonderful parable of Jesus that shows the sin of "at least." Two men—one a Pharisee, the other a tax collector—went into the temple. The Pharisee stood at a distance and prayed, "Thank God I am not like other people, especially this tax collector. I fast, I tithe, I do all the right things."

The tax collector, on the other hand, knew himself. He repented. He confessed and called himself a sinner. Jesus commended him (Luke 18:9–17). Most people miss the marvelous thing about this story in their hurry to get to the parable. It is in verse 9: He also told this parable "to some who were confident of their own righteousness and looked down on everybody else."

So the first step in repentance is to confess to ourselves that we are sinners desperately in need of a Savior. Barclay comments, "There is no one in all the world harder to face than ourselves; and the first step to repentance and to a right relationship to God is to admit our sin to ourselves."

Second, we must confess to those whom we have wronged. Jesus said that we must clear away human barriers before we come to the Father (Matt. 5:22–24). For most of us, it is easier to confess that we are wrong to God than to another human being. After all, the other person may not forgive us. He or she may agree with us that we are wrong and then we will be tempted to justify ourselves, to minimize our sin. One of the steps in Alcoholics Anonymous is to confess to people who have been wronged when it will do no further harm. Admitting our sin to another person has the wondrous effect of loosening its grip on us. Secret sins lose their power when they are not secret.

Third, we must confess to God. Echoing again the parable of the tax collector, Barclay notes, "It is not the man who desires to meet God on equal terms who will discover forgiveness, but the man who kneels in humble contrition and whispers through his shame, 'God be merciful to me a sinner'" (Barclay, *Mark*, p. 15).

A good example of a call to repentance is found in Isaiah 55:6–7: "Seek the LORD while he may be found; call on him while he is near. Let the wicked forsake his way and the evil man his thoughts. Let him return to the LORD, and he will have mercy on him, and to our God, for he will freely pardon." Jesus called everyone to repentance (Mark 1:15). This repentance calls for a change of the entire person, physically, volitionally, intellectually, morally,

and spiritually. Through repentance and conversion, humans dethrone themselves and place Christ on the throne as the rightful ruler.

R. E. O. White shows the link between repentance and conversion (or the
new birth in Christ): "In Jesus' openness and friendship toward sinners, the
loving welcome of God found perfect expression. Nothing was needed to win
back God's favor. It waited eagerly for man's return (Luke 15:11–24). The one
indispensable preliminary was the change in man from rebelliousness to
childlike trust and willingness to obey. That shown, there followed life under
God's rule, described as feasting, marriage, wine, finding treasure, joy, peace,
all the freedom and privilege of sonship within the divine family in the
Father's world" (*Evangelical Dictionary of Theology,* p. 968).

B. Baptism (1:5,8,9)

John the Baptist must have seemed bizarre, even dangerous, to the people
of his day. He came preaching repentance for the forgiveness of sins and then
he baptized Jews. We perhaps have lost sight of the meaning of his baptism.
Our own baptisms may have been surrounded with stained-glass windows
and white robes, or perhaps the fervency of a camp meeting. For some, perhaps, the ritual took place before we could remember it, let alone realize its
significance.

For the Jews, baptism was primarily a cleansing. The bronze basin in the
tabernacle represented this type of cleansing (Exod. 30:18–21). Cleansing
was necessary before the priest approached the altar. Barclay notes that symbolic washing and purifying was woven into the very fabric of Jewish ritual.
Gentiles, who were ritually unclean, needed to do three things when they
became proselytes: They received circumcision as the mark of the covenant
people; a sacrifice had to be made for the atonement of sin; and the proselytes
had to undergo baptism to symbolize their cleansing from the stain of their
past life.

John, however, was not urging Gentiles to repent and be baptized; he was
virtually demanding that the Jews be baptized. But they were Jews! They
were not supposed to need baptizing. After all, they had the priests who
made daily, weekly, and yearly sacrifices for them. Why did they need baptism? Barclay further points out that "John's baptism made sure that the Jews
realized that to be a Jew in the racial sense was not to be a member of God's
chosen people" (Barclay, *Mark,* p. 14). John denounced this kind of national-
ism, "Do not begin to say to yourselves, 'We have Abraham as our father.' For
I tell you that out of these stones God can raise up children for Abraham"
(Luke 3:8). Robert Guelich states: "Repentance connoted much more than
sorrow or remorse. It included the reorientation of one's total life . . . baptism
was both an acknowledgment of one's sins and one's desire to repent and an
acknowledgment of God's acceptance of that repentance. The ultimate goal of

repentance-baptism was the forgiveness of sins and acceptance by God in the coming day of salvation" (Guelich, *Mark*, p. 26).

In the New Testament, baptism became the primary rite of Christian initiation. It symbolized death and resurrection (Rom. 6:3–4). It symbolized washing, regeneration, and renewal (Titus 3:5). Spiritually, it is a work of the Holy Spirit based on what Christ has done through his own baptism of death.

The meaning of baptism in the New Testament is given by three Old Testament types: the flood (1 Pet. 3:19–20), the Red Sea (1 Cor. 10:1–2), and circumcision (Col. 2:11–12). These three types show us the different aspects of baptism. The flood and the Red Sea linked death and redemption, as does baptism into Christ's death and resurrection. It is a symbol that a person has died and is raised to new life. It is God's act of judgment and grace—judgment upon the old nature that has been crucified with Christ and grace with the bestowal of the new nature. Circumcision represented the divine covenant between God and Abraham. This act set aside Abraham and the Israelites as particularly chosen by God. They became a peculiar community, characterized by their obedience to God. Baptism is a sign that we have been adopted into a new community, a new family, and we are characterized by our obedience to God through Jesus Christ.

Mark states that Jesus was baptized by John. We know that Jesus did not need to repent. He had no sin from which to be cleansed. Why was he baptized? Barclay (*Mark*, p. 19) makes note of four reasons. First, it was the moment of decision, the launching of Jesus' ministry. Second, it was the moment of God's approval. At the baptism Jesus submitted his decision to God, and this decision was unmistakably approved. Third, at his baptism the Holy Spirit descended upon him, equipping him for the task ahead. Fourth, Jesus identified himself with sinful humanity.

G. W. Bromiley believes that identification with sinners is the true baptism: "This identification with sinners in judgment and renewal is what Jesus accepts when he comes to the baptism of John and fulfills when he takes his place between two thieves on the cross. Here we have the real baptism of the New Testament, which makes possible the baptism of our identification with Christ and underlies and is attested by the outward sign . . . Christ has died and risen again in our place, so that we are dead and alive again in him, with him, and through him" (*Evangelical Dictionary of Theology*, p. 113).

C. Baptized with the Holy Spirit (1:8)

The baptism with the Holy Spirit was originally, and I believe correctly, identified with judgment. John the Baptist was warning of coming judgment, of a purification that was both personal and national in nature. As Robert Alan Cole notes, "God's intervention, that was to result in the establishment of his rule upon earth, was at the very doors." Jesus Christ, the coming one

John referred to, ushered in the age of grace and judgment. Jesus stated this himself in the synagogue at Nazareth at the beginning of his ministry. He took the Book of Isaiah and read from it: 'The Spirit of the Lord is on me, because he has anointed me to preach good news to the poor. He has sent me to proclaim freedom for the prisoners and recovery of sight for the blind, to release the oppressed, to proclaim the year of the Lord's favor'" (Luke 4:18–19) (Cole, *Mark*, p. 58).

This is the age of grace. Of course, the scroll from Isaiah did not stop with those words. It continues, "And the day of vengeance of our God" (Isa. 61:2). While Jesus did not fulfill these words with his first coming, he will with his second coming. John the Baptist warned of a radical, fiery purification. The alternative he offered was to accept his baptism in water as a symbol of total repentance and reformation of life.

Some interpreters see the baptism of the Spirit as a judgment upon the temple and the sacrifices that are now made obsolete. Others see the baptism of the Spirit as a purification by the Holy Spirit that happens as the baptism of repentance occurs so that the two baptisms become synonymous.

This phrase should not be confused with "the baptism of the Spirit" found especially in Pentecostal and charismatic circles. This expression places less emphasis upon the indwelling of the Spirit, with the illumination of mind (John 14:26; 16:8–15), the refinement of character (Gal. 5:22–23, 1 Cor. 12:27–13:13), and the gifts of peace, power, and joy that the Spirit bestows. Instead, the phrase has become associated with the initial and continuing filling of individuals by the Spirit with miraculous powers, gifts, abilities, and emotional resources, manifest in spiritual healing, speaking in unknown tongues, prophesying, leadership, exuberant emotion, and other forms of equipment for Christian service. Some also indicate that this is a second baptism, an "in-filling," a second blessing that supplements conversion. Others argue that the gift of the Holy Spirit is for all believers and that the unique outpourings at Pentecost were for the purpose of launching the church and having it testify to God's work.

D. Kingdom of God (1:15)

John the Baptist was the herald of the king. If he had owned a horn, he could have blown it to announce the king's presence. When Jesus Christ came into Galilee and began saying, "The kingdom of God is near," he made reference to his own incarnation. He was saying, in effect, "God's rule has just broke into human history."

Basileia (kingdom) means, first, the authority to rule as a king and, second, the realm over which the reign is exercised. In the Old Testament, *male-kut,* when used of God, almost always refers to his authority. We may think of the kingdom as primarily God's realm, but it is first his authority. He has authority as the Creator. In the New Testament, the kingdom of God is the divine authority and rule given by the Father to the Son. When Jesus testified to Pilate that his kingdom was not of this world, he was not saying that he had no authority on earth. He was saying that his authority was not given to him by anyone in this world. God the Father had granted him the authority of the kingdom (Luke 22:29).

The Book of Isaiah pointed to the kingship, the authority, of Jesus: "For to us a child is born, to us a son is given, and the government will be on his shoulders. And he will be called Wonderful Counselor, Mighty God, Everlasting Father, Prince of Peace. Of the increase of his government and peace there will be no end. He will reign on David's throne and over his kingdom, establishing and upholding it with justice and righteousness from that time on and forever" (Isa. 9:6–7).

Jesus separated the present and future aspects of the kingdom. His incarnation, earthly ministry, death, and resurrection accomplished certain kingly objectives. When earthly kings invaded a land, they usurped the reigning power and released any prisoners that the king had captured. Christ's objective was to usurp Satan, redeem humanity, and deliver people from the powers of evil. Christ's present reign means the destruction of all hostile powers, the last of which is death. It brings to people "righteousness, peace and joy in the Holy Spirit" (Rom. 14:17) and deliverance from the "dominion of darkness" (Col. 1:13). It is accomplished by the new birth (John 3:3).

Christ will exercise his rule until he subdues all that is hostile to God and returns in glory. In the age to come, Satan will be defeated for all time (Matt. 25:41); the dead in Christ will be raised in incorruptible bodies (1 Cor. 15:42–50) which are no longer subject to death; every knee will bow before him; and every tongue will confess him as Lord (see Phil. 2:10–11).

E. Demons or evil spirits (1:23)

Earthly kings freed their subjects from enemy lands. It is no coincidence that Jesus' first recorded miracle in the Gospel of Mark was casting a demon out of a man. This was Mark's way of authenticating what he had just reported: The kingdom was indeed at hand, and the king was exercising his authority. Jesus' conquest in the desert becomes the pattern for the rest of the Gospel as they report the power of Jesus to heal the sick and cast out demons (Lyon, *Evangelical Dictionary of Theology*, p. 120).

Barclay points out that the era of Jesus' earthly ministry was a time filled with superstitions and fear. He notes that in ancient cemeteries skulls have been found in which a hole had been drilled. It was clear from bone growth that this boring had taken place during life. The reason? To allow demons to escape from the body. As Harnack says, "The whole world and the circumambient atmosphere were filled with devils; not merely idolatry, but every phase and form of life was ruled by them. They sat on thrones, they hovered around cradles. The earth was literally a hell" (Barclay, *Mark,* p. 33).

Scripture does not elaborate on the origin of demons. Two major themes emerge: the unnatural offspring of angels and women prior to the flood (Gen. 6:2; Jude 6); and Lucifer's original rebellion (Matt. 25:41; 2 Pet. 2:4; Rev. 12:7–9). The Jewish apocalyptic work 1 Enoch is a major source for the former view. Rabbinic tradition viewed demons as spirits who were left bodiless when God rested on the Sabbath or as the builders of the Tower of Babel who were punished and transformed into demons. Origen developed the later concept of a precosmic rebellion. All intelligent creatures were created with a free will. Lucifer rebelled against God. In his descent to hell, he took fallen angels with him. These became demons. This has become the prevailing Christian view, although Scripture does not speak definitively about this.

The Greek terms *daimon* and *daimonion* originally held no inherently evil connotation. They were used to specify a god or a minor deity, a personal intermediary believed to exercise supervision over the cosmos. Hebrew usage is more consistent in its uses of *sedim* and *se'rim*. The practices of idolatry, magic, and witchcraft were related to demonic forces (Deut. 32:17; Ps. 96:5) and were specifically prohibited by God (Deut. 18:10–14; 1 Sam. 15:23). Demonic activity in the Old Testament is a force opposed to God and his own personal intermediary beings, the *mal'akim* (angels).

Major characteristics of the recording of Jesus' encounters with demons include: (1) a statement concerning the physical or mental affliction caused by the possession, such as nakedness, mental anguish, masochism, inability to speak, blindness, lunacy; (2) the demon recognized and feared Jesus as the Holy One of God; and (3) Jesus' power is demonstrated, usually by exorcism, through the power of his word, or by Jesus' permission for them to depart. This power is also found in Jesus' disciples and is promised to all believers (Mark 16:17).

The Middle Ages saw many abuses of exorcisms, including witch hunts. The Lutheran church first restricted and then abolished exorcism by 1600. Calvinists renounced the practice as applicable only for Jesus' day. Although the power and duration of Satan's work is limited, Christians still feel the power of his hatred for the things of God. No matter what we believe of the origin of Satan or his minions, we can believe without question in what Scripture teaches—that Christians must be prepared to combat demons (Eph. 6:10–18). We can also take heart when we remember that we belong to the kingdom of God and that these beings are destined to share in the destruction which God has prepared for Satan (Matt. 25:41).

VII. TEACHING OUTLINE

A. INTRODUCTION

1. Lead Story: Lights, Camera, Action!
2. Context: In the first chapter of Mark's Gospel, he declares, "The beginning of the gospel about Jesus Christ, the Son of God" (v. 1). Mark does not mince words. He is straight and to the point from the beginning of his Gospel. Chapter 1 sets the stage for an action-packed drama that is about to unfold through the service and sacrifice of Jesus Christ the Messiah. The prophets foretold his coming; John the Baptist prepared the people for his coming; the Father blessed his coming; the Holy Spirit empowered him when he came and strengthened him for his mission. After gathering his team, Jesus was ready to proclaim the good news through words backed up by deeds.
3. Transition: As we look at this chapter, we see the care and compassion of Jesus Christ. We see his "servant" attitude and how quickly he sought to bring help and healing to those in need. We see Jesus as a man of authority, action, and passion to fulfill his mission of preaching the good news of salvation.

B. COMMENTARY

1. The Prologue (1:1)
2. The Ministry of John the Baptist Prepares the Way for the Sacrificial Servant (1:2–8)
3. The Presentation and Preparation of the Sacrificial Servant (1:9–11)
    a. Jesus submits to John's baptism
    b. Jesus receives approval from his father
4. The Testing of the Sacrificial Servant (1:12–13)
5. The Ministry of the Sacrificial Servant Begins (1:14–15)
    a. John the Baptist is imprisoned
    b. Jesus begins preaching the good news
6. The Calling of the Servant's First Disciples (1:16–20)
7. The Sacrificial Servant Begins His Ministry of Service (1:21–28)
    a. Preaching in the synagogue
    b. Casting out demons
8. The Sacrificial Servant Continues His Ministry through Healing Miracles (1:29–45)
    a. Healing Peter's mother-in-law
    b. Healing and casting out demons

    c.   Time to reconnect
    d.   Preaching and casting out demons
    e.   Healing a leper

C. CONCLUSION: SPECIAL TO GOD

VIII. ISSUES FOR DISCUSSION

1. Why is waiting so difficult in our culture? Name a time in your past when God's timing was perfect.
2. Define temptation. Is temptation sin? If not, why not? What was Jesus' main weapon against temptation? Name some key verses you might find useful when tempted.
3. How did Jesus "renew" himself after an exhausting time (1:35–37)? Why does busyness lead to barrenness? If you have a day off, do you rest? Are you restless? Why or why not? When is the best time for you to renew yourself?
4. Name two things you are trusting God for, even though nothing seems to be happening. Thank him right now for his perfect timing.

Mark 2

The Lordship of Christ

"Christ says 'Give me All. I do not want so much of your time and so much of your money and so much of your work: I want You. I have not come to torment your natural self, but to kill it. . . . I will give you a new self instead. In fact, I will give you Myself: my own will shall become yours.'"

C. S. Lewis

Mark 2

 IN A NUTSHELL

In chapter 1, Mark introduced us to Jesus. Chapter 2 picks up where chapter 1 left off as Jesus is performing miracles in the midst of large crowds, including religious leaders.

The Lordship of Christ

I. INTRODUCTION

A Larger-than-Life Hero

I recently read the book *Braveheart* by Randall Wallace. I love the action and the love story and the transformation of the characters. One part in particular stands out. William Wallace had won several skirmishes in Scotland's fight for freedom. These battles had been in Scotland. People wanted to know what he planned next—they were as caught up in their own story as we are! William Wallace says, "I will invade England. And defeat the English on their own ground" (Wallace, *Braveheart,* p. 149).

Did you catch that? He would not sit around and wait for the battles to come to him. He went in search of battle. People thought he was crazy. He did it anyway. And eventually Scotland was freed from English tyranny.

When I read Mark's Gospel, I get caught up in the story in the same way. There is action, romance, and transformation. And there is a larger-than-life hero who invades enemy territory to free his people from tyranny. Chapter 1 introduced us to the hero, but I believe that chapter 2 is where the action really gets going. In fact, I think if anyone wanted a good idea of what Jesus' mission was on earth, Mark chapter 2 sums it up well.

II. COMMENTARY

The Lordship of Christ

MAIN IDEA: *Through Jesus' ministry in Capernaum and the resulting controversies with religious leaders, Jesus claimed authority over sin, sickness, relationships, religious orders and the Law.*

A Jesus Is Lord over Sin and Sickness (2:1–12)

SUPPORTING IDEA: *While caring for all the details of our lives, Jesus is also aware of our deepest need.*

2:1–2. As this chapter begins, Jesus had already performed several miracles. In chapter 1, the text says that the whole city had gathered at Peter's house to see Jesus and that Jesus could not publicly enter a city. Chapter 2 begins as a continuation of this theme. Jesus was speaking and the crowds were so large there was standing room only.

Capernaum was the home of Simon Peter. This city was Jesus' base of operations in his Galilean ministry. It was a large city on the northern shore of the Sea of Galilee.

2:3–4. The paralytic was being carried on a bed or a small couch, probably with a friend on each corner. Mark is a master of understatement in these verses. While Palestinian homes would have been accessible to someone wanting to get on the roof, it was by no means a daily occurrence. The houses were low, usually with an outside stairway to reach the roof. The roofs were tiled and covered with thatch. The four men had to drag the cot up the stairs, tear up the tiles, and dig through the thatch. The hole would have to be large enough to get the cot through. Add to this the annoyance of the people below. Debris would be falling on them as they tried to listen to the words of Jesus. A further complicating matter would be the damage to someone else's property. We have no idea how the owner of the house, whether it was Simon Peter or someone else, reacted to the destruction of his property, but we can imagine that it came as quite a shock!

2:5. When Jesus saw their faith. Whose faith did Jesus see? The text says "their faith." He certainly saw the faith of the four men who would not let any barrier stand in the way of their friend's need. But I believe that Jesus also saw the man's faith. It took courage to lie calmly while people were hauling you up a flight of stairs and then lowering you through a hole in the roof. But perhaps there was even more evidence than that.

A friend of mine once went through a stressful period. Her landlady decided to sell the townhouse my friend was renting. Her mother was diagnosed with breast cancer. Her husband who had already had one back surgery was facing another. She was in a job that had a lot of deadlines. Everything seemed to be coming up at once. She was not sure where God was. She put a note in the prayer request box at her church, asking for prayers. The woman who ran the Stephen Ministry program at her church called the next day and asked if she would like a counselor while she was going through this tough time.

My friend has trouble asking for help sometimes. Don't we all? Don't we all like people to think we have it together, that we do not need anyone? My friend did the right thing—she swallowed her pride and said okay; it would be helpful to have someone to talk to. I think this is what the man on the pallet did. By letting his friends take him to Jesus, he was admitting his need. Sometimes this takes a lot of faith.

Son, your sins are forgiven. In the Greek, the word here is literally "child." Jesus claimed first a special relationship with the man—a relationship of love and care. The second thing Jesus claimed was the ability to forgive his sins. While not all physical infirmity is the result of personal sin (John 9:3), it seems in this case that it was. Jesus looked past the physical disability and saw the man's deeper need.

Mark's Gospel is filled with miracles of healing and exorcisms. This is the only place where a person's sin is forgiven. Some may take it that Mark views forgiveness as a lesser priority than healing. However, when this is looked at in context—that Jesus was claiming authority to forgive as well as heal—Mark is attesting to Jesus' identity as God. Without this authority to forgive, the miracles of healing and exorcisms are not as significant. Prophets were often said to heal, but only God could forgive.

2:6–7. The scribes were the keepers of the law (compare 1:22). If anyone knew the import of Jesus' words, they did. And they were right. By claiming to forgive sins, Jesus was claiming equality with God. Unless he spoke the truth, he was speaking blasphemy.

2:8–11. Jesus knew what the scribes were thinking. The text does not say whether he knew through omniscience or human reasoning. But he knew. The question **which is easier** was a difficult question for them to answer. On the surface, simply to mutter the words was as easy in one case as in the other. But to accomplish the actions of either, both were equally difficult. Further complicating the matter was the authority that Jesus claimed. If Jesus could perform the bodily miracle, he was claiming authority to perform the spiritual one as well. In that case, the scribes had no other option than to worship him as God. And that was something they were not ready to do.

Then, proving that he cared for the entire man—body and spirit—Jesus healed him, telling him to pick up his mat and go home.

2:12. The man verified that Jesus did indeed have authority to forgive sins by walking out of the gathered assembly, his mat in hand. As in 1:22, Mark reports the people were **amazed.** They had never seen anything like this. Jesus' inherent authority stood in sharp contrast to the borrowed authority of the scribes.

B Jesus Is Lord over Relationships (2:13–17)

SUPPORTING IDEA: *When Jesus claims our lives, old relationships and old perceptions come under his authority as well.*

2:13–14. The tax office is literally a toll gate, probably on the road between Damascus and the Mediterranean Sea. Jesus saw Levi and commanded him to **follow me.** Levi immediately got up and followed Jesus. In following Jesus, Levi (Matthew) left behind a very profitable business. Tax collectors were some of the most hated people in Israel. In order to be a tax collector, a person had to purchase the rights for this business from Rome. Since Levi was in Galilee, he would have been an agent of Herod. He could then charge whatever tax he wanted in order to recoup the money he paid to Rome for his privilege license. Tax collectors were considered traitors and extortioners. They were not allowed to be witnesses or judges in court because they were considered untrustworthy. They were excommunicated from the synagogue. And yet Jesus came to Matthew and invited him into fellowship.

As Christians, it happened to all of us. We who were once enemies of Christ are brought into an intimate relationship with him. And suddenly, what happened to Levi happens to us: The person we could not stand becomes in the most literal sense a brother or sister in Christ. Levi, in becoming a disciple, became a brother to the very people he had taxed in the past.

2:15. Most scholars assume that the house they came to was Levi's house. Many believe this was a meal given by Levi for his business associates and friends to introduce them to Jesus. It is plain from the text that once again a large crowd gathered and Jesus offended the religious establishment.

2:16. When we think of Jesus eating a meal with sinners, we generally think of these people as perhaps other tax collectors, prostitutes, people of questionable moral character. For the Pharisees, however, sinners were anyone who did not follow their interpretation of Scripture. For instance, the Pharisees had rigid laws of cleanliness and washing. Anyone, therefore, who did not wash his or her hands before a meal was a sinner. We can imagine their shock when Jesus went to dinner with a friend of Rome.

2:17. Jesus was not saying here that the scribes were not sick. He stated that a person needs to realize his own sickness and sin first. Doctors' offices are not generally crammed with healthy people clamoring to see the doctor. It is only when they realize their sickness that they turn to the doctor. So it is with the sin-sick soul and the Lord Jesus. It is ironic that Jesus seemed to point back to the miracle at the beginning of chapter 2. The man admitted his need, as did his friends, for they desperately wanted their friend healed. Only the scribes admitted no need and therefore received no healing.

Ⓒ Jesus Is Lord over the Law (2:18–27)

SUPPORTING IDEA: *Jesus did not come to reform Judaism, but to revolutionize it.*

2:18–19. Fasting was another of the Pharisees' interpretations of the law that the common people ("sinners") did not follow. Jewish tradition demanded a fast once a year: on the day of Atonement. For the stricter Jews, however, fasting was practiced much more frequently. The Pharisees fasted twice a week, on Mondays and Thursdays. These were generally twelve-hour fasts, from sunup to sundown. The Pharisees also made sure that people knew how spiritual they were by showing everyone they were fasting (Matt. 6:16–18).

Some people asked Jesus why Jesus' disciples did not fast. We do not know if this was an honest question or an implied accusation of unrighteousness. In reply, Jesus used an analogy common to the time—the bridal party.

Since engagements were often long (in some cases years), the actual wedding was a time of feasting and great joy. William Barclay notes, "In a hard wrought life the wedding week was the happiest week in a man's life. . . . There was actually a rabbinic ruling which said, 'All in attendance on the bridegroom are relieved of all religious observances which would lessen their joy'" (Barclay, *Mark*, p. 59).

The wedding celebration also symbolized the age of salvation. This verse also serves as a messianic reference with Christ as the bridegroom. Jesus' joy reminds us of Hebrews 12:2, "Let us fix our eyes on Jesus, the author and perfecter of our faith, who for the joy set before him endured the cross." Our salvation in Christ is a joyous event, not an irksome duty.

2:20. This is the first indication in Mark that Jesus was fully aware of his mission. Jesus' prediction here introduces a somber note that has been missing up to now in Mark's account of miracles and controversies. It reminds us that joy and suffering are often two different sides of the same coin.

2:21–22. Again, Jesus used analogies that the Jews of that day would have been familiar with. In sewing, if a piece of **unshrunk cloth** was used to patch an old garment, the patch would shrink when it was washed, making a worse tear of the cloth. **New wine** needs to be put in flexible skins so the skin has room to expand as it ferments. If it is put into an old, brittle skin, it will burst the skin. Jesus was making the point that the new order and the old order (symbolized either by the Pharisees or John the Baptist) are incompatible. Jesus' claim is that something new is happening. Verse 18 brought up John the Baptist and his disciples, who taught the need for repentence because the kingdom of God was at hand.

Jesus claimed that something new was happening, something incompatible with even John the Baptist. It was a message of salvation; and this echoed Jesus' proclamation of his mission in Luke 4:18–19. In these verses, Jesus did not finish the Isaiah quote, but stopped it here: "To proclaim the year of the Lord's favor." Something new was happening—and old, brittle wineskins would not be able to contain it.

It is interesting to note that in each case something is destroyed. God does not just *mend* our hearts; he gives us brand new ones. "I will give you a new heart and put a new spirit in you; I will remove from you your heart of stone and give you a heart of flesh" (Ezek. 36:26). He gives us a new nature, and we are new creatures in Christ. To try to put this kind of life into old, legalistic systems is to destroy the new life.

This teaching anticipates Paul's teaching that Christianity is not an extension of Judaism. Judaism cannot contain it. Jewish laws are not binding upon Christians. Paul took up this topic with enthusiasm in Galatians. The old order regulated behavior with rules; the new order regulates by relationship.

Jesus did not come to reform Judaism, as the prophets before him had. He came to introduce a new entity, the church.

2:23–24. In a continuation of the preceding confrontation with the Pharisees, Mark introduces a controversy that was at the heart of Judaism—the Sabbath. On this particular Sabbath, Jesus and his disciples were picking off the heads of grain and rubbing them between their hands to get rid of the chaff to eat the grain. The Pharisees interpreted this as reaping, winnowing, threshing, and preparing a meal; thus, the disciples were classified as law breakers. The acts of picking and eating the grain were not unlawful in themselves. Fields were harvested in such a way that the corners were not harvested. These corners with standing stalks of grain could be eaten by anyone as long as they did not put a sickle to the grain (Deut. 23:25).

2:25–26. In response, Jesus referred to King David's actions in 1 Samuel 21:1–6. The Pharisees and scribes would have been familiar with this passage. But they did not understand its significance. Matthew picks up this same story in Matthew 12:7 and adds a comment by Jesus: "If you had known what these words mean, 'I desire mercy, not sacrifice,' you would not have condemned the innocent" (compare Luke 11:42). Jesus cut through the posturing and pretense of the Pharisees and exposed their hearts.

2:27–28. Eventually, as Jesus noted (Luke 11:46), the number of rules became a heavy burden. Instead of freeing a day for humanity to rest from its labors, the Pharisees made the Sabbath into a day of burdensome rule-keeping. With Jesus' final statement in this chapter, he declared his lordship over the law. His Sabbath controversies, however, did not end.

MAIN IDEA REVIEW: *Through Jesus' ministry in Capernaum and the resulting controversies with religious leaders, Jesus claimed authority over sin, sickness, relationships, religious orders, and the Law. Through his authority, he truly is Lord.*

III. CONCLUSION

Jesus Is Lord of All

In Mark 2, Jesus acts like a king as he enters enemy territory and declares his lordship. And yet we as his disciples need to look at the places his lordship took him. His lordship brought him into contact with sick, hurting, and sometimes hostile people.

Often when we think of a king, we think of a man sitting on a high and lofty throne, far removed from his people. Think of the royalty we have now. In 1996, Princess Diana was killed in a tragic car accident. Princess Diana's death brought home to many people just how distant royalty can be. Outrage was poured out upon the royal family by the "commoners" because of their lack of reaction to the death of the princess. In contrast to Princess Diana, who was warm and approachable, they seemed chilly, remote, immune to the sufferings of the people around them. Rightly or wrongly, this royal family fits our conception of what human royalty is.

This is not a picture, though, of Jesus' royalty. As we saw in chapter 1, Jesus' lordship is that of a servant. His lordship took him to the streets, to touch lepers and call tax collectors friends. As his followers, we can do no less (Matt. 10:24). Another woman was in the spotlight of public scrutiny during the week of Princess Diana's death. Mother Teresa, a nun serving in Calcutta, died. Like Mother Teresa, our enslavement to the Lord Jesus will take us to minister to the poorest of the poor, the sick and downtrodden, the outcasts, even if they happen to be the people who live next door.

PRINCIPLES

- Every person can be forgiven by Jesus if they will come to him and ask for his healing.
- Every believer becomes part of a new family with new relationships.
- Every believer is freed from the law in order to serve the Lord.

APPLICATIONS

- Do not be afraid to go to the God who loves you and wants to heal you. Repent of your sins and receive his healing with thankfulness.
- When church politics or arguments begin to choke off your relationship with others, remember that they are family squabbles and that Jesus has paid the ultimate price for them as well as for you.
- Biblical exegesis, disagreements, and doctrinal differences cannot separate brothers and sisters.
- Recognize that Jesus is your Lord even if you have not yet given him all areas of your life.
- Ask Jesus where his lordship will take you. Look for opportunities to emulate your master.

IV. LIFE APPLICATION

A Different Person

When I got married, I thought Nancy was the most wonderful woman in the world. I know she thought I was a great man! Nancy was, and still is, beautiful, funny, a delightful companion. I knew all that when I married her. Once we got married, though, Nancy turned into a different woman. She is grouchy when she does not get enough sleep (so am I), she does not always agree with me, and she likes to get her own way.

Through the years we have spent together, I have learned other things about her as well. Some of them are big things that we fight about, like money or individual temptations and sins. Some are little things, like tooth-paste tubes, or that she does not like my mother as much as I do. I found out that she expects me to communicate more than I want to sometimes, and that she does not want me to watch football all day Saturday and then all day Sunday as well (we will not even talk about Monday nights!). What happened to the Nancy I married?

The answer is obvious. She did not really turn into another woman. She was all of that before. So was I. Life has a way of revealing things about another person, even one very beloved, that was not known before. It can astound us and sometimes frighten us.

But a part of this process is the process of intimacy. I know Nancy more intimately than I know anyone else in the world. And I can be my most vulnerable when I am with her. It is because we are truly known.

"Now I know in part; then I shall know fully, even as I am fully known" (1 Cor. 13:12). The word *know* in this verse is the same word that is used when we read that Adam *knew* his wife. It is a word that suggests a deep and abiding intimacy, the most complete intimacy possible. Jesus knows us like that now. Eventually, we will know him fully as well. Part of knowing him will be knowing all aspects of him, even as my knowledge of Nancy became more complete.

There is a controversy in some Christian circles about whether Jesus is Savior *and* Lord, or whether he becomes Lord after someone has been a Christian for a while. The Gospel of Mark is only one place in the Bible where this is answered definitively. Jesus is Lord over all, all the time. Yes, at the cross he chose to submit to the authorities of the day. But note in the Gospels who is in charge. Matthew records Jesus as saying that he could call angels down to rescue him, if he desired (Matt. 26:53).

How do we reconcile the lordship of Christ with his servanthood? A person chooses to be a servant. It cannot be forced upon him. Jesus did not become a slave. Only one who is in a superior position can submit and choose a lower position. As Philippians states, because he humbled himself, eventually *everyone* will acknowledge Jesus as Lord. Every knee will bow to Jesus in submission and every tongue will declare that he is Lord (Phil. 2:10–11).

He is our Savior and he is our Lord. We owe him everything.

V. PRAYER

Jesus, help me to realize my deepest need of you. Help me to be like the paralytic and trust that you will heal me. I want to take every area of my life and turn it over to your lordship. Let my tongue be in your control. Let my mind stretch through the reading of your Word. Let my eyes look on good and pure things. Let my ears listen to your praises. Let my strength be used in service to you, the Servant of all. Amen.

VI. DEEPER DISCOVERIES

A. Sin (2:10)

Most of the time when we think of sin, we think of an act of wrongdoing. She *stole* something. He *cheated* on an exam. She *lied* to her boss. We keep the list of the Ten Commandments in front of us and judge ourselves by its code. Some denominations have even stricter ordinances, and sin is defined as breaking these laws: he played cards, she danced. In some denominations, some rules are unwritten: They went to an R-rated movie; they are not going to have children.

The Bible, however, goes much deeper than acts of wrongdoing or rule-stretching. In fact, these are secondary—symptoms of the much larger problem. We can call these symptoms "sins," but they need to be distinguished from "sin."

Sin (*hamartia*) is a break in our relationship with God. It is alienation from the One who created us. The first sin is recorded in Genesis 3 when Adam and Eve disbelieved God and trusted in Satan instead. This is the essence of all sin. We turn our backs on God and on his promises and we reach instead for the false hopes, pleasures, and dreams that Satan offers us. What we do not realize, what Adam and Eve did not realize, is that Satan has no power to offer us any of the things he promises. Our true happiness is in believing God's Word.

The Bible teaches that sin is universal (Rom. 3:23) and that the wages of sin is death (Rom. 6:23). The concepts of sin, holiness, and forgiveness are bound together. It is hard to get a good picture of one without the others. In brief, God's holiness cannot allow sin into his presence. No matter how small the sin may seem from the human perspective, it is intolerable from God's perspective. So how can Jesus forgive our sins? Forgiveness for sins requires the shedding of blood, and perfect forgiveness requires a perfect sacrifice. Jesus Christ was given to be that perfect sacrifice (Heb. 10). It is only through Christ that we have forgiveness for our sins.

Like the sky at dusk, our sin keeps getting darker and darker, driving us further from God, but we may not be aware of it because it seems so gradual. However, when we come in contact with God and his holiness, our sin is revealed for what it is. Peter encountered Christ and said, "Go away from me, Lord; I am a sinful man" (Luke 5:8). Christ's presence illuminates sin.

Sin is personal, but it can also be collective. Many of the Old Testament prophets spoke against the collective sins of the nation; and nations were judged for their sins (see Ezek. 16:49, Isa. 1:4).

Talk of sin makes people uncomfortable. We hear much about tolerance. This is not a bad thing in itself, but we cannot use it as a reason to excuse sin. We also hear much about the sinner being "sick" or "having a disease." While this may be true to an extent, and therapy may be a useful tool to aid these persons, it still does not address the main nature of sin, which is rebellion and a stubborn disbelief in God. This sin cannot be overcome by human effort or a good twelve-step program, although both have their place. There is only one cure for sin, and this is available through Jesus Christ, who took the penalty of our sin upon himself.

It is through Christ and his redemptive work that we can overcome sin. When we come to him, he places a new heart within us. Through the process of sanctification, we can begin to overcome sin. At our glorification, we will be freed from our sinful natures.

B. Forgiven (2:5)

Forgiveness is at the heart of Christ's mission and message. The Old Testament uses three Hebrew words to denote forgiveness: *kipper*, meaning "to cover"; *nasa*, "to bear or take away"; and *salah*, "to pardon." *Kipper* is familiar to most of us in the phrase, *Yom Kipper*, the day of atonement.

The Greek words in the New Testament are *apolyein*, "to put away"; *charizesthai*, "to forgive sins"; *aphesis*, "forgiveness, sending away, letting go"; and *paresis*, "putting aside or disregarding." *Paresis* is used only once in the New Testament (Rom. 3:25). *Charizesthai* is linked closely with *charis* meaning "grace" and is used particularly about God's graciousness in dealing with sinners. *Apolyein* is used many times in the New Testament but only once in regard to the forgiveness of sins. Most of the time, the word is used in regard to "putting away" one's wife. The most common word for forgiveness is *aphesis*.

This word carries the sense of sending away or letting go. When we forgive someone, we let them go; we release their obligation to us. When God forgives us, he is releasing us from an obligation for sin. It is clear in the Bible that the initiative for forgiveness is with God (Hos. 14:4; Eph. 4:32; Col. 2:13; Heb. 10:17). God stands ready to forgive, as seen in Jesus' parable of the prodigal son (Luke 15:11–32). His forgiveness is given freely and immediately.

No other religion teaches forgiveness in this way. Christianity is truly set apart from the other great religions which teach that forgiveness must be earned by good works or repeated lifetimes. The Bible teaches, however, that forgiveness comes only through the shedding of blood (Heb. 9:22). Our great God, through his infinite mercy, has provided the way for us. He offered Christ to be our sacrifice (Heb. 9:26; 10:5–10). He is truly Jehovah Jireh, the God who provides (Gen. 22:8).

C. Authority (2:10)

Authority means rightful power. It is the right of a ruler to do what he or she wishes and to command obedience of others. Although the English word is not used, the concept of rightful power in the Bible is given to God alone. He is the ultimate ruler over all the heavens and the earth, over all humanity. Because God is the Creator, he has rights over his creation. There are many verses in the Old Testament that point to God's authority. God says that he is the potter and he can do as he wishes with the clay (Jer. 18:6). It is clear that he is the supreme authority who grants authority to earthly rulers and can take it away (Dan. 4:28–37). All authority comes from God (Rom. 13:1).

Authority can either be inherent or it can be bestowed, as when God bestows authority on human rulers. When Jesus Christ claimed authority, he was claiming it as God's representative on earth. He claimed authority over his own life and death (John 10:18). When Jesus was asked by what authority he acted (Matt. 21:23–24), the questioners were asking who had bestowed on him the right to do and speak as he did. They were assuming that his authority was external and not inherent.

When Jesus speaks with authority, he is speaking with the words of God. His words demand a response to God's authority. He validates his words and his claim to God's authority through his miracles. In this way, Jesus shows that he has authority or rulership over sin, sickness, disease, and demons. He has authority to forgive all sins as no other human has because he is God.

By Christ's victory over sin and death in his death and resurrection, the usurped authority of Satan in broken (Col. 2:15; Heb. 2:14–15; 1 John 3:8). Jesus' final authority will be seen by all when he returns in glory and finally subdues all of God's enemies. Then, as the rightful king of all, every knee will bow and every tongue confess that he is Lord, with authority and power over all.

In Mark 3, we read that Jesus granted his authority to his followers to act in his behalf. They were given the authority to heal, to cast out demons, and to preach. They were, in fact, to act as prophets, priests, and kings in service to the prophet, priest and king.

D. Sabbath (2:23–27)

It is hard for Western Christians to grasp the implications of the Sabbath. We may think of it as "a day of rest," and therefore do not work on the Sabbath. The Jewish conception of "do not work," however, was much stricter. More rules surrounded the keeping of the Sabbath than any other commandment. In the mind of the Pharisees, they were commanded to keep the Sabbath holy (Exod. 20:8–11). Think about their position a moment. How would you keep this command? The commandment says that on the seventh day, do no work. You are a good Pharisee and you desire to keep this command with all your heart. How do you do it?

If I do not go to work on the Sabbath, is that enough? But what about working around the house? Okay, no house work. No preparing meals because, as any cook can tell you, preparing a meal is work. Untying a sash is not work because it is relaxing something. Tying something, however, is work and is forbidden. What about walking? That can certainly involve work. So do I not walk at all? Or when does walking become work? How far can I travel and have it not be considered work? The Sabbath laws, and the purity laws, encompassed every moment of life. If you were a good Pharisee, there was not a moment of your life that you did not question whether what you were doing was violating either the Sabbath or the laws of purity.

The Jews were even forbidden to defend their lives on the Sabbath. Barclay discusses the wars of the Maccabees and how the Syrians finally overcame them by attacking on the Sabbath because they were not willing to break Sabbath laws (Barclay, *Mark*, p. 67).

And so the laws became more and more minute as the Pharisees, with the very best of motives, tried to define work. The fences they set around the Sabbath became larger and larger, encompassing more and more, as they tried to make sure the Sabbath was not broken. While setting up minute rules ensured that they kept the Sabbath, the Pharisees also became expert at finding the loopholes in their own law. Legalism in this context loses sight of the holy and becomes a way to "get away with" whatever you can. As we will see in Mark 3, their legalism led them to plot murder while vowing to keep the Sabbath holy.

E. Pharisees (2:16,18,24)

Mark 2:16 is the first place in Mark's Gospel that mentions the Pharisees. Today, we as Christians know that the Pharisees are the "bad guys" in the story and so we miss some of the impact of Jesus' dealings with them. For a moment, let's try to shed our presuppositions and look at the Pharisees as the people in Jesus' time would have looked at them. Philip Yancey, in his popular book *The Jesus I Never Knew*, says that the Pharisees were the party of the middle class. They were neither separatists, like the Essenes, nor collaborators, like the

Sadducees, nor rebels, like the Zealots. They held tightly to standards of purity and the law. The word *Pharisee* comes from the Aramaic word *perisayya*, meaning "separated." They regarded themselves as separate from the Gentiles, the common people and non-Pharisaic Jews. They were cautious men who were dedicated to protecting their religion.

When Jesus came to town, the Pharisees stood on the edges of the crowd, watching, waiting to see what he would do, testing him because they were not sure they could trust him. And they could not trust him. The primary goal of the Pharisees was to maintain their religion. Jesus' presence upset the status quo as he tried to get men and women, the Pharisees included, to seek a richer relationship with God. The Pharisees were distinguished from the scribes, also enemies of Jesus. The scribes were a certain class of people. The Pharisees were from all walks of life. Some were political, but most were not.

As Christians, we will often run up against pharisaism. In Mark 2:16, the Pharisees were identifying Jesus with those whom he associated with. In other words, he was guilty by association. A friend of mine volunteered for a time at Colorado AIDS Project. While she was in training to work with the AIDS patients, she did odd jobs at the project. One night while she was stuffing envelopes with a group of other people, a stranger walked in. My friend's first thought was, "What if this person thinks I am gay?" That is the risk we take when we associate with those who are not like us. It is the risk Jesus took and did not refute.

Another place we may run into pharisaism is in our own hearts. It is very easy to let zeal for God turn into judgmentalism against others. We must be zealous in rooting this sin out of our hearts, even if it means letting God break our hardened hearts.

VII. TEACHING OUTLINE

A. INTRODUCTION

1. Lead Story: A Larger-than-Life Hero
2. Context: Following the introduction of Jesus in chapter 1, chapter 2 leads the reader to view Jesus as a conquering hero. In this chapter, he runs headlong into confrontations with the religious leaders, confrontations that will follow him until his death. In this chapter, he sets himself up as an authority greater than the Sabbath, greater than the law.
3. Transition: As William Wallace did not wait for battles to come to him, so Jesus does not wait for controversy to find him. In some instances, he seems to instigate conflict! He does this as a king might conquer enemy territory, declaring his lordship over all.

B. COMMENTARY

1. Jesus Is Lord over Sin and Sickness (2:1–12)
   a. A need is presented (2:1–4)
   b. A deeper need is met (2:5)
   c. The stirrings of controversy (2:6–7)
   d. Jesus claims authority (2:8–12)
2. Jesus Is Lord over Relationships (2:13–17)
   a. The call of Levi (2:13–14)
   b. Fellowship with sinners (2:15–17)
3. Jesus Is Lord over the Law (2:18–27)
   a. Fasting (2:18–22)
   b. The Sabbath (2:23–27)

C. CONCLUSION: JESUS IS LORD OF ALL

VIII. ISSUES FOR DISCUSSION

1. How hard is it for you to ask for help? Do you find it easy or difficult to ask for help from God?
2. Do you think the body of Christ is too divided? How can Jesus' lordship over relationships help promote unity in the body of Christ?
3. In what ways are you pharisaical? Where do you draw the line between holiness and forgiveness?
4. How has the Jesus as Lord/Jesus as Savior controversy affected you? What areas of life are you holding on to that Jesus wants you to turn over to him?
5. Where is Jesus' lordship taking you?

Mark 3

A New Community

"Christianity means community through Jesus Christ and in Jesus Christ. No Christian community is more or less than this. Whether it be a brief, single encounter or the daily fellowship of years, Christian community is only this. We belong to one another only through and in Jesus Christ."

Dietrich Bonhoeffer

Mark 3

 IN A NUTSHELL

Jesus' conflicts with the religious establishment continue. But in the midst of these conflicts are several episodes that show what a premium Jesus placed on the community he was creating.

A New Community

I. INTRODUCTION

Jesus and His New Family

*S*ome friends of mine were trying to have a baby. Something that seems so easy for most people was stumping my friends. No matter what they tried, they could not conceive. They discussed whether they should begin the series of expensive fertility tests and procedures, but they decided against it. They had seen this put severe strain on others' marriages and they did not want to do that. They decided to begin adoption proceedings and, to speed up the process, selected a baby girl from China.

You guessed it. When the adoption proceedings were well underway, the wife became pregnant. Instant four-person family. They will be travelling to China to pick up the girl immediately after giving birth to what they know is their boy.

While they feel almost overflowing with joy, there is still a lot of tension involved. Social workers have recommended that the wife leave her son and spend a couple of weeks bonding with the Chinese girl because, being older and being from another culture, she will need time with her new mother to adjust. And yet, how can she leave a newborn son? She has decided that she will just have to take her son with her and, problems or no problems, they will have to bond as a family.

Jesus teaches this in chapter 3 of Mark. He institutes a new family and gives these new relationships precedence over the natural family. And sometimes our new family members have bad breath. Sometimes they annoy us, perhaps even hurt us. There is no emotion that a natural family experiences that the Christian family does not: happiness, anger, joy, sadness, exhilaration, tension, irritation, amiability.

II. COMMENTARY

A New Community

MAIN IDEA: *In this chapter, Jesus tells us what is truly important. We see the heart of the Servant as he states what his priorities are and what ours should be: people over rules; intimacy over familiarity; God's family over earthly families.*

A The Priority of Humanity (3:1–6)

SUPPORTING IDEA: *In a continuation of the conflicts with religious authorities in chapter 2, this chapter begins with Jesus establishing human need over religious law.*

3:1–2. Mark's use of the phrase **another time** suggests that this is not chronological but topical. Before chapter breaks to the Bible were added, this verse would have properly followed 2:28, which states "the Son of Man is Lord even of the Sabbath." Indeed, this story further illustrates Jesus' proclamation.

A man with a shriveled hand was there. This seems a simple declaration, but Mark, who knew his audience's familiarity with Jewish custom, built tension here like a master storyteller. If we remember how Job was treated, we can get a little glimpse of the tension. If infirmity hits, it must be due to sin in a person's life. People who were disabled, handicapped, or ill, no matter the reason, were ostracized from the community. Remember, Job's friends were trying to get him to confess his sin and be healed. If he did so, he would be welcomed back into community. If not—well, he got what he deserved.

With Mark's statement that this diseased person was in the synagogue comes the question, What is he doing there? Verse 2 gives us the answer.

Some of them were looking for a reason to accuse Jesus. The man might have been there by coincidence, but some interpreters speculate he might have been a "plant" by the religious leaders. They were testing Jesus to see what he would do. Yes, he allowed his disciples to pick grain on the Sabbath, but would he really do work himself? Jesus himself had given them the answer to this in 2:27–28. But they wanted to see how far Jesus would go.

They watched him closely to see if he would heal him on the Sabbath. The context suggests that the Pharisees believed that Jesus could heal. They did not want to know if he *could*; they wanted to know if he *would*. It is sad when we use our religion as a weapon and ignore human need just to prove a point.

3:3. Jesus could have easily waited to heal the man rather than to heal him on the Sabbath. As noted before, this was not life-threatening. Jesus could have told the man, "Come see me tomorrow." Jesus, however, did not back down from confrontation. The man's plight and Jesus' compassion contrasted sharply with the Pharisees' law.

There were three interlocking reasons for having the man stand in front of everyone. First, by doing this, the man would be admitting his need. Before people can be helped, they must acknowledge that they need help. Second, this miracle would further authenticate Jesus' message. Third, Jesus wanted to give everyone the chance to see that human need takes precedence over religious law. Here stood a man whom most of them knew, whom they had shunned because of his deformity. Jesus was giving them a chance to see the man through the eyes of compassion.

3:4. The one being tested became the tester as Jesus asked the Pharisees to interpret the law for him. It was an impossible question for them to answer, however. Like the question in 2:9, it was meant to expose the listeners' hearts. If they answered what the question obviously demanded, they would have to admit to more than they were willing to admit at this point.

This comes down to the question of sins of commission and sins of omission. By refusing to do good to a person on the Sabbath, the Pharisees were committing sins of omission and, in fact, doing evil. Further, because they were keeping the Sabbath law, they were in a position to call their evil good. Jesus' question pointed to the Pharisees' actions. While he was about to "do good" on the Sabbath by improving a man's life (and most likely giving him back his occupation and livelihood), the Pharisees were "doing evil" by plotting against Jesus.

But they remained silent. The word used here is *esiopon*. It has the sense of a determined, continuing silence. This was not the silence of one who had nothing to say, but the rebellion of one who refused to be touched.

3:5. Jesus' reaction was one that all believers should echo in the face of injustice and hatred, anger and sorrow. "Jesus regards his opponents with an anger that expresses the anger of God. In their concern for legal detail they had forgotten the mercy and grace shown by God for his children when he made provision for the Sabbath. In the name of piety they had become insensitive both to the purposes of God and to the sufferings of humans. But Jesus was also 'grieved.' His anger was tempered by a godly sorrow for men who could no longer rejoice in the tokens of God's goodness to his creatures" (Augustine Stock, *The Method and Message of Mark,* p, 118). We often hear the proverb "Hate the sin, love the sinner." It is a fine line to walk without falling into error on either side, but one that we must walk as followers of Jesus.

The phrase **stubborn hearts** is *porosei tes kardias,* meaning "hardness of heart." The term *porosei* is a medical term describing the process of mending a bone. In using this phrase, we get the picture of a heart so calcified that it can't be softened. The only remedy would be to break it.

Hardness of heart is a sin of attitude. It is a settled disposition against God. It is the sin that says, "I've already made up my mind." This statement foreshadows Mark 3:29 and Jesus' discussion of the sin against the Holy Spirit.

3:6. This verse shows just how far the Pharisees would go to see Jesus killed. The Pharisees under normal circumstances were very careful not to associate with Gentiles or those whom they considered unclean. The Herodians were followers of Herod the Great. They not only had contact with the

Romans, but they also desired to maintain the status quo of Roman rule. Jesus was a threat to the status quo. As the Pharisees know, he was also a threat to their religious rule. "Politics makes strange bedfellows," someone has said. So does hatred, and nothing bonds enemies quicker than a common enemy. Embodying the proverb "My enemy's enemy is my friend," the Pharisees began plotting with the Herodians to have Jesus put to death.

Jesus placed a high value on meeting human need. When human need comes into conflict with rules, humanity must take priority. If we do not choose humanity in these cases, we become less human ourselves.

B The Priority of Intimacy (3:7–19)

SUPPORTING IDEA: *Jesus and the crowds are contrasted with Jesus and his disciples.*

3:7. Jesus, perhaps aware of the plot against his life, withdrew from the synagogue. It was not yet his time to be handed over for crucifixion, so he avoids the ultimate confrontation. But with his growing reputation, the crowds grew and they followed him.

3:8–10. His reputation had grown so far as to include Gentile regions. We can be certain that even if the religious authorities did not want to acknowledge Jesus' miracles, the common people were taking note. The crowds were getting so large that a boat was made ready for Jesus. Anyone who has been in a large crowd can appreciate the wisdom of this. To be the very center of a large crowd is a dangerous position indeed. The people followed him, but their devotion to him did not go beyond what he could do for them. They were seeking a miracle worker. This is a perception that every believer struggles with. Even some of his disciples thought of him as a tool to release the Jews from Roman rule.

3:11–12. Like the people, the demons recognized something about Jesus. There is some disagreement among scholars about what the demons recognized specifically. Some commentators believe that the demons knew who Jesus was and gave testimony to him as the Son of God in its fullest expression. Others believe the expression **Son of God** in this instance means simply one who is close to God. This would be similar to the apostle Paul calling Timothy "my son." But the reaction of the evil spirits to the person of Jesus is best explained by their knowledge of who Jesus was and what he represented for their kingdom.

Jesus did not want the demons to give testimony to who he was. At other places, Jesus commanded people to give testimony to his work (Mark 5:19). "In Scripture God has ordained that only those who have experienced divine grace shall witness or testify of Christ and his saving power. He does not employ either evil spirits or the unfallen ones (angels) as witnesses" (Vos, *Mark,* p. 33–34).

3:13–19. In this section, we see Jesus calling a community together. This came at a pivotal point in Jesus' ministry. He had confronted the religious powers several times. After the confrontation in Mark 3:1–6, a plot was being hatched against his life. Crowds were following him, and yet, these were not close friends. It was a lonely time, a dangerous time. Jesus called twelve men to be his special companions. To them he granted power to perform miracles in his name. He gave them the message of the kingdom of God. If something happened to him—and he knew it would—there would be a band to take his message to the world. Luke 6:12 informs us that before Jesus appointed the Twelve, he spent the night in prayer.

Simon (to whom he gave the name Peter). In all four listings of apostles, Peter is named first. Peter was anything but "rock-like" in the Gospels. But Peter became the rock of the church in Acts as his preaching won a multitude of converts to the new faith.

James son of Zebedee and his brother John (to them he gave the name Boanerges, which means Sons of Thunder). John was a follower of John the Baptist, the author of the Gospel that bears his name, three letters, and Revelation. Tradition also states that it was John who leaned on Jesus' breast at the Last Supper. He was called the "beloved disciple" in the Gospel of John. He is generally considered to have been a teenager when following Jesus. He was the only apostle who did not die a martyr's death. John, James, and Peter formed the inner circle of apostles among the Twelve.

Sons of Thunder may have been a description of the fiery temperaments of these men. They were the ones who wanted to call down fire from heaven to consume the Samaritans (Luke 9:54), perhaps in imitation of the Old Testament prophets.

Andrew was first a follower of John the Baptist, and he was Simon Peter's brother (John 1:41). He evangelized Peter, introducing him to Jesus. Andrew also had contact with the boy who had the five loaves of bread and two fish (John 6:8–9). Later in John's Gospel, some Greeks came to Andrew, asking to see Jesus (John 12:21–22). **Philip** was also an early evangelist. He immediately told his friend Nathaniel about Jesus.

Bartholomew is not listed anywhere outside the Gospels. Because of his association with Philip, most scholars believe that Nathaniel and Bartholomew were the same person. **Matthew** is the Levi whose calling was recorded in Mark 2:14. Although he is called "Levi son of Alphaeus" in 2:14, most likely he was not related to James son of Alphaeus.

Thomas is called "the twin" or is known as "doubting Thomas" because of his questioning of the other apostles about the resurrection of Jesus. Thomas, though, is also the apostle who was willing to die with Jesus (John

11:16). He may have contained a mixture of courage and cowardice, of unquestioning faith and reluctant reason. In other words, he was like most of us.

James son of Alphaeus. It is probable that this James is identical to "James, the younger" in Mark 15:40. His mother, Mary, was present at the cross, and she was one of the women who cared for Jesus' needs. While **Thaddaeus** is mentioned in Mark and Matthew, he is not mentioned in other lists. Instead, "Judas, son of James," or "Judas not Iscariot" is mentioned. These are probably the same man.

Simon the Zealot. The Zealots were religious extremists who desired the overthrow of Rome. They would use any means to accomplish this purpose. As noted by Barbieri, it was amazing that Simon the Zealot and Levi the tax collector were part of the same family of followers of Jesus. They were miles apart in their political convictions (Barbieri, *Mark,* p. 85). As a tax collector, Levi was accustomed to Roman rule and in fact profited from it while the Zealots wanted nothing to do with the Romans. This is further evidence that when Jesus is the blood that flows through the family, every other barrier can be overcome.

Judas Iscariot, who betrayed him. Iscariot, literally translated, means "man from Kerioth," a town in Judah, although Stock believes that it derived from *ish sakariot,* meaning the man in charge of payments. This would fit Judas's occupation as treasurer among the apostles (Stock, *Method and Message,* p. 125). He was the only apostle who was not from Galilee. Judas represents the one barrier that could not be overcome by Jesus—the heart determined to be unregenerate. This foreshadows Jesus' later discussion of the only sin that will not be forgiven.

The calling of the twelve apostles represents the great need people have for companionship. There were many people crowding around Jesus, begging him to touch them, to heal them. The twelve apostles were the companions whom Jesus could teach at a deeper level and, at times, even draw some measure of strength from them (Mark 14:32–42).

C The Supreme Sin (3:20–30)

> **SUPPORTING IDEA:** *Through a parable, Jesus tells the people about the nature of Satan and the nature of the most evil of sins.*

3:20–21. Again, the crowds gathered. Jesus and the disciples could not take time to eat because of the pressure and the need of the crowds. His family heard about this and came to take charge of him, believing him to be out of his mind. They had probably heard about the crowds as well as his confrontations with Pharisees and scribes. They were concerned for the family name—something Jesus apparently cared nothing about. They were concerned for his safety—something that did not seem to concern Jesus. His permitting the crowds to engulf him "seemed to them an unwarranted absorption in an entirely visionary work" (Gould, *International Critical Commentary,* p. 61). They had probably seen many "messiahs" come and go. They could see where all of this was heading, so they went to seize him and bring him home.

Families can be a source of joy and support. But families can be possessive and even vicious. While a stranger's words may be barbed, it is the family's barbs that are dipped in poison.

3:22. The religious authorities were no longer silent. They began to accuse. The Greek word used here is *elegon,* which uses the imperfect tense. It has the sense that they were *repeatedly* accusing him of being possessed. **Beelzebub** is the Greek form of the Hebrew word *Baal-Zebub,* meaning "lord of the flies." It is a play on words here. In Ekron, where Baal was worshiped (2 Kgs. 1:2), the word *Baal-Zebub* meant "exalted Baal" or "Baal the Prince." The Hebrews mockingly changed the sound of the word to mean "lord of nothing more than a bunch of flies." Other commentators note that the word is also close to *zebel,* which means "dung." The word had come to be synonymous with Satan. Unable to deny that Jesus was casting out demons, the teachers accused him of being possessed by the highest demon possible and casting them out through Satan's strength.

Exorcisms were not uncommon in ancient Israel. Why were the religious leaders so upset over Jesus' exorcisms? It is possible that Jesus was doing this on a larger scale than others had done. He certainly was drawing the crowds. But their hatred was also at least partially due to the reaction of the crowds to Jesus. He spoke with an authority they had never seen before.

3:23–26. As Barbieri notes, it was unusual for Jesus to defend himself (Barbieri, *Mark,* p. 89). But this was an exceptional accusation. The seriousness of it was pointed out by Jesus later as he pronounced it to be the sin beyond forgiveness.

He asked his accusers a logical question: **How can Satan cast out Satan?** He then used two familiar images to drive home his point—the kingdom or nation and house or family. If it were true regarding nations and houses, which they knew by their experience to be true, how could it not be true of Satan? If he was casting himself out, dividing himself, it would be suicide: **his end has come.** They could see, however, that Satan had not been defeated, that he was still active in their midst.

3:27. Jesus suggested that it took someone stronger than Satan to cast out Satan. By his actions, he was proving to them who that "someone stronger" was. His power and authority were freeing people from their enslavement to Satan and his demons.

3:28. I tell you the truth is a way to introduce a very serious topic. By this phrase Jesus was saying, "What comes next is of great importance, so pay attention." Jesus said that all sins and all blasphemies will be forgiven. This is a great promise, one that we as Christians can rest firmly upon. But, as is often the case in Scripture, this great promise is linked with a solemn warning.

3:29–30. The one sin that would not be forgiven, Jesus said, is blasphemy against the Holy Spirit. The scribes and Pharisees were guilty of **an eternal sin.** Through their superior knowledge and study of the Old Testament, the scribes, Pharisees, and religious leaders should have recognized Jesus. Rather than plotting to kill him, they should have been leading people to him. When faced with Jesus' love, compassion, and authority, they attributed them to Satan. "When a man so steels his heart against God's love, there can be no hope for him; for only to a broken and repentant heart can forgiveness come, and this is the way that he himself has consistently refused to take" (Cole, *Mark,* p. 78). Their sin was eternal because they would not accept the only remedy for their sin. Instead, they attribute God's work to the devil.

Ⅾ The Priority of God's Will (3:31–34)

SUPPORTING IDEA: *Those who do God's will are the true family, and they must take precedence even over our earthly family.*

3:31–32. While Jesus was discussing with the religious leaders whether he was related to Satan, Jesus' family arrived. Because of the press of the crowds, they could not get to Jesus. So they sent word to him inside that his **mother and brothers** were waiting for him.

3:33. Jesus had overthrown many conventions in this chapter, so why not one more? He asked a rhetorical question: **Who are my mother and my brothers?** While this may seem a harsh question, it was not meant to be. Jesus' aim was not to destroy family. Jesus loved and cared for his mother, even at his death (John 19:27). But family must be viewed in light of higher priorities. Jesus' life and mission revolved around the will of God. When Jesus asked, "Who are my family," he was stating that there are some matters and some relationships that transcend the normal blood relations known as "family."

3:34–35. Notice the phrase, **Then he looked at those seated in a circle around him.** The first thing to be noticed is Mark's literary usage of this phrase. It is a pause—a way to build tension and contrast. Notice also that those who were seated around Jesus were disciples. The place for a disciple is at the Master's feet. While the text does not state it in so many words, there is no doubt that the teachers of the law were not seated at his feet. Jesus' next proclamation was not for them.

Then, in words that seem to sweep across the page even as they sweep across all previous relationships, Jesus established a new priority in family. He stated that blood relationships are not enough, just as he declared in Matthew 3:9 that being a child of Abraham is not enough. His mothers and brothers are those who do the will of God—those who believe in Jesus and put their trust in him.

> **MAIN IDEA REVIEW:** *In this chapter, Jesus tells us what is truly important. We see the heart of the servant as he states what his priorities are and what ours should be: people over rules; intimacy over familiarity; God's family over earthly families.*

III. CONCLUSION

A Relationship Without Boundaries

Have you ever watched siblings when they are young? A couple of brothers might roll around on the ground, punching each other, and yelling. You would think they hated each other. But let anyone else try to join in the fight and everything changes! You will hear things like, "Don't talk like that to my brother," or "You leave my brother alone."

It was like that in my family. I could pick on my sisters and they certainly picked on me. But no one else could. After all, we were *family*. But it went further than blood. It was a relationship that crossed all boundaries. And I know that even now, if my family needed me for anything, I would not hesitate to cross physical boundaries to help.

When I became a Christian, though, other relationships supplanted my family relationships. Though I still dearly love my family, my Christian family is more important. We are knit together by something stronger than human blood: the blood of Jesus Christ.

I may not like some of the people in my new family. Some of them are the most irritating people I have ever known! But my life is bound up with theirs. I am to laugh when they laugh and mourn as they mourn. When they are persecuted for Jesus' sake, I should feel a sorrow as though it were my own brother being persecuted and wronged. I am to rise to their defense when I can. As Micah 6:8 says, I am to "act justly." This means that I work for justice for my brothers and sisters. I do what I can to relieve their suffering, just as Jesus did.

I may wish at times that these people were not in my family. There will always be people in this family whom I am closer to than others. Nevertheless, in the words of the popular song, "we are family."

PRINCIPLES

- When people are confronted with human need and suffering, an appeal to law will not win their hearts.
- While we can have many acquaintances, we need people who know us intimately.
- No matter who else in our family believes in Christ, we must claim this relationship for ourselves.

APPLICATIONS

- Try to look beyond people's sin to the hurting person underneath. While we cannot excuse or ignore sin, we can offer love and compassion to sinners. They may come closer to Christ because of our charity.
- If you do not have a close, intimate friendship with someone, pray that God will prepare one for you. Keep your eyes and your heart open.
- Examine your life for places where you put family, work, church, and amusements above Christ and his love. Ask for his forgiveness and strength to enable you to do his will.
- Submit your life and desires to Christ and allow his unfailing love to melt the hard spots in your heart.

IV. LIFE APPLICATION

A Changing Allegiance

The daughter of a friend of mine went to an Arab country to do some missionary work. My friend and his wife traveled to visit her and meet some of her friends. She met them at the airport and talked excitedly of the things she had learned and the people she had met.

Then she told them some very distressing news. Through the friendship of a woman there, she had decided that Christianity was false. She had converted to Islam. Although she appreciated the way her parents had raised her and loved her, this was a decision she had to make, and she knew they would understand.

But they did not understand. How could she throw away everything they had taught her? Through the night they prayed, pleaded with her, tried to show her the error of her thinking, and cried. But nothing changed her mind. She had given it too much thought. She had seen more clearly than she ever had before that Islam was true and Christianity was false. Although she loved them dearly and hoped they would continue loving her, she was now a Muslim.

Finally, her parents fell silent. There was nothing left to say; their hearts had been broken. Then their daughter told them the truth. She had not really converted to Islam. Her faith in Jesus Christ was just as strong as it had ever been. Her parents were shocked. Why, they wanted to know, had she done this to them? She told them that her friend had just converted to Christianity. "I wanted you to understand," she said, "what she and her family are going through."

As we saw beginning in Mark 2 and continuing in chapter 3, when we come to Jesus, when he claims our lives for his own, our relationships become his relationships. Our allegiance to family changes.

V. PRAYER

Jesus, when you drew me to yourself, you became my brother as well as my Lord. Rather than facing God as my rightful judge, I can now come to him as my heavenly Father. Thank you for your magnificent work in my life. Instill in me a love for my brothers and sisters in Christ and a delight in the privilege of worship with them. Amen.

VI. DEEPER DISCOVERIES

A. Anger (3:5)

We generally think of anger as a negative emotion. It is not pleasant to be around someone expressing this emotion. And yet, it is such a necessary emotion! There is something wrong with a person who never gets angry.

The word *anger* is used in the Old Testament most often about God. It is a reaction to those things that violate his holiness. True repentance turns away God's wrath. For those who do not read Scripture very often, it seems as if God is angry in the Old Testament, but not in the New Testament. Yet there are many places in the Old Testament where God yearns for his people Israel and speaks of them in tender terms (in Isaiah, for example). And in the New Testament Jesus often became angry. He was "indignant" when the disciples would not allow the children to be brought to him (Mark 10:14).

In chapter 3 of Mark, Jesus was angry with the hard-hearted synagogue leaders. Peter drew Jesus' wrath when he rebuked Jesus for viewing his Messiahship as one of suffering and death. In righteous anger, Jesus drove the moneychangers from God's house of worship. He called the religious leaders hypocrites and fools (see Mark 12:24–27; Matt. 23:13–36).

Laura Davis, who writes about sexual abuse, tells a story from her childhood. She recounts how at one time when she was a child there were many contractors around their house. There was one who tried to molest her. She told her mother. Her mother became furious. She went directly to the man and began hitting him with her broom. She ordered him from her house, and he was fired on the spot.

For Laura Davis, this was a defining moment (one which, sadly, a lot of victims do not have). Her mother's anger had been the means of her protection. She felt loved and safe. She felt important because her mother had taken this kind of action. This is a good example of righteous anger. Benny Hester, a popular Christian songwriter, has a song with the refrain, "Whoever touches you, touches the apple of my eye." God is angry when his children are mistreated, persecuted, and martyred.

While God created us with emotions, our emotions are fallen and our expressions of our anger can be sinful (Eph. 4:26,31). The answer, however, is not to suppress our emotions or pretend we do not have them. As D. G. Benner notes, this can also be sin because it violates what our emotions were given to us for (Benner, *Evangelical Dictionary of Theology*). All of our emotions are to lead us to action, to response. Joy leads to worshiping God and praising him for his goodness. Sorrow and compassion lead us to acts of mercy. Anger leads us to right wrongs. As with everything in our lives, we must put our emotions under the authority and lordship of Christ for him to use to his glory.

B. Apostles (3:13–19)

The Greek word for apostles is *apostolos,* which means "messenger" or more literally "one who is sent with the authority of another." It is closely related to the verb *apostellein,* "sent out," and it carries the connotation of being commissioned. Mark lists two reasons for the appointment: to be with Jesus and to be sent out. These twelve would be his close companions. Barclay notes: "It is significant that Christianity began with a group. The Christian faith is something that from the beginning had to be discovered and lived out in a fellowship. The essence of the way of the Pharisees was that it separated people from others. The name *Pharisee* means "the separated one." The essence of Christianity was that it bound people to others, and presented them with the task of living with each other and for each other" (Barclay, *Mark,* pp. 73–74).

After Christ's death and resurrection, the apostles were given the responsibility of preaching, teaching, and administration. There were two requirements for being an apostle: (1) Christ's teachings must have been received by the apostle firsthand, (2) the apostle must have been an eyewitness to his resurrection (Acts 1:22). Administration meant that they were primarily responsible for the life of the body and the distribution of funds (Acts 4:37). They were responsible for this until it became burdensome. Then they appointed others to take over this task. The apostles were the leaders of the early church. They were responsible for its discipline, healing, and conflict resolution.

Paul became an apostle through the direct appointment of Christ (Acts 26:16–18; 1 Cor. 9:1; Gal. 1:1). Never claiming to be one of the Twelve, he nevertheless was accepted by them as a true apostle. Paul viewed his commission as a call to service rather than an opportunity to lord it over others in the leadership position (1 Cor. 15:10).

The New Testament mentions other apostles, but it seems that these were apostles only in a limited sense or for a limited time. For instance, Barnabas was called an apostle in Acts 14:4, but was not regarded as an apostle in Acts 9:27. He may have been sent as an apostle by the Antioch church, but this was finished when his mission was complete (Acts 14:27).

C. Blasphemy against the Holy Spirit (3:28–29)

Of all the things that Christians worry about, this is one of the most common. Their question is usually, "What is this sin and how do I know I have not committed it?" I know of a man who in a moment of extreme pain cursed the Holy Spirit. Although this man has consulted with counselors and teachers, his life is still haunted by the belief that he cannot be forgiven. He is a sad specimen as he goes from counselor to counselor, teacher to teacher, pastor to pastor, looking for assurance that he is not beyond forgiveness.

In the Old Testament, blasphemy meant to insult, mock, or doubt God. Because it detracts from the glory of God, blasphemy is the exact opposite of praising and worshiping God. This sin was punishable by stoning. In the New Testament, the meaning was expanded to include blasphemy of persons. Human beings are made in the image of God and therefore should not be mocked. This sin, while very serious, is forgivable.

Blasphemy against the Holy Spirit, however, is treated differently. Jesus said that while every other sin will be forgiven, this sin will not. Jesus' solemnity demands that we take this sin seriously. It is listed in the other two Synoptic Gospels (Matt. 12:30–32; Luke 12:10). In all three Gospels, the saying comes in the context of the Beelzebub controversy. When the leaders attributed Jesus' works to Satan, they were rejecting his ministry and his very person as God incarnate. To reject Jesus is to reject forgiveness.

How are we to understand the "sin against the Son of Man" which may be forgiven? This can be taken to mean Jesus in his earthly life. As noted by G. M. Burger in The *Evangelical Dictionary of Theology,* it was a time of ambiguity even for the disciples. During this time, an unknowing criticism of Jesus as a man was pardonable. After Easter, however, this is no longer the case.

The verb in verses 29–30 is the imperfect tense, suggesting that the action is continual. "They were saying" refers to a repeated or habitual action. The unpardonable sin should not be viewed as one sin against the Holy Spirit. It does not refer to an act so much as it refers to a steady disposition against God. This is a continued hostility to God even after one has been exposed to the truth of God in Jesus Christ. "The sin is to recognize a supernatural power at work in Jesus and yet to call that power unclean or evil. The sin is unforgivable because it rejects the very agent of God's healing and forgiveness" (Gould, *International Critical Commentary*, p. 68).

C. S. Lewis said that there were two types of men, those who said to God "Thy will be done," and those to whom God in the end says, "*Thy* will be done." There is nothing so frightening as a man having his wish granted when his wish is for God to leave him alone. This is the sin beyond forgiveness.

Someone once said, "If you are worried about it, you have not done it." The unforgivable sin rules out a troubled conscience. People who have not received the forgiveness of Jesus do not worry about it. On the other hand, everyone who seeks will find. As noted in verse 28, for those who seek, nothing is beyond God's grace. Forgiveness is there for the asking. Jesus never turns down anyone who asks from a repentant heart for forgiveness.

VII. TEACHING OUTLINE

A. INTRODUCTION

1. Lead Story: Jesus and His New Family
2. Context: As the conflicts with the religious community continues, Jesus appoints twelve apostles. These twelve will be with him and learn from him in a way that his natural family cannot.
3. Transition: Jesus begins instituting a new family and tells what this means for his followers. Through this chapter, we see what Jesus considers of prime importance.

B. COMMENTARY

1. The Priority of Humanity (3:1–6)
2. The Priority of Intimacy (3:7–19)
   a. The crowds follow Jesus (3:7–12)
   b. The twelve disciples are appointed (3:13–19)
3. The Supreme Sin (3:20–30)
   a. The accusation of the leaders (3:20–22)
   b. Jesus' response in a parable (3:23–27)
   c. A severe warning (3:28–30)
4. The Priority of God's Will (3:31–34)

C. CONCLUSION: A CHANGING ALLEGIANCE

VIII. ISSUES FOR DISCUSSION

1. Who are the "undesirables" today? How should Christians respond or reach out to those who have been labeled as outcasts?
2. What are the areas of your life that you would like Jesus to touch, to heal?
3. What do you find most difficult about being in a new family?
4. Discuss the differences between the twelve apostles and the larger group of Jesus' followers. What similarities do you see? How does this relate to your life?

Mark 4

Are You Listening?

Quote

"*W*eavers' fingers flying on the loom,

Patterns shift too fast to be discerned

All these years of thinking

ended up like this

In front of all this beauty

Understanding nothing."

B r u c e   C o c k b u r n

Mark 4

IN A NUTSHELL

*T*hrough the use of parables, Jesus tells the crowds what the kingdom of God is like. He explains them in further detail to his disciples. But everyone is admonished, "He who has ears to hear, let him hear."

Are You Listening?

I. INTRODUCTION

Hearing and Understanding

A man consulted a doctor and told him that his wife was going deaf. "I ask her what we are having for dinner and she doesn't answer."

"Bring her in," the doctor said. "I'll examine her."

So the man brought his wife in. The doctor had her stand fifty feet away. He said to the man, "Go ahead and ask her what's for dinner."

"Hey, honey," he said, "what's for dinner?"

Next, the doctor had the woman stand forty feet away.

"Hey, honey," the man said, "I said, what's for dinner?"

After going through this routine several times, the doctor finally had her stand five feet away.

"Hey, honey," the man said, "for the sixth time, I said, what's for dinner?"

The wife looked at the doctor and then back at her husband. "And for the sixth time, I said, spaghetti!"

This man thought his wife had a hearing problem, but he was the one with the problem. Sometimes we can be so sure of ourselves, so sure of something that we are hearing or not hearing, that the real message does not get through. That's why in conflict resolution, it is important for the person listening to repeat back what he thought he heard. Conflicts often happen because of misunderstandings.

But hearing involves more than the ears. It also involves an act of the will. Real hearing involves taking action. In this chapter, Jesus tells his disciples about the kingdom of God. He wants them to understand as well as to hear physically but to take action when necessary.

II. COMMENTARY

Are You Listening?

> **MAIN IDEA:** *Through parables, Jesus tells his disciples what the kingdom of God is like. Through these parables, the disciples are to examine their own lives and bring them into conformity with the standards in the parables.*

Ⓐ Listen! The Key to the Parables (4:1–9)

SUPPORTING IDEA: *Jesus introduces the teaching method known as parables, the first of which is the parable of the sower.*

4:1. Surrounded as usual by the crowds, Jesus taught from a boat while the people listened from the shore of the lake. This would allow a greater number of people to see and hear. He sat in the boat. Teachers traditionally sat when they taught.

4:2. The word *parable* literally means "to throw alongside." Thus, a parable is an extended metaphor comparing a spiritual truth with something from the listeners' everyday world. The phrasing here means that Jesus' speaking in parables was a repeated action, something that took place on more than just this occasion.

4:3. The word **Listen!** introduces the rest of the parables in the chapter. It invites the listeners to participate, drawing them into the story. It arrests people, stops whatever other conversations are going on. It says, "Pay attention because this is important."

This first parable is the key to the other parables. It does not describe the kingdom of God as the other parables do. Rather, it describes the condition of the hearers. As with all parables, but this one especially, the key is not to ask, "What does this one thing signify?" but "What does this mean for me? Where am I in this parable?" This first parable also followed directly on the heels of the religious leaders' misunderstanding of the person of Jesus. Jesus was describing their spiritual condition. He set the scene by referring to something his hearers were familiar with: a farmer sowing seed.

4:4. Sowing during this time period was done by hand rather than machine. Therefore, it is easy to see how some seed would end up on the path. There was nothing there for the seed to grow in, so the seed remained on the path until the birds ate it up.

4:5–6. Nothing would grow on rocks. So it was important for farmers to remove the rocks from their fields before planting. No matter how diligent a farmer was, however, it would be almost impossible to get them all out. Seeds scattered on the rock would spring up quickly in the shallow soil that covered the rock. However, when the sun scorched the seedlings, they would die because they did not have a root system.

4:7. Some of the seed was scattered among thorns and weeds. Again, these seed grew because of the life of the seed, but they yielded no harvest.

4:8. Good soil produces good crops with an abundant return. This is truly a sign of the kingdom of God. There will be a glorious return on the scattered seed, a literal filling of the storehouses of heaven.

4:9. Because this parable describes the hearers, Jesus gave it this special ending. This ending sets the tone for the entire chapter. Everything that follows must be seen in the light of this verse. While this verse is only listed once in this chapter, each parable has the feeling of the words of the verse. It is a phrase that seems to be echoed throughout the entire New Testament. This verse calls for the hearers to evaluate their own response. What does Jesus mean by the parable? And if they know, the next question becomes, What kind of soil am I for the word of God?

B A Parable Explained (4:10–20)

SUPPORTING IDEA: *Jesus provides a key to understanding the parables, thereby inviting listeners to examine their own hearts and to respond to his message.*

4:10–11. As soon as the disciples got Jesus alone, they asked him why he was teaching in parables and what this particular parable meant. Jesus acknowledged that the mysteries of his kingdom were being revealed to them and not to everyone. The disciples were privileged to hear Jesus interpret this parable. This was not because of their superior spiritual state, but because the Lord Jesus had chosen them.

For every parable there are two levels of understanding: the physical and the spiritual. Everyone received the parable at the physical level, but the disciples were granted understanding at the spiritual level. The disciples—and this now includes us as believers—had been chosen, as were the chosen people of God in the Old Testament. We have been given a sacred responsibility.

4:12. The outsiders Jesus referred to are probably the religious leaders who accused him of acting by the power of Beelzebub. They would not understand; they would not hear. Barbieri notes, "The parables themselves became judgmental, for although the instruction was parabolic the truth had been communicated" (Barbieri, *Mark,* p. 99). They were responsible for the truth they had heard and rejected.

Some interpreters have questioned the authenticity of these words of Jesus because they sound particularly harsh as though Jesus did not want his unbelieving hearers to be forgiven. The controversy exists because of the Hebrew word *hina* in Isaiah 6:9–10 which is translated in Mark as **so that.** Some commentators believe the correct translation should be "as a result." This would make Jesus' words descriptive of a condition rather than prescriptive.

The theme of secrecy runs throughout Mark's Gospel, and it is no different here. Parables, which typically revealed truth, are shown in this context to conceal it. Is this a contradiction? No, because parables are more than illustrations; they are also spiritual tests. They hide the truth from those who do not seek truth, but they reveal truth to those who seek it.

4:13. Jesus' question was a gentle rebuke to the disciples. If they did not understand this parable, the key to all parables, how would they understand the rest of them?

4:14. The **word** that the sower sowed may be understood in two ways. It may be the word of God that Jesus had been preaching. This was the message of John the Baptist: Repent for the kingdom of God is at hand. *Word,* however, may also refer to the person of Jesus. The word sown would therefore be the people's response to Jesus: would they accept him or not? At this very moment, Jesus was sowing the word. He was preaching to the people. His miracles had preached to them. What kind of soil would they prove to be? Note that there are really only two types of soils—productive and nonproductive. But Jesus gave three examples of the nonproductive type.

4:15. The word of God never makes an impact on **some people**. It rests on the hardened soil of their hearts until Satan comes and snatches it away. These are the people who will never even think to question their response to the gospel.

4:16–17. The seed sown on rocky soil is like those who hear the word and accept it gladly. Their faith seems to shoot up overnight, and they have great joy in the Lord. Some of Jesus' audience may have been in this category. These are the people who followed Jesus from place to place and longed to have him heal them or feed them.

But Jesus' teaching eventually became too demanding for them (compare John 6:66), and they turned away. There was not much moisture in their soil. When the going got tough, they got going. Persecution, trouble, or even hard teaching shriveled the word until it became as nothing in their hearts.

Some people might think that this means Christians can lose their salvation. The parable, however, does not teach this. The parable actually encourages those who will be sowing the word in the future. Jesus was saying that we are to sow without looking at the results. Sometimes the results will be snatched way and sometimes the results will be shriveled because of circumstances. But at other times, our efforts will mesh with God's divine activity and a rich harvest will result.

4:18–19. The seed sown among weeds at first grew and looked like a healthy plant. But worldly things choked the life out of this hearer. Worries represent a lack of faith—unbelief in the One who said not to worry because God would take care of us. Wealth gives people a sense of self-sufficiency and little need of God. We are to ask God for our daily bread and live in the knowledge of his mercies which are "new every morning." Wealthy people do not need to live hour to hour because they believe their needs are taken care of. Likewise, their desire for the things of this world crowd out the things of the heavenly world. Jesus declared that we cannot serve two masters. The soil or wealthy hearer in this parable had chosen what master it would serve.

4:20. Others hear the word and act upon it. They produce fruit by increasing numbers. God will take what we give him and produce a bountiful crop from it. The average yield of a crop is seven and one-half times more than the seed that were sown. The huge numbers reported here—thirty, sixty, or even one hundred times what was sown—show that the harvest provided by the Lord is miraculously abundant.

The harvest is typically symbolic of divine activity, and here we have the key to the parable. The parable encourages Christians who have not fallen away, those who remain at Christ's side—then as well as now. While we may get discouraged that our evangelistic efforts are not producing the fruit we would like, we can be encouraged that God is working in the harvest and that it will be a rich harvest. The emphasis in the parable is not on the soils but on the harvest. In spite of failures, setbacks, and even persecution, there will be an abundant harvest for those who remain faithful to God.

C A Description of Responsibility (4:21–25)

> **SUPPORTING IDEA:** *Jesus warns his disciples through parables that people are responsible for the truth they receive.*

4:21–23. Most interpreters take these verses as individual parables with no connection to what has gone before or what comes after. Barclay notes that these verses are all repeated in Matthew but not in one unit.

Cole gives an interesting interpretation (*Mark,* p. 93) which focuses attention on the literary context of Mark's Gospel. Cole believes the preceding parable must have troubled the disciples as it has troubled modern readers. Can the soil change? Does this passage teach a double predestination where God has damned certain souls to certain soils? Does Jesus' teaching in parables deliberately keep certain people from understanding the truth?

These parables would be obscure for those who failed to seek the truth in them. For those who will not accept Jesus Christ, there is no understanding of spiritual things. The passage does not teach that each person is predestined to a certain soil. Jesus is reminding us that we are sowing seeds and spreading light to a dark and difficult world. We are not in a country club where each person has his or her own opinion and nice people do not argue about them. No, we are in a war, a spiritual battle, against evil. God guarantees that though some people will be destroyed in the battle, God will win.

Jesus' words here declare that a person is responsible for the light or knowledge he or she has received. One does not take a lamp and hide it. Therefore, a person does not take the truth and deliberately obscure it. If that is true of humans, it is even more so with God. But whatever is hidden will be revealed. In fact, the disciples found things they did not understand revealed fully with the coming of the Holy Spirit at Pentecost.

Stock notes that Mark uses a definite article before the word "lamp," so it should be translated "the lamp" rather than "a lamp." The literal phrasing of the verse is, "The lamp does not come." If this is true, Jesus is the lamp, the light of the world (Stock, *Mark*, p. 150). Jesus is the light that is hidden from some eyes because they refuse to see, but he will be revealed in glory to all: to the disciples in their lifetimes and to the Pharisees at the final judgment.

4:24–25. Notice the phrase, **Consider carefully what you hear.** "Hear" in the Bible also carries the meaning of "act upon." Jesus was telling us to pay attention to what we hear and beware how we act upon it. These verses came after Jesus' confrontation with the religious leaders when they accused him of acting by Satan's power.

Maybe you have heard the story about two men, one a baker and the other a butcher. Rather than charging each other, they would trade their goods to each other. But the butcher became angry because the pound of flour he was given for his pound of meat always came up short of a pound. He confronted the baker. The baker told him, "I don't have a measurement on my scale, but a balance, so I always used your pound of meat on one side of the balance." His point was clear. The butcher had been trying to cheat him by giving him less meat, but he did not want the same standard of measurement used against him!

What measure were the religious leaders using? If they were using the Law, then the Law would become their judge, because the Law pointed to Jesus Christ. If we use the truth we have received to condemn others instead of attracting others to Jesus, this measure will be used upon us. To those who use the truth they have been given appropriately, more will be given. As with the good soil, their crop will increase to a hundredfold. But to those who oppose the truth—and the Pharisees must be counted in this condemnation—whatever they have will be taken away. Their love of the Law will disintegrate, and they will be left in darkness.

D Two Kingdom Parables (4:26–34)

SUPPORTING IDEA: *Jesus describes what the kingdom of God is like.*

4:26–28. This parable and the next expanded the parable of the sower while serving as parables in themselves. They expanded the parable of the sower by describing what the good soil was like and what it would be in the final days. The kingdom of God will come in its fullness when God reigns over the earth: "Your will be done on earth as it is in heaven" (Matt. 6:10). Like the parable of the sower, this parable also encourages those who will be sowing God's word. God works even when our work is done.

The point of this parable is the passivity of the person who scatters and the power of God in acting apart from any human contribution. The sower scatters and then it is out of his hands. He does not even understand the process that the grain takes. The verbs **sleeps** and **gets up** denote activity that is repeated continuously, signifying a long process.

4:29. This verse can be viewed in an eschatological sense. Many people expected Jesus to overcome Roman rule and establish his kingdom on earth. This verse highlights that when the time is right, when the harvest has come, then the sickle will be put to the grain in the harvest. We can be assured that growth is taking place by God's good grace and that his harvest will eventually come to fruition.

4:30–32. This verse also describes what the reign of God is like. The mustard seed was the smallest of all the seeds in Palestine. But the Jews recognized that even from this small seed a large plant—large enough to give shade to a man—could grow. Such is the beginning of the church. It had its small beginnings in a band of fishermen. But like the mustard seed, it will grow until birds can take shelter in its branches.

In parts of the Old Testament, birds represented messengers of Satan. This has led some interpreters to speculate that this is a negative parable. Some think that this parable represents the lost mission of the church. The church was intended to be an itinerant movement. By becoming institutionalized (becoming rooted), the bush grew large and acted like a tree. Therefore, some interpreters think this parable warns against church growth.

The actual text, however, does not bear out this kind of interpretation. The bush is seen as giving good things to others. The text speaks of what God can do with small beginnings. It is an assurance of harvest. The birds of the air may represent different nations (see Ezek. 17:23; 31; Dan. 4:12). Perhaps Jesus was telling the disciples to get ready—that many different people would become a part of his kingdom. The parable may be interpreted as a reference to worldwide mission and growth.

4:33–34. These verses conclude the parabolic section by repeating that Jesus told many parables and explained them to his disciples. This drew a distinction between Jesus' followers and those who refused to hear and understand.

⑤ Jesus Validates His Claims (4:35–41)

SUPPORTING IDEA: *In order to validate the truths he has just spoken, Jesus performs four miracles that demonstrate his lordship.*

4:35–37. After the time of teaching, the disciples got into the boat that Jesus had been teaching from and headed to the other side of Lake Galilee. Mark's Gospel is the only one that mentions that other boats were with them. Of these, Cole says, "It thus becomes a miracle of mercy on a wider scale than the mere salvation of the Lord's own boatload of frightened disciples. We might perhaps compare the closing words of Jonah, 'and also much cattle' (iv. 11), with its undertone of the infinite mercy of God" (Cole, *Mark,* p. 96). While Jesus was concerned with his disciples, he was also concerned with people beyond the narrow context of his disciples. This mention of other boats in verse 36 shows that God's grace extends to the entire world, that his grace falls on the just and unjust, that it rains (or in this case does not rain) on everyone.

While they were out on the boat, a squall blew up. Mountains surround the Sea of Galilee. Violent storms, rising without warning, are very common. In this particular storm, the waves were so strong they were breaking over the bow of the boat.

4:38. Jesus was sleeping on a cushion. He was not bothered by the storm. There is no doubt that he was physically exhausted, but more than this is probably communicated in this event. Because of Jesus' words to the disciples about their lack of faith, it is clear that Jesus was sleeping because of his faith. He was not worried about the storm but was resting in God. The disciples, however, interpreted Jesus' faith as lack of concern for them. They awakened him and rebuked him for his unconcern.

4:39. Jesus, the Creator of the universe, told the wind to stop—and it did. How could they not obey the One who had created them? Jesus' command to the wind to be quiet was the same command he issued to a demon in Mark 1:25. This may mean that there was a demonic element in the storm. Whether there was or was not, the result was the same. The noise of the wind and the water and the shouts of the disciples suddenly stopped. The calm must have been as peaceful as Jesus' rest had been.

4:40–41. Jesus rebuked the disciples because of their lack of faith. He had told them to go to the other side of the lake. Did they not believe that he had the power to see them safely across the water?

They were terrified. The words are literally, "They feared a great fear." Some translations read that the disciples were "filled with awe." A moment before they had feared for their lives, and now they had been delivered by One who was stronger than the waves.

MAIN IDEA REVIEW: *Through parables, Jesus tells his disciples what the kingdom of God is like. Through these parables, the disciples are to examine their own lives and bring them into conformity with the standards in the parables.*

III. CONCLUSION

Obedience Is the Point

Henri Nouwen says, "When we learn to listen, our lives become obedient lives." He points out that we get our word for *obedience* from a word akin to the Latin word *audire,* which means "listening."

The act of hearing, of listening, is inextricably entwined with action. For instance, a mother may tell her child to clean her room. The child may hear. However, if an hour later her room is still not clean, the mother will wonder whether her daughter really heard her. And she will not be happy with the response, "Yes, I heard you." She will not question the daughter's hearing ability, but her obedience.

Mark portrays Jesus as the suffering servant. We see in Jesus his humble obedience to the will of God—a continual submission of his own will to that of the Father. Because Jesus is our teacher, our Master, our Savior, we owe him the same type of obedience. But first we must learn to listen.

PRINCIPLES

- Good soil will produce a good crop.
- The hidden things of God will eventually, in the fullness of time (Gal. 4:4), be revealed.
- Christian growth is a process involving time and spiritual nurture.
- Christians sow the seeds of the gospel, but God is responsible for the growth.

APPLICATIONS

- Because God is responsible for the growth of the gospel, be bold in your testimony and witness for Christ.
- Turn a discerning, critical eye upon yourself, first and foremost.
- Examine your "root system." Feed yourself through Scripture and prayer so that in times of drought your roots will go deep into the soil.
- Cultivate a time of listening to God.

IV. LIFE APPLICATION

Our Master's Voice

The Rocky Mountains in Colorado are beautiful, but they can sometimes be deadly. People will sometimes wander off from their party, thinking they know where they are going, and then they cannot find their way back. Mountains and valleys look remarkably similar to other mountains and valleys. When someone gets lost in the mountains, search-and-rescue teams are pulled together to cover the area. It is particularly harrowing when the missing person is a child.

A woman was frantic when she discovered her daughter was missing in the Rocky Mountains. She thrashed through the woods, screaming her daughter's name. She went back to the campsite and called for help. Within half an hour, a search team had been organized. It began sweeping the area, calling out at regular intervals for the little girl.

The woman sat down on a rock for a moment to rest. How would she ever find her little girl? The beauty of the mountains surrounded her, and yet she was blind to it all. Birds sang, but all she could hear was the volunteer search team pounding through the woods, calling to her daughter and to one another. Suddenly she decided that she and the other searchers were making so much noise that they could not hear the girl if she was yelling or crying.

She relayed this information to the others and in moments everyone was silent, standing quietly. The woman listened. Nothing. She listened harder. Every pore of her body, every fiber, every muscle strained to hear the one voice she would recognize above all others. Then she heard her little girl calling for her. By carefully listening and following the sound of her voice, the woman was reunited with her daughter.

God is speaking to us, trying to get our attention, trying to tell us of his love. Most of the time we are making too much noise to hear him. We fill our lives with physical noise—television, radio, and movies. Or, we fill them with psychic noise—work, too many "leisurely" activities, too much busyness. We thrash through the woods of our lives, encompassed in darkness and despair.

And yet God calls us to listen. When we "come . . . to a quiet place" (Mark 6:31), we prepare ourselves to hear. When we rest from the busyness and turn off the noise, we enter into a holy place. Be like that mother whose daughter was lost and yearn to hear God's voice. Delight in his voice. When you hear his voice, act on what he tells you. It may not be a command like "leave everything and go to a country that I will show you." It may not be, "Give away everything to the poor." Perhaps God just wants to tell you that he loves you. While we cannot be sure that everything in our "quiet times" is from God, we can be assured that God is waiting for us to shut off our noise long enough to enjoy him.

V. PRAYER

God, I want to hear your voice. I want to hear what you have to say to me. You gave me breath and you sustain me by your mighty power. You alone are worthy of my attention. And now, I give over my noise to you. I want to listen to you.. (Spend the next few minutes listening like that mother did for the voice of God.) Amen.

VI. DEEPER DISCOVERIES

A. Parables

The word *parable* is made up of two Greek words, *para* meaning "alongside," and *ballo* meaning "to throw." The literal meaning of the word is "to throw alongside." The parable acts as an extended metaphor. It uses a familiar truth to illustrate or illuminate God's truth.

Sometimes the best way to get people's attention is to tell them a story. C. S. Lewis once talked about his own fiction in this way. He said that he could write about doctrine and teach philosophy, but only certain people would get his meaning. Some would get his meaning but be unaffected by it. Others would ignore what he had to say. But by telling them a story, the message would slip past the "watchful dragons" of reason and philosophy and get to the emotions that we often try to hide.

The parables are just such stories. They slip past the justifications that people make for their unbelief. But more than that, they call for a response. They get people involved in the story and demand that they make a judgment, not only on the people in the stories but on themselves. For instance, in the well-known parable of the prodigal son, the people listening knew exactly what Jesus was talking about. There were no hidden meanings. Jesus was setting up the listeners. They knew the younger son had acted despicably. They were waiting for him to be punished by the father.

Instead, the father ran down the road, taking on his son's humiliation, and then offered him a feast and a full welcome back into the family. Then the older son acted despicably toward the father. Again, the listeners were waiting for the rebuke from the father. But the father's speech was full of compassion and love. It ended with a question. Jesus used this device so the listeners would put themselves into the story and answer the question. The question was meant for them. It led them to examine their own hearts and answer the question.

A similar technique is found in the parable of the good Samaritan. Again, there was nothing hidden in this parable. Those who lived at that time and knew the culture knew exactly what Jesus was talking about. The bad guys in the story were the religious leaders. But that was okay, because Jesus was talking to common people. So they fully expected the good guy to be a commoner like them. Again, Jesus had set them up. Instead of giving them what they expected, Jesus turned the tables. The good guy in the story was a hated

Samaritan. Jesus made his point again by using a question at the end of the parable.

This is the beauty of parables. They cause people to think for themselves. As Barclay notes, "Truth has always a double impact when it is a personal discovery. . . . He presented them with truth which, if they would make the right effort in the right frame of mind, they could discover for themselves, and therefore possess it in a way that made it really and truly theirs" (Barclay, *Mark*, p. 87).

B. Word

In the New Testament, *word* refers to the word of God. It is the saving message of Jesus Christ. This can be embodied in three ways.

First, this is the word that is spoken of in Acts 6:7, where the "word of God spread" or in Acts 4:31, when the disciples spoke the word of God "boldly." It is also called the "word of truth" in Colossians 1:5. This is the gospel that we preach today. It is the gospel or good news of Christ's redeeming work on the cross and our subsequent relationship with God as our Father. Until Scripture was recorded, the word of God was the oral preaching or oral tradition of telling God's acts and commandments to the world.

Second, the word of God is the Word in holy Scripture. Paul refers to Scripture as "God-breathed" in 2 Timothy 3:16. Jesus referred to the Scripture of the Old Testament in John 10:35 when he stated that the word of God could not be broken. Throughout the history of the church, early and late, orthodox believers have believed that the written word in the Bible is the Word of God. Augustine stated, "What is the Bible else but a letter of God Almighty addressed to his creatures, in which letter we hear the voice of God, and behold the heart of our Heavenly Father?"

Third, *word* is used of Jesus Christ. John speaks of him as the *logos* of God. He is not just the word of the Lord; he is *the Word*. The prophets spoke of the word of the Lord. They uttered God's words to the people. Jesus Christ, though, embodies the message. He is himself the message. While God revealed something of himself through the words he gave to the prophets, his self-revelation in the person of Christ was total. As Christ said to Philip, "Anyone who has seen me has seen the Father" (John 14:9). The revelation of God was complete in Jesus.

This is an important distinction, one that other religions do not have. Allah has his messenger in Mohammed. Buddha is a messenger. Only Christianity says that the message is the Messenger. God became incarnate. He entered human history and walked among us as a man.

In these parables, where the seed is sown, we can interpret word of God to mean all three of these definitions. The good news is scattered on the soil either through preaching or through reading the Scriptures. The seed that is scattered is the *Logos* of God, Jesus Christ.

C. Faith

In the Greek language, the word for faith is *pisteuo,* and this noun corresponds to the verb "believe." This is the term used most often to denote trust in God. The word is used in a broad variety of ways. James used this word to describe intellectual assent (2:24–26) and noted that this type of faith is inadequate. Paul used it in Galatians 1:23 and 1 Timothy 4:1 to denote a body of truths believed, "the faith." Jesus used the word for an exercise of trust that works miracles.

In the Old Testament, faith meant to rest, trust, and hope in God. Faith was an unswerving trust in God to save his people from their enemies. Faith also implied that what God had promised would come to pass. In the New Testament, faith is not divided from the person of Christ. This is another place where Christianity departs from other religions. Other religions encourage their believers to have faith in God. Only Jesus Christ says, have faith in *me.*

Faith in Christ (believing in, coming to, and receiving him) involves acknowledging him as God incarnate (John 20:28). His death on the cross is the sole means of our atonement and salvation. His resurrection secured eternal life for us (John 5:24; 17:3). It is this set of beliefs through which we receive eternal life. While some people may think that faith automatically means "blind faith," it is illogical to think of it this way. We take things into consideration, we reason, we look at alternatives. We do not place our faith blindly, but we place it in the things that deserve our faith.

For example, let's assume you take an elevator every day to the eleventh floor of your office building. You have faith that the elevator will indeed take you to the eleventh floor and not the twelfth and that it will not go crashing down to the basement. If, however, you go to work tomorrow and there is a sign on the door saying "out of order," your faith is placed in something different: the sign. If the sign remains there for a week, you may begin to question the reality of the sign. Did maintenance put it there or did someone place it there as a prank? You begin an investigation. You act, then, on the results of your investigation.

There are many competing truth claims in today's culture. The pervasive feeling is that "whatever is good for you is okay but don't push it on me." Some people worship Jesus, some believe that Jesus is a great spiritual Master who can teach all of us to become spiritual masters, some do not believe in him at all. Others follow Buddha or some form of Buddhism, Hinduism, and its westernized New Age beliefs. The Bible does not ask us to follow Christ blindly. Even Thomas was invited to check the evidence.

So we look at the evidence. We look at Christ's claims for himself. What did he say? Further, what did he do? Did the miracles prove that he was who he said he was? What kind of historical basis can we find for the crucifixion? What about the resurrection? When all the evidence is in, it is clear that Christianity is the religion that best fits the evidence and best fits how we as humans live. It is this God in whom we place our faith.

But faith does not end when we accept Christ. We also need faith to continue to grow in sanctification. How does a search for evidence help here? We search to find what kind of God we are serving. If my investigation leads me to a God who does not care, does not show compassion, does not take care of the birds and the lilies of the field, then perhaps this God is not trustworthy. However, in Scripture we find a God who cared so much that he sent Christ. We find a God who heals outcasts. We find a God who weeps over the unrepentant. We find a God who feeds the hungry with a few pieces of bread and fish. If this is the kind of God we serve, we can trust him to calm the storms or go through them with us.

VII. TEACHING OUTLINE

A. INTRODUCTION

1. Lead Story: Hearing and Understanding
2. Context: Jesus' teaching style is shown in this chapter as he teaches his disciples through parables. Several parables are put together as topical rather than chronological to teach what the kingdom of God is like.
3. Transition: Remember the joke about the man who thought his wife was deaf while it was he who had the hearing problem? Often our perceptions of what God is saying need to be modified. We can hear but we often fail to obey. Obedience is hearing in the truest sense of the word.

B. COMMENTARY

1. Listen! The Key to All the Parables (4:1–9)
2. A Parable Explained (4:10–20)
   a. The secret is given to the apostles (4:10–12)
   b. The parable is explained (4:13–20)
3. A Description of Responsibility (4:21–25)
   a. The lamp (4:21–23)
   b. The measure (4:24–25)
4. Two Kingdom Parables (4:26–34)
   a. The seed grows (4:26–29)

     b.   The mustard seed (4:30–32)

     c.   Epilogue (4:33–34)

5. Jesus Validates His Claims (4:35–41)

     a.   The first miracle (4:35–41)

     b.   The other validating miracles are in Mark 5

C. CONCLUSION: OUR MASTER'S VOICE

VIII. ISSUES FOR DISCUSSION

1. Of the three "bad" soils, which is most a problem for you? How can you become transformed?
2. Compare Mark 4:24 with Matthew 7:1–5. Is Jesus asking people not to be judgmental? How does this compare with the gift of discernment?
3. What kind of faith is Jesus asking the disciples to have in verse 40? Why is fear the enemy of faith?
4. If hearing involves obedience, what do you hear God asking you to do as you read through this chapter?

Mark 5

The Transfiguration of the Outcasts

Quote

"The miracles in fact are a retelling in small letters of the very same story which is written across the whole world in letters too large for some of us to see."

C. S. Lewis

Mark 5

IN A NUTSHELL

Through his contact with three outcasts, Jesus demonstrates true compassion while teaching us what to think about the physical human body.

The Transfiguration
of the Outcasts

I. INTRODUCTION

Fooled by Illusions

I will never forget the first time I saw a mirage. My family was driving down the street on a hot summer day. I was in the back seat, not paying much attention to anyone in the car, just kind of daydreaming and looking out the window. Then up ahead I saw a body of water across the road. I thought it was strange because it was hot outside and there were no clouds in the sky. It did not look like it had rained and gathered into a puddle. And it was so clear! I could see the reflection of the trees in the water.

I asked my mom about it and she told me it was a mirage caused by the heat, the sunshine, and the rocks on the road. I was amazed! I could not believe how something that looked so real was not there in reality.

Some illusionists go to great lengths to make your eyes think they see something that is not really there, or they make you think that something that is really there has disappeared. Some religions unknowingly do the same. The belief has been around for a long time that human beings are nothing more than spirits trapped by physical bodies—kind of like the genie in Aladdin's lamp. The Bible, however, teaches that God created the spirit and the body. Jesus Christ was incarnated in human flesh. But perhaps, some might say, the body is less important than the spirit. Let's see what Mark 5 has to say about our physical bodies.

II. COMMENTARY

The Transfiguration of the Outcasts

MAIN IDEA: *Jesus' compassion is evident in his treatment of three outcasts.*

A Jesus Restores a Man's Mind by Casting Out a Demon (5:1–20)

> **SUPPORTING IDEA:** *When Jesus encountered a man whose body and mind were being tormented by demons, he acted out of compassion to heal the man.*

5:1. If this story does indeed follow chapter 4, then it must have been late in the evening or night. The apostles had struck out across the Sea of Galilee and had encountered Jesus, whom they thought was a ghost. Then when they landed, they came to a place of tombs and caves, where they encountered a demon-possessed man. They were in the land of the Gerasenes, an area inhabited mainly by Gentiles.

5:2–5. The man who approached Jesus had been suffering a long time as evidenced by the many "treatments" given him by the townspeople. He had often been bound with chains, but they could not restrain him. He was violent, and according to the account in Matthew 8, no one could pass safely along the road where he lived.

Mark painted a picture of a man in a pitiable state. He could not live with his family, so he lived alone (or with another demon-possessed person, according to Matthew) in a graveyard. He was strong enough to break the chains that bound him, but not strong enough to expel the demons from his body. His shrieking was heard throughout the countryside. He was even violent toward himself and cut himself with stones. He was naked and most likely covered with scars. Even after the Fall, the image of God, the *imago dei*, resided in humans. Demons, in this case and others, did what they could to destroy the image of God.

5:6–8. When the man saw Jesus, he **fell on his knees in front of him**. Literally, he worshiped him. This was an acknowledgment that someone greater than him was in his presence (compare Phil. 2:10). The demon knew that it must relinquish its hold on the man in the presence of God: "The reason the Son of God appeared was to destroy the devil's work" (1 John 3:8).

An interesting note in the NIV states that the phrase **What do you want with me?** carries the sense of "Mind your own business." With this phrase and the following encounter, we see a wrestling match going on over one man's soul. The demon may or may not have known all the implications of the title Son of the Most High God. It was surely an acknowledgment of sovereignty. Lane suggests that this may have been an attempt to gain control over Jesus (Lane, *Mark,* pp. 183–184). People in the first century believed that to know someone's name was in a sense to control him.

The demon tried to bind Jesus with a vow, **Swear to God that you won't torture me!** The phrase **for Jesus had said to him** gives the impression that Jesus had already spoken to the man. It is possible that Jesus, upon departing from the boat, immediately assessed the situation of the man and commanded the demon to leave. This could have caused the man to rush toward the boat and bow before Jesus.

5:9–10. Jesus commanded the demon to identify itself. Cole suggests that this was not for the demon's sake but for the man's and those gathered around. Confession releases shame and enables healing to happen. Cole states that "in the Bible, *name* stands for 'nature': so the man was virtually asked to confess the nature of the powers of evil by which he was enslaved. His reply is not only a confession of human impotence, but a vivid expression of the might and destructive force of the demonic powers by which he was gripped" (Cole, *Mark*, p. 98).

The word **legion** may have differing meanings. Stock, following Jeremias, believes that the word should be translated "soldier" because the demons were a great host and were waging war upon the man. Other interpreters believe this means that a legion of demons inhabited the man. Because more than one demon can inhabit a person (see Mark 16:9; Luke 11:26), this is probably the meaning here—many demons, with one demon who spoke for the entire group of evil spirits.

A legion consists of six thousand soldiers. This may not have been the number of demons in this one man, but it was clear that an army of demons had taken possession of him. They continued to beg Jesus not to send them back to the abyss (Luke 8:31; cf. Rev. 9:1–12), perhaps sensing that the battle had been lost.

5:11–13. The demons begged to be allowed to enter a herd of pigs that were feeding nearby. No one knows for sure why Jesus allowed this, but conjectures are plenty. The demons may have asked because pigs were considered unclean animals and Jesus was more likely to grant their request. Demons did great violence upon leaving a person. Perhaps Jesus allowed this so the violence was done to the pigs and not to the man. Jesus could have allowed the demons to enter the pigs to let those watching—including the man—know for sure that the demons were gone and that the man was healed. With this visible proof, he would now be accepted back into community by his fellow citizens. Or, perhaps Jesus wanted to show that the demons wanted nothing less than the complete destruction of anyone they inhabited. It may have been all or a combination of these reasons. In any case, the pigs ran down the bank into the lake and drowned.

One thing in this passage is clear and should not be overlooked in concern for the pigs. The demons had to ask permission of Jesus before they could enter the pigs. Again, Jesus was their superior and they knew it.

5:14–17. The people tending the pigs were not the owners, but they must have known how the owners were going to react to the loss of two thousand pigs. An even larger crowd gathered, and they were greeted by an astonishing sight. This man was now calm, dressed, and rational. Stock mentions the man now being clothed and notes how clothing lends identity to a person (Stock, *Mark,* p. 168). For example, in the parable of the good Samaritan, those who passed by the man could not tell who he was because he was naked. He might have been a Gentile. There was no way to know since he had been stripped of his clothes by the thieves. Clothing also lends dignity. During Jesus' passion, they stripped his clothes off as a way of mocking him and taking away his dignity.

Now this man, whom they knew as a raging maniac, was clothed and sitting with Jesus. It was an astounding sight and an even more astounding tale they heard about Jesus. Afraid, they asked Jesus to leave the region. Were they more concerned for their financial loss than for the restoration of the man? Or were they fearful of the great power exhibited by Jesus? In either case, Jesus gave them what they wanted and departed.

5:18–20. But the man knew the wonderful gift that he had received. He begged Jesus to take him with him. Jesus denied his request. Why? He left the man there as a witness to the region as well as a constant reminder of his judgment against them if they refused his gift. Jesus told the man to return to his family and tell everyone what God had done for him. The man did so. In his mind, God and Jesus were equal. This realization comes only through the Holy Spirit (1 Cor. 12:3). Note this was a situation where Jesus did not tell the healed person to remain silent. Perhaps he did so because this was a Gentile region where messianic expectations did not exist among the people.

B A Religious Leader Seeks Jesus (5:21–24)

SUPPORTING IDEA: *Jairus pleads with Jesus to save his daughter.*

5:21. Jesus and his disciples crossed back across Lake Galilee, probably returning to Capernaum, Jesus' base of ministry. Note the contrast between two different shores of the lake. Crowds were gathered on both shores. One group urged Jesus to leave, while the other welcomed him.

5:22–24. Jairus was a synagogue ruler. This was a respected and honored position in the community. He did not serve as a priest, but it was his responsibility to take care of the administrative details of the synagogue. This included making arrangements for public worship and inviting visitors to teach. Despite his high position, Jairus cast his dignity aside and bowed at the feet of Jesus. His twelve-year-old daughter was dying. Note Jairus's description of her as his **little daughter.** A twelve-year-old is not "little." However, this shows how precious she was to him. Jairus knew that if Jesus would come and touch his daughter, she would live. Jesus needed no convincing. He went with Jairus, and the crowds followed.

A Small Subplot (5:25–34)

SUPPORTING IDEA: *While on his mission of mercy for Jairus, Jesus had time to heal and speak kind words to an outcast.*

5:25. A woman was in the crowd that followed Jesus. Mark states that she had been subject to bleeding for twelve years. It is not clear what her bleeding was. Some suggest a uterine discharge. Others suggest that this was not a continual bleeding but excessive bleeding that had continued off and on for twelve years. She probably suffered from physical exhaustion as well and possibly pain. An even greater source of pain would have been the interruption of daily social activity because of her disease. Anyone coming in contact with her would be made ceremonially unclean (Lev. 15:25–30). She herself was unclean and would not be allowed to participate in communal feasts and sacrifices. She was just as much an outcast as the demon-possessed man had been.

5:26. Adding to the woman's physical disorder was her financial distress. For twelve years she had made the round of doctors, and none of them could help her. Many of the cures listed in the Talmud and probably tried on her—such as carrying the ashes of an ostrich egg in a cloth—would seem like superstitious magic to us. She did not get better but only grew worse.

5:27–29. This woman had heard about Jesus, and she acted upon what she had heard. She desired to touch his clothes, believing that this would heal her. Some interpreters believe this was an act of humility on her part—that she did not want to disturb Jesus on his mission. Some compare her to the centurion (Matt. 8:8), who asked Jesus to give the word of command so his servant would be healed. Others see this as a demonstration of the belief that a holy person's clothes carried power.

Barbieri has the right interpretation (*Mark*, p. 124). This woman was an outcast. Because of her condition, she would not have been allowed to approach Jesus. To talk to him would be unthinkable. So she approached him in the only way she could—secretly. And it was enough. At once, she was freed from her distress.

5:30. This question has puzzled many people. Did Jesus not know who touched him? Doesn't he know everything? Why did power go out from him when it did not go out from the apostles when they healed in the Book of Acts? There are some things that Jesus did not know, such as the day and hour of his return. Some interpreters feel that Jesus did know who touched him, but he did not want her to remain anonymous. Faith always requires confession. This would allow him to restore her to community as well.

5:31–32. The disciples were astounded that Jesus even asked such a question. The Lord, however, would not be deterred.

5:33. Under the ceremonial law of the Jews, this woman was considered unclean. She had made Jesus unclean by touching him. It was no wonder that she came to him trembling with fear. Like Jairus and the demon-possessed man, though, she knew her place was at his feet.

5:34. The first thing we note in this verse is that Jesus called her **daughter,** a word used only in this passage in the New Testament. He claimed the same special relationship with her that Jairus had with his little daughter—infinitely precious, unbearably sorrowful at the thought of loss. She had come to him as an outcast, fearful of rebuke because of her status. Instead, she had found not only physical healing but spiritual healing as well.

Your faith has healed you. Not magic or superstition, but faith in the person of Jesus had healed her. The word for "healed" is the same as the word for "saved," indicating the physical and spiritual aspects of her healing. **Go in peace**. Only now could she go in peace—a bodily peace from which all traces of disease had been removed and a spiritual peace in which all hostilities with God had been removed through the work of Christ.

We learn something, as well, from what is not said in this section. Jesus did not rebuke the woman for touching him. As with the Sabbath laws, Jesus was giving the Jews a message about his kingdom. As Stock notes, "The story subtly shatters the legal purity system and its restrictive social conditioning" (Stock, *Mark*, p. 172). If Jesus is Lord of the Sabbath, then he is Lord of the purity laws as well.

Ⓓ Raising the Dead (5:35–43)

SUPPORTING IDEA: *Jesus comes into contact with another outcast, and he proves to those who may have doubted that the material body is of great worth.*

5:35–36. We now return to Jairus and his daughter. Even while Jesus was speaking to the woman he had just healed, men came up to Jairus and told him his daughter had died. What must have gone through this synagogue ruler's mind? Shock, sorrow, maybe even bitterness that this woman had been healed at the same time that his own daughter had died.

Jesus, who knew what he was about to do, comforted and encouraged Jairus. He told him to **just believe.** The Greek *monon pisteue* denotes continued action. Jesus was asking Jairus for more than a single act of belief. He was telling him to have a continuous, steady, ongoing faith—a "no-matter-what" type of faith, the type all Christians are called to exhibit.

5:37. Jesus took with him the inner circle of the twelve apostles to see Jairus's daughter. These three—Peter, John, and James—are also mentioned at the Transfiguration and in Gethsemane. These were important events that revealed something of Jesus' nature.

5:38. When Jesus arrived upon the scene, the professional mourners were already there. Mourning customs among the Jews included wailers, flute players, the rending of clothes, and the tearing of hair. Even the poorest person was required to hire at least one mourner and two flute players. Since Jairus was a synagogue ruler, there were probably several of these mourners on the scene when Jesus arrived.

5:39. The word **asleep** can sometimes mean "dead." Jesus used the same word of Lazarus in John 11. We often speak euphemistically of death as "sleep," "resting," or "passing on." These words point to a deeper spiritual meaning—that death is not permanent. Jesus, however, in his statement to those gathered, was clearly saying that the girl was asleep.

5:40. The mourners' laughter at this point seems out of place. If they were truly grieving and expressing concern for the family, we would expect them to be angry or outraged over the hurt being done to the family. But they laughed. It was the laugh of unbelief, and this unbelief kept them from witnessing Jesus' great miracle. He ordered them all out of the house. Jesus never performed for the unbelieving crowds. The only ones who would witness this miracle were three of his disciples, Jairus, and Jairus's wife.

5:41. In another blow to the purity laws, Jesus took the dead girl's hand. He was not concerned with ritual defilement. As Cole notes, Jesus is purity himself (Cole, *Mark,* p. 105). He is the source of holiness. With his touch, all that defiles is gone. *Talitha koum* ("child arise"). Mark's Gospel is the only one that uses these Aramaic words. This is probably because this account of Jesus' miracle came directly to Mark from the apostle Peter. Peter was impressed with Jesus' tenderness, his lack of concern about the purity laws, and his power.

5:42–43. Jesus, who had already proved his authority over disease and demons, now proved his authority over death. Immediately, the girl's life was restored. Jesus told those gathered not to tell anyone. He was again in Jewish territory where his messiahship could be easily misconstrued and misunderstood. He told the girl's parents to give her something to eat. Jesus is concerned about the physical dimension of our lives.

MAIN IDEA REVIEW: *Jesus' compassion is evident in his treatment of three outcasts.*

III. CONCLUSION

The Physical Body Does Matter

The Gnostics believed that the God of the Old Testament was evil because he created matter. Jesus Christ was good because he taught people how to transcend matter. Death released spirits from the prisons of their bodies. Some cults believe the same thing today. There is no such thing as matter, they say. There is no sickness. We must give priority to mind over matter. If you just believe that you are well, you will be well. Some of the more extreme charismatic denominations believe the same thing. The mind, or spirit, is supreme.

But Jesus taught that the whole of our existence, spirit and body, is valuable and real. Paul declared that we are a temple of the Holy Spirit. And the Bible teaches that our bodies, not just our souls, will be resurrected. While it is true that Jesus' resurrected body could walk through walls, it could also be touched and could take in food. Our bodies are important to God.

PRINCIPLES

- The human body and spirit are linked; God created both.
- When we admit our need to God, he forgives and heals us.
- Our relationship to Christ must not be secret. No matter the cost or the risk, we must acknowledge Jesus.
- For Christians, death is a passage to joy.

APPLICATIONS

- Use different body postures when praying and see how it affects your prayers. For example, lift your hands in worship, kneel or prostrate yourself when confessing sin.
- Take care of your body because it is the temple of the Holy Spirit (1 Cor. 3:16–17).
- Be willing to give your schedule to God when opportunities for ministry present themselves.

IV. LIFE APPLICATION

Myths about the Body

The young woman I was counseling was bright and energetic. Smiling the entire time we talked, she could only be described as bubbly. I would not have been surprised to learn that she had been a cheerleader. She seemed the type with her lilting voice, bouncy step, and perky manner.

The problem was that she would not stop smiling while she told me story after horrific story about her childhood. I wanted to cry, and yet she smiled. I wanted to weep when she told me the things she would do to her own body in order to feel something. It had started with just pummeling her body with her fists and scratching herself with her nails. But that was not enough.

Eventually, she took razor blades and cut herself repeatedly around her breasts, her stomach, her thighs—all the places that people could not see.

This woman had disassociated herself from her body. She did not think of her body in any terms relative to her, unless she hurt herself. This is what the Bible teaches we should not do. Our bodies are good because they were created by God.

Of course, some people fall into the opposite extreme—thinking that nothing but the body exists. To them, there is no such thing as spirit. These people do not consider the despair that this belief brings. Instead, they make the most of the life they have. "You only go around once, so go for all the gusto you can," they say. "Eat, drink and be merry for tomorrow you shall die," is the way the Bible puts it. If life ends with the grave, why not party hardy? Why not work out at the health club until your rock-hard muscles gleam with sweat?

We can fall into two errors regarding the body. We can either ignore it or we can worship it. To do either is to sin. God created our bodies for our use and for his glorification. We must not ignore the messages our bodies give us, including the need to worship God with our bodies. But worship belongs to God alone, so we dedicate our bodies to his service. Because we are more than a physical body, we work to relieve the physical suffering of others as well as lead them to life in Christ.

V. PRAYER

Lord, thank you for creating my body. You have made all of creation and called it good. I thank you that one day your creation will be redeemed. My body will be glorified, and I will live without pain and sickness. Thank you, also, for gathering the outcasts to yourself. We live in a lonely world, full of hurting people. But you have transformed our loneliness. With you, we are never alone, we are never outcast. Amen.

VI. DEEPER DISCOVERIES

A. Fear (5:15,33,36)

In all three of the miracles in this chapter, fear is mentioned. In the first and second miracles, the people and the woman were afraid of Jesus. In the third miracle, Jesus told Jairus not to be afraid. We can fear many things. If I go to court for a speeding ticket, I may be afraid that the judge will not look leniently on my circumstances and will punish me to the full extent of the law. I may be afraid of spiders or snakes or the dark. When my wife comes home late, I may be afraid that something has happened to her.

Some fear is good—especially the fear of the Lord. This is a reverential fear that may also be called "awe." I am afraid of the judge at traffic court because I know the judge has full authority over me and I broke the law. God is our lawgiver and we do well to fear his retribution. However, if we accept the terms he has offered—the atoning death of his Son—we do not need to fear.

I may fear snakes because I have a healthy respect for the damage they can do. I may be allergic to spider venom, so I respect the damage that spiders can do to my body. I may fear the dark because I cannot see as well, and by walking across a dark field, I may fall into a hole and break my leg. Sometimes, though, these fears become irrational. If I run screaming every time I see a spider or snake, or if my fear of the dark is because I fear the monsters that may be hiding in the dark, my fear is not based on respect but on irrationality and imagination.

Another type of fear would more properly be called worry or anxiety. It may also be irrational because nothing can be accomplished by worrying. This type of fear shows a lack of trust in God. Jairus exhibited this type of fear that Jesus calmed with the words "Do not be afraid." Jesus encouraged Jairus to trust in him.

The people who saw the man who had been possessed by demons sitting with Jesus exhibited the second type of fear—fear of the unknown. But instead of letting this fear lead them to an awe of God and what he had done, they drove Jesus from their midst.

The woman with the hemorrhage exhibited the first kind of fear. She knew what she had done, she knew her status, and she knew that Jesus was infinitely more powerful than she was. Her fear, however, was overcome by Jesus' kind words and his proclamation of her healing. It is this kind of fear that leads to worship of God.

B. Peace (5:34)

The Hebrew word for "peace" is *shalom* and the Greek word is *eirene*. It carries the idea of completeness or wholeness. When Jesus told the woman, "Go in peace," he was making a statement about her entire being. The word *peace* also refers to an absence of strife. For the Israelites, the promise of peace was a messianic blessing. They were a warring nation, as were those around them. To have peace meant to be the one in power, to establish the peace. When the Messiah came, he would establish peace.

Christians experience peace with God. There is no longer any hostility between God and human beings. Christ's mission was to bring spiritual peace with God (Isa. 9:6; Luke 1:79; 2:14; John 14:27). This may seem to contradict Christ's statement in Matthew 10:34 that he came not to bring peace but a sword. This apparent contradiction is due to our misunderstanding of the concept of peace. When we think of peace, we generally think of a feeling. We may struggle with a hard decision. When we finally make a decision, we say that we have "peace" about it. We are referring to a lack of internal conflict.

While peace is experienced as a feeling, it is more than this. Peace is a state of affairs or a reality, no matter how we feel about it. It is a reality even when there is still fighting. For example, in a war the leaders of a country may talk about a cessation of hostilities and eventually sign a peace treaty. Peace is established. The fighting, however, may continue until each soldier is given the word that fighting has stopped. Their feelings have not changed. But their position has. And if there are some who do not accept their leaders' agreement to peace, fighting may continue for a time.

How does this apply to Jesus' statement? First, we need to understand the nature of the hostility. God is a God of holiness. He cannot allow sin into his presence. And yet we as humans are sinful. Our natures are hostile to God and his rule. God, because of his nature, could not allow us into his presence without a sacrifice. God made peace with us by sending Jesus to be our sacrifice. Hostilities have indeed ceased for those who accept this substitutionary atonement.

The problem is that not everyone accepts this sacrifice, this cessation of hostilities. Thus Christ's statement that he brings not peace but a sword. There will still be fighting among Christians who have surrendered to Jesus and those who will not accept him. These may be members of the same family. Peace brings conflict because of our fleshly nature. While we as Christians were given a new nature, the old is still active and the two natures war against each other.

Another who did not accept Christ's rule and never will is Satan. He is still active in the world, and he tries to get Christians to sin against their Savior and Lord. Christians must be active in fighting against Satan. Remember, our battle is not primarily against flesh and blood but against the ruler and principalities of darkness (Eph. 6:12).

Such is the nature of peace. While there are still battles to be fought, the peace has been won. We are assured of our salvation in Christ, and this is the greatest assurance of peace that can be given.

C. Women

It is difficult to appreciate the full depth of Jesus' compassion for the woman with the issue of blood without understanding something of the treatment of women during his day. The Jewish attitude at the time of the New Testament was discriminatory. Rabbis would not teach women or even speak to them. Pharisees were instructed not to touch them. To touch a woman when she was menstruating would be to become unclean. Since there was no way of telling when a woman was menstruating, it was better not to have contact with a woman at all. It was also believed that sin came from woman. Women were viewed as temptresses, anxious to lead men astray.

When the Gospels record Jesus speaking to women, touching them, allowing them to sit under his teaching, and being the recipients of his blessing, it stands in sharp contrast to how women were generally treated in that time. Jesus often referred to women in his parables, something that was unthinkable among the Jews. He healed women as well as men. In fact, the three incidents of raising someone from the dead involved women to a large degree. In the present story, it was a girl who was dead. In John 11, Lazarus was raised, but the story is told from the perspective of Martha and Mary. In Luke 7, the son of the widow of Nain was raised. Luke gives the impression he did this out of compassion for the grieving mother.

VII. TEACHING OUTLINE

A. INTRODUCTION

1. Lead Story: Fooled by Illusions
2. Context: This chapter continues chapter 4. These miracles are a continuation of Jesus' teaching ministry in chapter 4. They validate what he had said about the kingdom of God. He who has ears to hear, let him hear.
3. Transition: A popular belief in today's New Age world is that the body shackles the soul. Some day, the New Agers say, the body will suffer death and the soul will be freed of its chains. But Jesus taught that the body has great dignity and significance. He taught this by coming in contact with three outcasts, three unclean people, and transforming them into healthy bodies and spirits.

B. COMMENTARY

1. Jesus Restores a Man's Mind by Casting Out a Demon (5:1–20)
   a. The man's description (5:1–5)
   b. The man's confrontation with Jesus (5:6–13)
   c. The town's response (5:14–17)
   d. Jesus' response (5:18–20)
2. A Religious Leader Seeks Jesus (5:21–24)
3. A Small Subplot (5:25–34)
   a. The woman's description (5:25–28)
   b. The woman's confrontation with Jesus (5:29–33)
   c. Jesus' response (5:34)
4. Raising the Dead (5:35–43)

a. The death of a daughter (5:35–36)
b. The mourners' response (5:37–39)
c. The miracle (5:40–43)

C. CONCLUSION: THE PHYSICAL BODY DOES MATTER

VIII. ISSUES FOR DISCUSSION

1. Which of the three healings by Jesus in this chapter do you most identify with? Why?
2. How public is your confession of your need? Or are you like the woman, hoping to go unnoticed?
3. How often do we as Christians let our own notions of purity stand in the way of human need? What are some of these unwritten purity laws? What would Jesus' response be?
4. Reread verses 15–17 of Mark 5. How is this rejection of Jesus happening today?

Mark 6

The Good, the Bad, and the . . .

I. **INTRODUCTION**
A Dramatic Contrast

II. **COMMENTARY**
A verse-by-verse explanation of the chapter.

III. **CONCLUSION**
Empowering Leadership

An overview of the principles and applications from the chapter.

IV. **LIFE APPLICATION**
Follow the Leader

Melding the chapter to life.

V. **PRAYER**
Tying the chapter to life with God.

VI. **DEEPER DISCOVERIES**
Historical, geographical, and grammatical enrichment of the commentary.

VII. **TEACHING OUTLINE**
Suggested step-by-step group study of the chapter.

VIII. **ISSUES FOR DISCUSSION**
Zeroing the chapter in on daily life.

"The light shines in the darkness,

but the darkness has not understood it."

J o h n   1 : 5

Mark 6

IN A NUTSHELL

After many controversies with religious leaders and after the healings in Mark 5, Jesus goes home to Nazareth, but he is rejected and mocked by his own people. The chapter finishes with two miracles. In between these two sections of the chapter is the story of the execution of John the Baptist by Herod. Mark contrasts the leadership styles of Jesus and Herod.

The Good, the Bad, and the . . .

I. INTRODUCTION

A Dramatic Contrast

*R*andall Wallace's book *Braveheart* tells the story of Scotland winning its freedom from English tyranny. Wallace does this by contrasting several characters. Perhaps the strongest contrast in the book is between William Wallace, the leader of the Scottish rebels, and Edward the Longshanks, king of England and oppressor of Scotland. King Edward showed his ruthless and brutal attitude toward his subjects. He granted lands and titles to the lords even though his people were starving. He sacrificed his own men in battle.

In vivid contrast to King Edward the Longshanks is William Wallace, who fights without compromise for the freedom of the "sons of Scotland." He would not accept Longshanks's offer of gold, land, and title because it would mean betraying his people. Even while being tortured to death, he would not recant his determination for his people to be free. Nothing else mattered to him.

Contrasts help to highlight opposing characteristics. The beauty of a diamond shows up best against a dark background. Sometimes Christian growth occurs dramatically during times of persecution or tribulation. Such is the case in this chapter of Mark. Jesus had been viewed in previous chapters against the backdrop of the Jewish religious authorities. But in this chapter, Jesus is viewed in contrast to a political leader. His compassion pronounces severe judgment on the weakness and harshness of Herod.

II. COMMENTARY

The Good, the Bad, and the . . .

> **MAIN IDEA:** *Through his encounters at Nazareth, with the Twelve, with the people, and even with nature, Jesus' leadership is compared with the kingship of Herod.*

A The Climate of Unbelief (6:1–6)

> **SUPPORTING IDEA:** *Jesus himself chooses when to use his power.*

6:1–2. From what we know of Jesus' life before his public ministry, he spent most of his time in Nazareth. It is to Nazareth that he now returned with his disciples. But this was not just a time of visiting his family. The presence of the disciples implies that he came as a rabbi, a teacher followed by his students. It was only natural, therefore, for the synagogue to invite him, a visiting rabbi, to teach. Again, he amazed the listeners.

6:3. The listeners **took offense at him**. They were offended, not at what Jesus said or what he did—as was the case with the Pharisees and scribes—but at who he was. They began mocking him. These people had known Jesus for thirty years. They knew his earthly family. Some of them had perhaps hired him to do work for them. It is often hard to recognize greatness when we are confronted with it daily. As Stock notes, "Many are on the verge of asking the right question about Jesus but cannot bring themselves to believe in the greatness or in the mission of a local boy, a neighborhood kid" (Stock, *Mark*, p. 176).

The word **carpenter** (Gr. *tekton*) means "a worker in wood, stone or metal." This word denotes a craftsman. Jesus was a common worker, a blue-collar laborer. He had no formal training; he was not a scholar. And the people in his hometown knew this. There may be none so quick to judge our fitness and competence as those with whom we grow up.

The phrase **Mary's son** suggests that Joseph was probably dead at this time. Because Jesus was the oldest son, responsibility for the family fell to him upon his father's death. Perhaps their mockery of him was due in part to the impression, however misguided, that he was abandoning his duties to his family as the eldest son. This also may have been an insult to Jesus, referring to his apparent illegitimate birth.

6:4. Jesus repeated a well-known proverb of the time. He was clearly identifying himself with Old Testament prophets who were often ridiculed, not listened to, and sometimes even put to death.

6:5. Jesus healed people through compassion, not on demand or as a performance. Our human minds may think, *If he had performed a miracle here, perhaps they would have believed*. Jesus, however, knew their hearts. They had been presented with many opportunities to see, to hear, and to believe. Some people have made up their minds and do not want to be confused with the facts. "The performance of miracles in the absence of faith could have resulted only in the aggravation of human guilt and the hardening of men's hearts against God. The power of God which Jesus possessed could be materialized in a genuinely salutary fashion only when there was the receptivity of faith" (Lane, *The Gospel of Mark*, p. 204).

We need to consider the purpose of Jesus' miracles. They pointed to his claims of divinity and his offer of salvation. Some people would not believe, even if Jesus raised a person from the dead. Doing a miracle in these circumstances could only harden hearts and make a mockery of the gracious God who heals physically and spiritually.

While it is not "faith" that heals, the presence of faith does have positive effects. And the opposite is also true. The absence of faith hinders receptivity to God and his activity. Healing takes place in many different forms in the Bible regardless of the faith of the person involved, but healing is never granted as a reward for having enough faith. For example, Luke recounts the story of Jesus seeing a dead man being carried away. He was the only child of a widow. Jesus raised the young man with no evidence of the faith of the widow, the crowds, or the dead man (Luke 7:11–15).

As Christians, we can rest assured that our sovereign God knows what is best for us. For some people, the "best" is to be healed, and we can praise and thank God for its occurrence. For others, the "best" is to remain as they are without healing. We can praise God for his continual presence in our lives and his graciousness, whether or not this results in physical healing. Mark's statement **except lay his hands on a few sick people** indicates that there were some who were willing to admit their need and come to Jesus for help, even though he is a carpenter.

6:6. Jesus was **amazed at their lack of faith.** Only one other time is the word *amazed* used about Jesus. In that instance, he was amazed at someone's faith (Luke 7:9). Jesus then went to other villages teaching.

B Winning a Kingdom (6:7–13)

SUPPORTING IDEA: *Jesus gives his disciples kingdom authority.*

6:7. Jesus had called the apostles for the purpose of preaching (3:14), and the time for them to do this had now come. He sent them out in teams of two—a practice still followed by many door-to-door evangelists and cultists. The reason may be that in Israel, the law demanded two witnesses for any testimony (Deut. 17:6). The sharing of a common task by two people would also help bind the Twelve into a more cohesive group. The strength of two is more than doubled: "Two are better than one, because they have a good return for their work: If one falls down, his friend can help him up. But pity the man who falls and has no one to help him up! Also, if two lie down together, they will keep warm, but how can one keep warm alone? Though one may be overpowered, two can defend themselves. A cord of three strands is not quickly broken" (Eccl. 4:9–12).

Jesus gave the disciples authority over evil spirits. They did not go under their own authority but the power and authority of Jesus.

6:8–9. Jesus gave the apostles specific instructions so they would know they were dependent on God for their provisions and success. They were to take no bread, no bag, or no money so they would be dependent upon the hospitality of those to whom they went. The tunic would normally be worn as a cloak during the day and as a blanket at night. They were not to take an extra tunic to remain warm. They were not to take supplies or money to purchase supplies. They needed to depend on God and the hospitality of others for their housing and food.

6:10–11. When the disciples found a home that was receptive to them, they were to stay there until they left the town. If they observed this principle, they would not bring offense to their message by searching out better accommodations than what they had already accepted. "The spread of the gospel has the priority over personal likes and dislikes" (Hendriksen, *Mark,* p. 230).

The Jews considered Gentile country to be defiled and unclean. When an orthodox Jew returned home after visiting a Gentile area, he was supposed to shake every bit of dust from his body because the Gentile land was unclean. As Barclay notes, "It was a pictorial formal denial that a Jew could have any fellowship even with the dust of a heathen land" (Barclay, *Mark,* p. 143).

Jesus was saying that if the people to whom they preached shut the door in the disciples' faces, if they refused to listen, there could be no fellowship between them. This would serve as a further message to the unreceptive to consider carefully their actions. "The action . . . was not to be performed in a contemptuous or vindictive spirit, but with a view to its moral effect; either it would lead to reflection and possibly repentance, or at least it would justify God's future judgment" (Swete, *Mark,* p. 118).

6:12–13. The apostles took healing of spirit and body to the neighboring cities. They carried out the command of Jesus. They brought first a message of repentance, forgiveness of sins, and the need for the people to turn to God. The second message they brought was that of physical healing. God cares for the total person—body and spirit. God frees his people from sin that leads to death, and he frees them from the physical infirmities and demons that haunt their bodies and souls. Physical infirmities, poverty, and starvation are part of Satan's dominion. Therefore, we do well to fight against Satan by taking care of people's physical needs as well as their spiritual needs.

C In Comparison . . . (6:14–29)

SUPPORTING IDEA: *In contrast to Jesus, Herod is manipulated to use his power; he is not motivated by compassion but by lust; unlike Jesus, he bows to the wishes of the crowd.*

6:14–15. The miracles and teaching of Jesus, and now of the disciples, brought him to Herod's attention. But Herod was uncomfortable at what he heard about Jesus. These verses prefigure the central event of Mark's Gospel: the confession of Peter in 8:27–30. Some people thought Jesus was John the Baptist raised from the dead and that he was granting Jesus the power to perform miracles. This notion may also have arisen from the fact that Jesus' message and the disciples' message were a continuation of John's message of the need for repentance.

Elijah is mentioned in Malachi 4:5 as returning before the Day of the Lord. Jews understood this as the day when God would conquer Israel's enemies and bring peace and prosperity to their land. Messiah was the one who would lead this restoration of Israel.

He is a prophet, like one of the prophets of long ago. Israel had not had an important prophet in more than three hundred years. They had seen minor prophets (not to be confused with the books called the Minor Prophets). But they were looking for prophets from God who spoke authoritatively for God. Those prophets called for repentance and announced God's judgment on those who turned away. Could it be that Jesus was one of their line?

6:16. Herod, however, thought he knew exactly who Jesus was: John the Baptist raised from the dead. A guilty conscience can be a terrible thing. It makes one look suspiciously at everything and everyone. The belief that "everyone knows" permeates every thought, creating anxiety and worry. Such was the condition of King Herod.

6:17. This verse begins a discussion of John the Baptist's death at Herod's hands. According to the Jewish historian Josephus, John the Baptist was imprisoned at Machaerus, a Roman fortress overlooking the eastern shore of the Dead Sea. It is a bleak, grim place where the dungeons still stand today. Herod had imprisoned John because John rebuked him for marrying Herodias, his brother's wife. While Jewish law required that a man marry his brother's wife if the brother died in order to carry on the brother's line, no such event had taken place. Philip, Herod's brother, was still living. Therefore, Herod was in violation of Levitical law (Lev. 18:16; 20:21).

6:18. John had shown tremendous courage by rebuking Herod publicly. Herod was a powerful Roman ruler who could have John executed whenever he pleased.

6:19–20. These verses present a contrast between Herod and Herodias. Herodias hated John and wanted to put him to death. Herod, on the other hand, recognized John as a righteous man who spoke the truth. Apparently, Herod even liked listening to John. Therefore, he refused to have him executed. Unfortunately, he did not allow his respect for John to blossom into repentance.

6:21. Herodias harbored great hatred in her heart for John. She waited for an opportune moment to move against him. Sinners often have great patience in waiting, watching, and planning. Herod's birthday banquet gave her the opportunity she had been waiting for.

6:22–23. The **daughter of Herodias** is listed by Josephus, the Jewish historian, as Salome. The word translated "girl" (*korasio*) means a young girl of marriageable age. She was probably a teenager. Her dance was a suggestive, indecent dance, meant to incite the lust of Herod and his guests.. Whether or not this dance was instigated by Herodias, she knew it was taking place. Herodias's hatred of John the Baptist led her to prostitute her own daughter in an effort to gain John's death.

Herod was pleased with Salome's performance, and he vowed to give her whatever she wanted. Scholars generally agree that his promise to give her **up to half my kingdom** is hyperbole. It was meant to show Herod's greatness and generosity to those leaders who were attending the party.

6:24–25. When Herodias got her opportunity, she told Salome to ask for John's death. Salome added two further requests to that of her mother. She wanted John's death to take place at once and she wanted his head on a platter. Her cruelty was a mirror of her mother's.

6:26–28. In this situation, Herod stood in pathetic contrast to Jesus. Jesus never played to the crowds. Herod, however, could not deny the girl's request, no matter how much it went against his wishes. He had taken a rash oath. Rather than lose face in front of his guests, he granted Salome's wish. Hendriksen notes that Herod could have escaped the vow he made (Hendriksen, *Mark,* p. 241). He could have said, "I promised you a gift, not a crime." He could have repented as John had urged him to do. Instead, he sinned against God as well as his better judgment. The request was granted, and the bloody gift was handed to Salome and eventually to Herodias.

6:29. John's disciples gave him the burial he deserved and reported this event to Jesus (Matt. 14:12). Most of them probably joined Jesus' ministry. John certainly would have approved of this move. About thirty years later, during Paul's ministry, there were still some people who knew nothing about Jesus, but only the baptism of John. Under the counsel of Paul, these followers became followers of Jesus (Acts 19:1–7).

Ⓓ A Simple Banquet (6:30–44)

SUPPORTING IDEA: *In comparison to Herod's banquet, this miracle of Jesus shines with its simplicity and Jesus' surpassing compassion.*

6:30–31. With this verse, Mark resumes his narrative about the disciples whom Jesus had sent out. The disciples returned and they had an exciting tale to tell. But the crowds were increasing by such large numbers (partly due to the disciples' actions) that they had not even had a chance to eat. The large crowds suggest that Jesus and his disciples were probably in Capernaum.

Jesus knew how tiring ministry can be. He knew what it felt like to heal people, to have the press of the crowds upon him, to preach from town to town until his voice was hoarse, to get so caught up in God's business that daily needs were forgotten. His compassion reached out to the disciples, and he encouraged them to come away from the crowds to get some rest.

6:32–34. They got into a boat and tried to reach a quiet place. Luke 9:10 implies that they were going to the northeastern side of the Sea of Galilee. But too many people saw them leave, and they ran to catch up with them. This was a distance of four or five miles on foot, and it would not be hard to meet the boat on the other side, particularly if the boat was sailing into a strong wind. Jesus did not view the crowd as an inconvenience. Although there may have been some disappointment and weariness on the part of the disciples, Jesus felt compassion for the people, viewing them as sheep without a shepherd.

No animal is as dependent upon a shepherd as a sheep. Without the shepherd, sheep wander aimlessly and get lost. Without the shepherd to show them to the good places to graze, sheep do not eat. Without a shepherd to lead them to water, sheep die of thirst. Without the shepherd, wolves can devour the sheep. Jesus viewed the people as helpless sheep. Herod and the religious leaders could have viewed their followers like this and granted them good guidance, but they were lost themselves. Because of Jesus' compassion, he began teaching the crowds.

6:35–36. By this time, it was getting late in the day. The disciples became concerned about the people being in this remote spot. But it was not so remote that the people could not leave and get something to eat in the nearby towns.

6:37. Jesus' command to feed the people probably startled the disciples. They immediately began to calculate that it would cost approximately two hundred denarii to feed all these people. They had already forgotten that they had just returned from a mission trip that saw much success.

6:38. Jesus asked the disciples to count their resources. They were woefully inadequate. The parallel passage in John 6:8–9 reveals that the loaves were not the bread loaves that we would typically see in the supermarket. They were small barley cakes—not much bigger than a roll—generally eaten by poor people. The disciples must have thought there was no way these meager provisions would feed a crowd. But when we are with Jesus, we do not have to rely on human means. "God does not lead us to see a need, unless it be in his mind to use us to meet that need, be it by prayer or otherwise" (Cole, *Mark*, p. 114).

6:39–40. Jesus told the disciples to have the crowd **sit down in groups.** This would make for an orderly distribution of food. At least, the disciples had faith enough to obey Christ's instructions.

6:41. The Jewish people normally looked downward when asking a blessing, taking a stance of humility. But this was not a normal meal. Jesus was doing more than thanking God for provisions. "[It is] an appeal to the

Father for the extraordinary power necessary to meet the people's need" (Stock, *Mark,* p. 195). This also prefigured the day when Jesus himself would be the bread that is offered up and broken to meet people's need.

Jesus blessed the bread and the fish. He wanted to make sure that those witnessing the miracle remembered that God provides. Some interpreters believe the people did not know where the food was coming from. This seems in disagreement with John 6, where the people, after the miracle, were ready to seize Jesus and make him king. The disciples participated in Christ's work by handing out the food. They had recognized the need and were used by Jesus in meeting the need. God uses people who put themselves at his disposal.

6:42–44. There was enough food for everyone to be satisfied. Kingdom resources do not run out. Mark notes that five thousand men were fed. Matthew notes that there were also women and children. The number is a rough estimate based on the number of people in each company.

Some interpreters have noted that the twelve baskets of leftover bread correspond to the twelve tribes of Israel. But this may communicate a deeper message. There were twelve disciples, and each disciple had a basket. Cole notes that this was probably the disciples' provision for the next day. Christians must be good stewards of God's gifts and not waste anything.

E Lord over Nature (6:45–56)

> **SUPPORTING IDEA:** *Jesus' lordship and compassion are victorious over the forces of nature.*

6:45. After this miracle, everyone was exhausted. Jesus sent the disciples in the boat on ahead to Bethsaida. He dismissed the crowd—no small feat, considering there were at least five thousand people—and they flocked to Jesus like moths to a light. There may be another explanation for his sending the disciples away. In John's record of this miracle, the people tried to seize Jesus and make him their king. They had seen miracle after miracle, but none like this. They reasoned that if Jesus could feed this many people on a few pieces of bread and fish, he must be the Messiah. Jesus may have sent the disciples away to keep them from getting caught up in the middle of this nationalistic spirit regarding the Messiah..

6:46. Jesus needed to get away by himself for prayer to his Father. Luke's Gospel tells us that before this miracle occurred, John the Baptist's disciples had come to Jesus and told him of John's death. Jesus' mind would have been filled with sorrow for the death of his cousin and friend. There was much to pray about.

6:47–48. In the miracle of the feeding of the five thousand, Mark notes that the people sat down on "green" grass (v. 39). The grass is green in

Palestine only in mid-April. That point becomes important now. This was the time of the Passover, which was always held during a full moon. The full moon let Jesus see clearly what was happening on the lake. He could see the disciples struggling with the oars against the crashing waves. Jesus was filled with compassion for them. He left his prayers and his own troubles behind and set out to help them.

6:49. The phrase **pass by them** does not mean that Jesus was going to pass by and ignore his disciples in the boat. The phrase is also used in the Old Testament when God "passed by" Moses, revealing himself to him. Jesus' appearance would serve as a reassurance to the disciples. He had sent them out on the water; he would see them through their troubles.

But the disciples feared they were seeing a ghost. Sailor stories about ghosts and supernatural figures were numerous. There was a Jewish superstition that ghosts seen at night foretold destruction and disaster. No wonder the disciples were afraid.

6:50–51. Jesus did not let them labor long in their distress. He immediately spoke a word of comfort. The wind died down and the sea became calm. The parallel story in Matthew tells of Peter getting out of the boat and walking toward Jesus. If Mark was the recorder for Peter, why is this not mentioned here, in Peter's Gospel? Perhaps Peter wanted the focus of the story to be on the actions of his Lord rather than Peter's actions.

6:52. The disciples did not understand Jesus' miracles. If they had understood the miracle of the feeding of the multitude, they would have understood Jesus walking on the water. They should have understood that Jesus is the Lord of creation. He had primacy over the Sabbath, the purity laws, the bread they ate, and the water upon which they sailed.

6:53–56. Mark notes that when they landed, they were again besieged by people. Jesus could not go anywhere now without being recognized. They went through the countryside, telling everyone that Jesus was present. The sick were brought out in droves for him to touch or for them to touch him. News of Jesus' previous miracle had preceded him.

MAIN IDEA REVIEW: *Through his encounters at Nazareth, with the Twelve, with the people, and even with nature, Jesus' leadership is compared with the kingship of Herod.*

III. CONCLUSION

Empowering Leadership

We hear a lot about leadership these days. The old way of doing things is out; the new leadership is in. It involves being part of a team rather than having a boss. It involves letting people discover their giftedness and then letting them go, rather than telling them what to do and continually making sure it gets done. It involves letting people stretch their wings and fly rather than clipping their wings to conform to management's image. The best leaders empower their team to reach goals. They give them what they need to succeed.

This is the new leadership. And yet, it is a leadership style that Jesus exhibited as he gave his disciples authority to preach and heal in his name. It is a style that Herod knew nothing about. Herod led through fear. Concerned with public opinion, he allowed others to make decisions for him. He could not admit to making a mistake. He would not allow godly men like John the Baptist and Jesus to make an impression on him when they came into conflict with his earthly appetites.

PRINCIPLES

- Jesus calls us to be a part of his ministry to the world, but our provisions always come from him.
- Jesus is aware of our needs and comes to us in our distress. We can be assured that the waves will not overtake us. He is watching and praying for us.
- A good leader does not depend on public opinion but is confident in God's power.
- Good stewardship demands that we not waste God's resources.

APPLICATIONS

- Our top priority is to tell people to repent and turn to God. We must also bind their wounds, feed their hunger, quench their thirst, and cast out their demons.
- Establish a "quiet place" to be with Jesus so he can restore your soul and help you cope with the burdens of ministry.
- Depend on God to meet your needs.

IV. LIFE APPLICATION

Follow the Leader

I was watching the neighborhood kids play "Follow the Leader." The snow was piled high, with huge drifts covering bushes and cars. In fact, on most of the cars, only the antennas sticking up gave any indication that vehicles lay beneath the snow.

The "leader" was leading the other kids in a maze through the cars and bushes. Sometimes he would take his sled and slip down the slope. At other times, he plowed through huge drifts. Then he began digging a tunnel. At one point, he plopped down in the soft stuff and tried to make a snow angel, but the snow was too deep and he sank. Nevertheless, the followers lay down and waved their arms up and down in faithful imitation of their leader. Then the leader climbed on the branch of a low tree and let himself fall into the soft snow. The others, with varying degrees of confidence, followed his lead.

Jesus calls us to follow him. We go where he leads, confident that he is not leading us to a place where he has not been. And he has promised his presence, even if he leads us in the dark at times. The darkness, whether it be through persecution or suffering, can highlight the growth and the beauty of the life within us. But follow we must. It is challenging. Sometimes it is scary. Sometimes it is fun. By the end of the game, we know more about ourselves, even as we learn more about our leader.

V. PRAYER

Lord, I thank you that your light shines brightest in dark places. Let me be a light for you. I see your work in so many areas. Sometimes I am not thankful enough. Sometimes my heart is hardened and I do not recognize your power in my life. Forgive my ungratefulness and soften my heart. Help me meet human need with your love, compassion, and mercy. Take my life and let me be the kind of leader who glorifies your name. And let me lead, knowing that I am still and always a follower. Amen.

VI. DEEPER DISCOVERIES

A. Prophet (6:15)

The word *prophet* comes from the Greek *prophetes,* meaning "to speak." The prophet is one who speaks for God. The prophet of the Old Testament was not a magician like some of the pagan practitioners of the day. The prophet was called by God. God initiated his utterances, sometimes to the prophet's distress! God spoke to the prophet, and the prophet spoke exactly what God had told him or her to say (the Old Testament does mention prophetesses).

The prophets were as important to Israel as the king. In fact, it was the prophet who anointed the king, signifying God's blessing. God also gave the Israelites word through the prophet Moses that an ideal prophet would come (Deut. 18:14–22). This prophet would be like Moses. After four centuries of prophetic silence, John the Baptist began his ministry as the forerunner of Jesus. Jesus identified himself as a prophet in this passage in Mark. The gift of prophecy continues in the New Testament with such people as Agabus, Jude, Silas, and the four daughters of Philip.

Jesus Christ fulfilled a threefold role—prophet, priest, and king. In his prophetic role, he brought the Father's message to the people and he foretold the future. His prophetic work continued as he revealed to us the will of God.

Prophecies can be divided into three main categories: (1) the nation of Israel; (2) messianic prophecies; and (3) last days. The prophecies about Israel were of two types—a foretelling and a forthtelling. The forthtelling was the main part of any prophecy even though we today may focus on the more spectacular foretelling. Forthtelling was an exhortation, a rebuke, an encouragement. It called Israel back to its purpose, to God. This type of prophecy was practiced by Jesus and should still be practiced in the church today. We need to hear words of rebuke when we are far from God and words of encouragement when we face persecution and martyrdom.

Some prophecies for the nation of Israel and the messianic prophecies have been fulfilled. Because we know the God whom we serve, we can be assured that the prophecies that have not yet been fulfilled will be some day. These are the last-day prophecies of which the Book of Revelation is a part.

B. Anointing with oil (6:12)

Anointing with oil signifies the presence of the Holy Spirit. This practice does have medicinal value, but the religious import of such anointing would have been more significant for the Jews. It was a symbol of God's grace being poured on them. It also signified that the one who applied the oil was a conduit of God's grace and healing power.

Anointing was a common practice in the ancient Near East. Anointing oil was often used as perfume. It was put on wounds, corpses, and released captives. In the Book of Exodus, a special oil was prepared to anoint the furniture that was placed in the tabernacle (40:9). This became a means of setting something apart for God's service. The greatest number of references to anointing are to the anointing of a king. This supposedly assured the king of a royal line. The prophets spoke of a king to come. This would be the Anointed One, the Messiah, the Christ.

The church carried through with the practice of anointing its leaders. Bishops and kings were anointed in the eighth and ninth centuries because they were considered to be the vicars of Christ. Bishops are still anointed today.

C. King Herod (6:14–26)

Although Mark refers to Herod as "king," this was his popular title. He was actually the Roman tetrarch, or governor, of Galilee. The marriages of the Herodian line are so intertwined and entangled that it is hard to keep track of who's who. Herod Antipas was the son of Herod the Great, the king responsible for the slaughter of the male babies under two years of age in Bethlehem.

Herod the Great was an insane man and in his later years he put many of his own sons to death, fearful that they would usurp his throne. One of his murdered sons had a daughter, Herodias, who was married to one of Herod's other sons, Herod Philip. They had a daughter, Salome.

Herod Antipas was another son of Herod the Great. On a visit to Herod Philip in Rome, Herod Antipas seduced Herodias and stole her away from his half-brother. As Barclay puts it, "By marrying Herodias, his brother's wife, Herod had broken the Jewish law and had outraged the laws of decency and of morality" (Barclay, *Mark,* p. 150). John the Baptist rebuked Herod publicly for this sin.

Luke 23 records Herod's trial of Jesus. He had long anticipated meeting Jesus. Luke records that Herod wanted to see a miracle. Herod had no interest in God. He just wanted to be entertained. But Jesus would never allow himself to be put on display. He performed no miracles for Herod.

Herod Antipas was eventually banished to Spain by the Roman emperor Caligula. Caligula released Herodias from her marriage to Herod so she would not have to share in his banishment, but she refused and went into exile with her husband.

VII. TEACHING OUTLINE

A. INTRODUCTION

1. Lead Story: A Dramatic Contrast
2. Context: After working the miracles in chapter 5, Jesus goes to his hometown where he is rejected. He sends out the Twelve, and their ministry brings them to the notice of Herod Antipas. A brief account of John the Baptist's death at the hands of Herod shows the contrast between his leadership and that of Jesus.
3. Transition: The beauty of an object is often seen best in contrast with something else. A jeweler will place a diamond on a black background so the customer can see the color and how it reflects the light. Mark shows Jesus in contrast with Herod Antipas, the tetrarch of Galilee. Jesus' beauty, compassion, love, and leadership are dramatically different from Herod's weakness and worldliness.

B. COMMENTARY

1. The Climate of Unbelief (6:1–6)
2. Winning a Kingdom (6:7–13)
3. In Comparison . . . (6:14–29)
   a. Herod hears of the apostles' ministry (6:14–16)
   b. Herod's relationship with John and Herodias (6:17–20)

     c.   Herodias's plot (6:21–25)

     d.   Herod's weakness and John the Baptist's death (6:26–29)

  4. A Simple Banquet (6:30–44)

     a.   A statement of need (6:30–37)

     b.   Jesus provides (6:38–44)

  5. Lord over Nature (6:45–56)

     a.   The disciples' distress (6:45–47)

     b.   Jesus provides (6:48–56)

C. CONCLUSION: FOLLOW THE LEADER

VIII. ISSUES FOR DISCUSSION

1. What other contrasts do you see between Jesus and Herod? What similarities do you see between the death of John the Baptist and the passion and death of Jesus Christ?

2. What ministry has Jesus called you to? How has he empowered you for this ministry? How do you need to be dependent upon him?

3. Has there been a time in your life when Jesus calmed the storm? Read the parallel to this story in Matthew 14:22–33.

4. How have you experienced the proverbial saying of Jesus in Mark 6:4? What insight can you gain from this saying?

Mark 7

Breaking Down Barriers

"*I do not want a religion I have to carry . . . but one that carries me.*"

H a d d o n   R o b i n s o n

Mark 7

IN A NUTSHELL

*I*n chapter 7, Mark points out that the gospel is a matter of the "heart." Jesus' controversial encounter with the teachers of the law over the disciples not washing their hands highlights the emptiness of religious performance. The observance of religious rites does not produce "righteousness" in a person. It's what's on the "inside" that counts. The healing of the Syrophoenician woman's daughter and the deaf man shows that they may not have been acceptable from the outside because of their race, culture, and physical handicaps. But they were acceptable to God because of their "heart" attitude. Jesus finds them more than acceptable.

Breaking Down Barriers

I. INTRODUCTION

Spiritual Adrenaline

I love homemade pizza, especially the kind my sister made when we were growing up on the farm. She would put everything but the kitchen sink on her pizzas. None of the national pizza chains had anything on my sister's pizzas.

I distinctly remember one time when my sister needed some mushrooms to put on the pizza she was making for dinner. She asked me if I wanted to go with her to the back part of our farm, affectionately known as the "back forty." I resisted until she commented that I would not get any pizza unless I went. I called my little dog, and he went with us. At the time his going with us did not seem to be a big deal until something happened that almost cost us our lives.

To get to the "back forty" we had to go down a dirt road for about a mile and then climb over a five-foot fence. My sister wanted to go to this particular place because mushrooms grew there. We climbed over the fence and started picking mushrooms. In that same vicinity there was a large bull with about thirty other cattle. I cautiously looked around and did not see the bull, so I figured we were O.K. My sister insisted we needed more mushrooms and ordered me to the top of the hill to get some she had seen. You guessed it! There was the two-thousand-pound bull and all his buddies. The bull became very agitated.

This is where my dog came into the picture. This bull and my little dog had met before, and they remembered each other. I slowly looked down to my right and there he was—my faithful little mutt.

The bull began to stomp the ground, snort, and bellow as if all two thousand pounds of him was upset. My little dog began to growl and paw the ground as if all forty pounds of him was upset. Me—I was just upset. I looked around to see where my sister was. She was climbing over the fence, leaving me all by myself. Suddenly, I lost my taste for pizza.

When the bull charged, I wheeled around and sprinted wildly through the pasture with my dog right beside me. Suddenly, I realized that a five-foot fence was coming up—fast. I leaped with all my might and cleared the fence like a track star. The dog went under the fence, and the bull almost went through the fence—but fortunately he stopped.

There's no way I could jump a five-foot fence under normal circumstances. But because of something called "adrenaline"—a kind of emergency power source in my body—I was able to clear a barrier I normally could not jump. The adrenaline gave me the power I needed to clear that five-foot fence and preserve my life.

You might say that the gospel, the good news, is like spiritual adrenaline. It is the gospel's power that not only sustains and strengthens us but also gives us what we need to overcome barriers in our life. In this chapter of Mark, we see Jesus, the sacrificial servant, setting people free through the gospel's power. Jesus shows us that there is no barrier—whether physical disability, racial difference, or religious traditionalism—that cannot be overcome by the gospel's power. He has come to set us free.

II. COMMENTARY

Breaking Down Barriers

MAIN IDEA: *Jesus, the sacrificial servant, teaches that our relationship to God is not based on religious formality but a radical faith in him.*

A The Busyness and Barrenness of Religious Tradition (7:1–8)

SUPPORTING IDEA: *Jesus teaches that doing religious activities on the outside does not mean a person is right on the inside.*

7:1–2. It was not uncommon for Jesus to have "religious hit men" from Jerusalem—the scribes and Pharisees—following him just watching for something to criticize. This was the second time that these **teachers of the law** had come **from Jerusalem** to find fault with Jesus' teaching. Jesus, in his previous encounter (Mark 2:23–3:5) with these religious leaders, had not taken the party line. In fact, he had opposed it. This encounter was no different.

The religious leaders discovered that Jesus' disciples did not wash their hands before eating. These washings had nothing to do with personal hygiene nor were they commanded in the law. The scribes and Pharisees were upset because Jesus' disciples were not following the "rules" for ceremonial washings that they had established as additions to the law.

7:3–4. Mark felt the need to explain to his Gentile readers the Jewish custom of ceremonial hand washing that was based on the **tradition of the elders.** The tradition of the elders was a set of ceremonial practices, such as hand washing, that were added to the law and handed down from generation to generation. The original purpose of these practices was to help people know God's will in specific situations. These "practices" ended up being more binding than the law itself.

These religious leaders felt their identity and authority were at stake. Whenever the Jews practiced these ceremonial washings, they were declaring that they were God's special people and that other people were "unclean." These "traditions" reminded the Jews that they were God's special people and that they should not be contaminated by the world around them. Yet, these traditions gradually degenerated into empty ritual and religious isolationism.

Mark gives an example of the custom of "washing" in verse 4 when he points out what a Jewish person would normally do when coming from a trip to the market. If a Jew went to the marketplace to buy food, they might come in contact with Gentiles and be "defiled." Therefore, Jews observing these practices would wash themselves, even their pots and pitchers, to make sure they were ceremonially clean from the contact with "unclean" Gentiles or Samaritans.

7:5–7. The religious leaders were angered and threatened by Jesus' departure from religious traditionalism. To them, this was a question of authority. In essence, they were asking Jesus, "Who are you to disregard centuries of Jewish tradition?" Jesus gave them the answer in verse 6 by quoting from Isaiah 29:13. Jesus called the religious leaders **hypocrites** and then used the Scripture to back up his charge. A "hypocrite" is someone whose worship is merely outward and not from the heart. Jesus made it clear in the Sermon on the Mount (Matt. 5) that true purity and worship is a matter of inward love and a right attitude and not just outward actions and associations. Jesus taught that you could do all the right things and still not do them for the right reasons. True defilement takes place in the heart prior to the actions.

Jesus quoted Isaiah because this prophet's words of condemnation of the religious leaders of his day fitted those of Jesus' day, although the circumstances were different. The religious leaders' outward appearance of piety was a lie. It was not accompanied by a lifestyle of true "heart" commitment to God

7:8. Jesus made it clear there was a big difference between **the traditions of men** and **the commands of God**. True worship must come from the heart. It must be directed by God's truth, not a set of ideas. These "traditions" were supposed to help the people keep God's law, but they actually usurped God's law and drove people from God. The *Mishna*, a collection of Jewish traditions in the Talmud, records, "It is a greater offense to teach anything contrary to the voice of the Rabbis than to contradict Scripture itself." This is a clear example of how the "traditions of the elders" had become more important than the law—God's Word.

Ⓑ Cultural or Biblical? (7:9–13)

SUPPORTING IDEA: *Jesus teaches that if there is a conflict between culture and Scripture, the believer should follow Scripture.*

7:9. Jesus was tired of these religious leaders' false piety. He showed them that they used God's Word like a wheelbarrow—they pushed it wherever they wanted it to go. Selective obedience is not really obedience at all—it is merely convenience. Jesus called them hypocrites and showed them in verses 10–13 that by obeying their traditions, they were breaking God's law.

7:10–13. Jesus exposed the hypocrisy of the religious leaders by showing how they were breaking the fifth commandment—honoring your mother and father—in keeping one of their traditions. Jesus pointed out the penalty of the law by saying, **Anyone who curses his father or mother must be put to death.** Jesus pointed out the seriousness of breaking this command. The death penalty was decreed for those who cursed their parents or treated them with contempt. We may not like what our parents do, but they deserve respect. Jesus died for them as well.

Jesus then illustrated how the fifth commandment was broken by the Pharisees in observing the "traditions of the elders." Part of honoring one's mother and father in the Jewish family was to take care of their needs when they got older. Yet, one of the ingenious ways to get around this command was to pronounce something as **Corban.** The word *Corban* literally means "an offering or gift dedicated to God." Here is how it worked.

According to this tradition, if a person pronounced over any property or money the word *Corban,* it could not be given to any other person—even your parents. But here was the real kicker. The money or property dedicated to God could still be used by its owner for personal gain and gratification. Therefore, by keeping the traditions of the elders a person was breaking one of the Ten Commandments—God's law. Even if people who claimed Corban had a change of heart and wanted to help their parents, they could not.

This is what Jesus meant when he said in verse 12, **You no longer let him do anything for his father or mother.** If a person were to go to one of the religious leaders to undo or arbitrate his case so he could help his parents, he would be turned down because of this vow to God in dedicating his goods. The religious leaders based their rigidity in this matter on Numbers 30:1–10. Numbers 30 speaks of making vows to God. It teaches that a vow made to God supersedes any personal commitments, including parents. Jesus categorically rejected the practice of using one biblical text to negate another. He showed how we can make the Bible say whatever we want if we do not take the time to understand the spirit and purpose of the law.

Jesus was disgusted with the traditions of the scribes and Pharisees. By observing the traditions of men, they neglected the greater law of love. Jesus showed the peril of being content with outward observances while the heart is full of selfishness and sin. Tradition had replaced truth.

ⓒA Matter of the Heart (7:14–23)

SUPPORTING IDEA: *Jesus teaches that the purity of a person is not determined by external actions but an internal heart attitude.*

7:14–15. Jesus cut to the heart of the matter. He called the whole crowd to him and announced that the source of godly living was from "within and not from without." Notice that Jesus took the religious leaders to a deeper level in answering their objections to "unwashed hands" by proceeding to talk about "unclean foods." Jesus in essence was rejecting the religious leaders' approach to God's Word. They were concerned about surface piety and purity, while Jesus was concerned about internal purity. This alone brings true godliness.

7:17–19. Jesus gave a general announcement to the crowd about the source of true holiness, but he gave a more detailed private explanation to his disciples. Jesus' statements to the disciples seemed to puzzle them. These statements ran counter to their Jewish upbringing about dietary restrictions and godly living. Jesus said, **Don't you see that nothing that enters a man from the outside can make him unclean? For it doesn't go into his heart but into his stomach, and then out of his body.** He was declaring that true obedience results from a love of God from the heart— not the outward acts of keeping the rules. True holiness is internal. Jesus said, "Blessed are the pure in heart, for they will see God" (Matt. 5:8). Our heart attitude—not the keeping of rules—determines the purity and power of our relationship to God.

Notice the phrase, **In saying this Jesus declared all foods "clean."** This indicates the source from which true defilement originates. The Jewish dietary laws were about ceremonial impurity. Jesus was saying that the food we eat is digested and the waste is eliminated, but sin begins in the heart and produces true impurity in our lives. Jesus implied that our fellowship with God is not affected by unclean hands or unclean foods, but by personal sin.

7:20–23. Jesus showed how the observance of external rules does not correct the "nature" of the heart. The heart is the core for motivation, deliberation, and intention. He gave a list of behaviors and characteristics that come from the heart.

Evil thoughts is the spring from which all the other "bad" attitudes and activities arise. Jesus was making it clear that doing the right things does not mean that a person is "right" on the inside. No amount of hand washing can change the selfish nature of the heart or make it clean. There is only one way. His name is Jesus. By trusting in him for our salvation, we can be changed from the inside out.

Ⓓ The Power of Persevering Faith (7:24–30)

SUPPORTING IDEA: *Jesus shows that a radical, persevering faith in God's grace gets God's attention.*

7:24. Note that this encounter of Jesus with the Syrophoenician woman came on the heels of a major conflict with the religious leaders about ceremonial uncleanness. Jews normally did not have any contact with Gentiles because this made them ceremonially "unclean" according to Jewish tradition. Jesus showed by example that "it's what's in the heart" that matters. He showed the absurdity of the tradition of the elders by making contact with this Gentile woman. Mark also wanted to emphasize the mission and inclusion of the Gentiles in God's plan of salvation. The gospel of God's love and his kingdom are not limited to Israel, even though Jesus showed that Israel must have the first opportunity. By using the example of the Syrophoenician woman, Mark wanted his Roman (Gentile) readers to realize that the good news was also for them.

Only one other time had Jesus crossed into Gentile territory (Mark 5:1–20) Yet, this time Jesus stayed in Gentile territory for quite some time. He traveled to Phoenicia (now Lebanon), where the city of Tyre was located. Jesus had not gone there for public ministry. He was looking for a place to rest with his disciples as well as to escape the persecution of the religious leaders who were always following him. He knew they would not want to defile themselves by going into Gentile territory. Yet, in his attempts to get some rest, **he could not keep his presence secret.**

7:25–26. A Gentile woman sought Jesus. Mark shows the incredible cultural and gender boundaries that existed between Jesus and the woman. First, she was a Gentile. The Gentiles had not always treated the Jews kindly, and they often dominated them. There was a gender issue. Men dominated women during this time. Also, a rabbi (teacher) was not supposed to have any direct contact with a woman. By nationality she was a Syrophoenician (during this time Phoenicia belonged to Syria). Yet, the desperate need of her daughter and her radical faith in God's goodness caused her to humble herself before Jesus and risk crossing all these barriers.

7:27–28. Jesus probably spoke to the woman in her language, which was Greek. He said to her, **First let the children eat all they want . . . for it is not right to take the children's bread and toss it to their dogs.** Jesus was not being sarcastic or uncaring. His mission centered on the "lost house of Israel." Jesus implied that there was a place for the Gentiles. It just was not then. Their turn would come later. The reference to **dogs** was not to scavengers on the street but to the little dogs that wait eagerly under the table of their master for the scraps and crumbs to fall from the table. The children of the household indicated the privileged position of Israel in hearing the gospel, and the "little dogs" indicated the less privileged position of the Gentiles.

This did not deter this woman of faith. Jesus left an opening, saying that the Gentiles would have a turn at hearing the gospel and benefiting from his ministry. Why could not that time be now? As far as she was concerned, it was time to "seize the moment." This woman agreed that Israel was first but she had a radical faith that refused to believe she was excluded. She replied, **even the dogs under the table eat the children's crumbs.** This shows her persevering faith and her belief in God's goodness. The barriers of race, culture, and gender are surface issues. The real need is true healing on the inside, and only the gospel can cross these barriers to bring such healing.

7:29–30. This woman's faith must have pleased and surprised Jesus. He not only saw her quick thinking ability but her great faith as well. Jesus responded with compassion. It is significant that the Gospels refer twice to people of "great faith"—this woman and the Roman centurion in Matthew 8:5–13. Both these people were Gentiles. In both instances, Jesus healed at a distance. Jesus will test our faith, just like he did with this woman, but he will reward our faith when we persevere in the process.

Amazing Grace, How Sweet the Sound (7:31–37)

SUPPORTING IDEA: *Jesus demonstrates through the healing of a deaf man that there are no barriers—racial, cultural, or physical—beyond the grace and goodness of God.*

7:31–32. Jesus left the region of Tyre, crossed the Sea of Galilee, and returned to the area of Decapolis, where he had previously cured a demon-possessed man. During this visit, he was asked to perform a miracle on a man who was **deaf and could hardly talk.** The people begged Jesus to heal him. This showed their concern for their friend, since he could not make the request himself because of his speech impediment. Jesus responded with compassion to their faith.

7:33–35. Jesus took the man away from the crowd so the healing would be private and the man would not attract public attention. Then Jesus communicated with him in a way that he could understand. Is not this like Jesus? He meets us where we are so he can take us where he wants us to go. Notice that Jesus placed his fingers in the man's ears. This seems to indicate his hearing would be restored. Saliva on the tongue indicated that his tongue would be healed so he could talk. Jesus then looked up to heaven, indicating the source of his power for healing (see John 11:41; 17:1).

Jesus then gave **a deep sigh.** This showed the incredible empathy of Jesus. This was an inward groan indicating Christ's compassionate response to the needs of this man. He not only felt for him—he felt with him (see

Rom. 8:23; 8:26). Jesus uttered a one word prayer—*Ephphatha*—which is Aramaic for "be opened." Mark felt the need to explain this to his Roman readers. Jesus' prayer was answered immediately. This man's ears were opened, his tongue was loosed, and his speech impediment was gone. This miracle is recorded only in Mark. Mark's Gentile readers could rejoice because the good news was for them as well.

7:36–37. Jesus **commanded** the people to keep this miracle to themselves, but they did not. The more he insisted, the more they talked. Jesus' desire to keep this miracle quiet was probably for the same reason he did so in Mark 1:44. He did not want to gain the reputation of being just a miracle worker.

But these people were overwhelmed with what they had witnessed. The statement **He has done everything well** is the same statement God made in Genesis 1:31: "God saw all that he had made, and it was very good." Only Jesus can restore us to the position and purpose for which God created us. The words **He even makes the deaf hear and the mute speak** reflect a similar saying in Isaiah 35:5–6, which refers to the healing power of the coming Messiah. The Messiah had come, and Mark wanted to show that he had come for the Gentiles as well.

> **MAIN IDEA REVIEW:** *Jesus, the sacrificial servant, teaches that our relationship with God is based not on religious formality but on a radical faith that transcends all barriers.*

III. CONCLUSION

It's What's on the Inside that Counts

The Queen Mary was the largest ship to cross the oceans when it was launched in 1936. She served through four decades and a world war until she was retired and anchored as a floating motel and museum in Long Beach, California. During the conversion, her three massive smokestacks were taken off to be scraped and repainted. But once placed upon the dock they crumbled. Nothing was left of the thick steel plate from which the stacks had been formed. All that remained were more than thirty coats of paint that had been applied over the years. The steel had rotted away. The smokestacks appeared to be solid, but they had no substance.

In essence, Jesus was saying the same thing to the Pharisees about their "traditions." He was showing them that externally everything about their traditions looked great, but on the inside there was no substance to their rituals. Instead of bringing them closer to God, their traditions were driving people from God. Life has a way of stripping us down and revealing us for what we are. The Pharisees hung on to their traditions and external rituals, but in the end were condemned by God. Yet, the Syrophoenician woman and the deaf man showed a "heart" of faith in God that was richly blessed and honored.

PRINCIPLES

- The mere performance of religious acts does not produce personal purity and holiness.
- Humility, coupled with faith, is pleasing to God and invokes his favor.
- The Lord speaks to us in "our" language so we will understand his desires for us.
- Religious legalism can lead us away from God.

APPLICATIONS

- Ask the Lord to make your worship of him meaningful rather than mechanical.
- Be aware of your own personality style and then see how God "communicates" to you in that way.
- Rejoice that there are no barriers that keep God from meeting your needs.
- Search yourself to see if you have any prejudices about race, culture, or gender. Ask God to help you see people as Jesus sees them.

IV. LIFE APPLICATION

Looking Beyond the Obvious

Dodie Gadient, a schoolteacher for thirteen years, decided to travel across America and see the sights she had taught about. She launched out in a truck with a camper in tow. One afternoon, rounding a curve on I–5 near Sacramento, California, in rush-hour traffic, the water pump on her truck blew. She was tired, exasperated, scared, and alone. In spite of the traffic jam she caused, no one seemed interested in helping. Leaning up against the trailer, she prayed, "Please God, send me an angel . . . preferably one with mechanical experience."

Within a few minutes, a huge man covered with a long beard and tattoos drove up on a Harley. With an incredible air of confidence, he went to work on the truck. He flagged down a larger truck, attached a tow chain to the frame of the disabled Chevy, and whisked the truck and camper off the freeway onto a side street, where he continued to work on the water pump.

The school teacher was too intimidated to talk—especially when she read the words on his leather jacket: "Hell's Angel's—California." As he finished the task, she finally got up the courage to say "thank you" and to carry on a brief conversation. Noticing her surprise, he looked her straight in the eye and mumbled, "Don't judge a book by its cover. You may not know who you're talking to." With a smile, he closed the hood of the truck, straddled his Harley, and was gone as fast as he had appeared.

Given half a chance, people will often crawl out of the boxes into which we have relegated them. Life is a contact sport. We have opportunities to make contact with people every day to enrich their lives and allow theirs to enrich us. But how many times have we avoided someone because of the appearance of their clothes, the color of their skin, or their social class.

The Pharisees based everything on appearance. They were very picky about who they associated with. But Jesus became "flesh and dwelt among us." He touched those who were considered untouchable and crossed the boundaries of race, culture, and gender. Underneath the skin, all of us have the same need for salvation and redemption. If we are followers of Jesus, we must follow his example in how we relate to all people—without prejudice or discrimination.

V. PRAYER

Jesus, help me not to have a "checklist" mentality when I spend time with you. Every time I pray at a meal, or have a quiet time, or go to church, may I see these as "fresh" opportunities to connect with you. May I be more concerned with my heart attitude toward you than trying to impress others with my religious acts. I want more than anything to love you with "all" of my heart. Like the psalmist, I pray that you will "search me, O God, and know my heart; try me and know my ways and see if there be any wicked way in me. Then lead me in the way everlasting, O Lord." Amen.

VI. DEEPER DISCOVERIES

A. Tradition of the elders (7:3)

The Pharisees wanted to conform to God's will in all details of life. They added to Scripture in order to accomplish this objective. Their desires were commendable, but the "tradition of the elders" actually conflicted with Scripture. Jesus showed this contradiction between Scripture and their traditions by citing the example of "Corban" found in Mark 7:9–13.

Jesus called their additions to Scripture the "traditions of men" (v. 8) rather than the tradition of the elders. The Pharisees had added six hundred "traditions" to be followed in addition to the Scripture itself. The result was that the Word of God considered burdensome rather than a blessing by the people.

B. Unclean hands (7:5)

The phrase "unclean hands" centers on the issue of purity. The Mosaic Law gave detailed instructions called "purification rituals" for three distinct categories of uncleanness. They were for leprosy (Lev. 13–14), bodily discharges (Lev. 15), and contact with a dead body (Num. 19:11–19). Yet, in Mark 7:5 the Pharisees were concerned about Jesus' disciples having "unclean hands" that had not been washed before eating. Where did this "command" come from, since it is not among the biblical mandates given for purification from uncleanness? It came about as an addition to the Scriptures known as "the tradition of the elders" (Mark 7:3). These "traditions" were added to the actual law (Old Testament Scriptures).

Exodus 30:19–21 required only the priests serving in the tabernacle to wash their hands. The law also required the priests to regard as holy the portion of the sacrifices that they were allowed to eat. The priests and everyone in their family could share in this food only when they were ceremonially clean (Num. 18:8–13). The Pharisees decided this practice should be extended to all Jewish people—not just to the priests and their families—as well as to all foods—not just the food of the priests.

The Pharisees' desire was that all Jewish people—not just the priests and their families—should strive for holiness. They literally believed that a man's home was his temple. Therefore, he and his family should strive to be holy because God is holy (Lev. 19:2). The washing of one's hands, then, became a symbolic and concrete reminder to all Jewish people of their need to strive for holiness. These unwritten oral laws tried to fill the gaps in the purity laws found in the books of Leviticus and Numbers.

C. Dogs (7:27)

In Jesus' conversation with the Syrophoenician woman, the word *dogs* was used. In ancient Israel, the dog was not seen in a very favorable light. In fact, calling a person a "dog" was equivalent to calling him or her "the scum of the earth." The Bible mentions dogs often, and most of these references are negative. In New Testament times, the Jews called the Gentiles "dogs," referring to their cultural practices. They thought of them as racially inferior. The term *dog* also referred to a male prostitute (Deut. 23:18). In the Book of Revelation, those who are not a part of the New Jerusalem (Rev. 22:15) are also called "dogs," or unbelievers. Jesus' association with Gentiles and his love for all people made the religious leaders of Israel angry.

VII. TEACHING OUTLINE

A. INTRODUCTION

1. Lead Story: Spiritual Adrenaline
2. Context: In Mark 7 the religious leaders try to trap Jesus, and it back-fires on them once again. Jesus shows these religious leaders how they have made their "traditions" more important than the Scriptures. He also points out that their teaching contradicts Scripture. His reprimand of these teachers of the law goes against religious rituals that have been practiced for centuries. By ministering to the Gentiles, Jesus also declares that God is more concerned with what is on the inside (a good heart attitude) than with what we do on the outside (religious rituals).
3. Transition: As we look at this chapter, we see how God is concerned with "why" we do what we do. What you see is not always what you get. People may see the outside, but God sees the heart. Through Jesus' interaction with the teachers of the law, the Syrophenician woman, and the deaf man, we realize that God is not impressed with religious acts but with righteous hearts.

B. COMMENTARY

1. The Busyness and Barrenness of Religious Tradition (7:1–8)
2. Cultural or Biblical? (7:9–13)
3. It Is a Matter of the Heart (7:14–23)
4. The Power of Persevering Faith (7:24–30)
5. Amazing Grace, How Sweet the Sound (7:31–37)

C. CONCLUSION: LOOKING BEYOND THE OBVIOUS

VIII. ISSUES FOR DISCUSSION

1. Are there certain "traditions" that you practice in your family or personal life? If so, what are they? How do you keep them meaningful? How do you keep from getting into a "religious" rut in your times with God?
2. Define "cultural." Name some ways our "culture" can conflict with Scripture.
3. Is there a difference between "cultural" Christianity and "biblical" Christianity? If so, what is it?

4. Are there certain people groups (racial, cultural, or gender) that you might consider "unclean" or have hang-ups about? If so, who and what are they? Where did these beliefs in your life come from? What needs to change?

5. Are there any "barriers" that need to come down in your life? Ask the group to pray for the "walls" to come down.

Mark 8

Mid-Point

Quote

"To have experienced the Christ, to have encountered Jesus of Nazareth, to have run headlong into the person of God in the flesh must have been like stepping into the path of a hurricane."

Martin Bell

Mark 8

IN A NUTSHELL

This is the mid-point of Mark's Gospel and we can anticipate Jesus' ministry and teaching to look different from what has gone before. In this section we see various stages beginning to take shape in Jesus' teaching and miracles.

Mid-Point

I. INTRODUCTION

Conflict and Resolution

A friend of mine who is a scriptwriter told me about the writer's creative process. A similar structure is used in stories and novels as well as films and plays. In script writing, each play has three acts. Act one sets the scene, introduces us to the characters, and introduces the conflict. Act two is the majority of the play. It develops everything that was introduced in act one and prepares us for the resolution by the climax which thrusts us into act three. Act three is the resolution.

An interesting plot development is called the mid-point. Generally, it takes place at the exact middle of the script. While it is not climactic, it is an important turning point. It lets the audience or the reader know that life will be different from this point on.

We see this exemplified in Robert Frost's poem, "The Road Less Traveled." The author while walking came upon a fork in the road. His conclusion, "I took the one less traveled by. And that has made all the difference." The fork in the road was Frost's mid-point. Life brings you to a certain point and then changes direction. Life goes on, sometimes to climactic and exciting places, but it is the turning point that make this possible.

Chapter 8 of Mark's Gospel is the mid-point, the turning point, in the Gospel. It is the middle chapter. The more I read his Gospel, the more I am convinced that Mark was intentional in what he was doing! We can expect the things happening to Jesus at mid-point to be of great importance. Mark does not let us down.

II. COMMENTARY

Mid-Point

> **MAIN IDEA:** *Mark shows us in this chapter that everything is a process. Salvation, healing, the growth of the kingdom often take place in stages.*

A The Second Feeding (8:1–13)

> **SUPPORTING IDEA:** *Through another miracle of feeding a large crowd, Jesus introduces the second stage of kingdom growth.*

8:1. This feeding of the crowds is generally considered to be a separate event rather than a repeat of the first feeding. Jesus mentions the two in verses 19–20, and there are enough differences between the two to believe that they are separate accounts.

This time, the crowd was gathered not by Lake Galilee but in the region of the Decapolis. He had been in Tyre and Sidon in chapter 7. As we have seen previously in chapter 5, this region was populated by Jews and Gentiles. Barclay makes an interesting point about the crowds gathered here. In chapter 5, after the healing of the demoniac, the crowds urged Jesus to leave, but the restored man stayed behind. It is possible that the people now gathered were a result of his witnessing to Christ's intervention in his life (Barclay, *Mark*, p. 184).

This miracle probably included numerous Gentiles. While Jews had been the recipients of the first miraculous meal, the Gentiles were fed this time. This symbolizes a time when all people, regardless of race or national origin (Gal. 3:28), will share in the Lord's Supper. The two feeding miracles emphasize that the kingdom will be made up of Jews and Gentiles. In between the two feeding miracles are miracles to Gentiles and Jesus' miracle for the Syrophoenician woman. Jesus' discussions in chapter 7 had been about "clean" and "unclean." The miracle of the feeding of the four thousand validates his teaching that only God can decide who is clean and who is unclean.

8:2–3. Jesus' teaching had filled a spiritual hungering on the part of these people. So intent were they on his words that they had not eaten for three days. This is reminiscent of Ezekiel's experience of eating the scroll of the word of the Lord. It tasted as sweet as honey in his mouth (Ezek. 3:3; cf. Ps. 119:103). "This audience had proved their right sense of spiritual values by three days of eager listening to the Lord's preaching. It is not just that they were hungry, but that they were hungry in God's service: and so theirs was to be an experience of 'seek ye first the kingdom of God . . . and all these things shall be added unto you' (Matt. vi. 33)" (Cole, *Mark*, p. 127).

Jesus had probably gone without food for this time as well. But it was for his flock that he was concerned and felt compassion. He was also concerned about sending them home. Many of them had traveled great distances and might not make it home without fainting or becoming ill.

8:4. This location was more remote than the location of the previous feeding miracle. In that place, there had been nearby towns where the people could buy food if necessary. This place was too desolate. Some interpreters take the disciples' question as evidence of a lack of faith and a failure to remember the previous miracle. Other interpreters feel that the disciples were acknowledging there was no way for them to feed the crowds and that they were looking to Jesus in faith for another miracle.

8:5–7. As in the previous miracle, Jesus asked the disciples to determine the amount of food they had. Again, it was inadequate. But Jesus took what they had—seven loaves and a few small fish—blessed them, and gave them to the disciples to distribute. As before, Jesus took a little and made much of it. In Jesus' hands, there is no such thing as too little.

8:8–10. Again, all the people were satisfied and the fragments were gathered. As Cole points out, it is not necessary to affix a spiritual meaning to the number of baskets of fragments picked up. There were probably twelve baskets because there were twelve disciples and each had a small basket. On this feeding occasion, four thousand men were present. After feeding the crowd, Jesus dismissed them and then left, returning to Galilee.

8:11. Stock notes that in returning to Galilee, Jesus was returning to a discussion with the Pharisees. "In contrast to the faith encountered in Gentile territory, Jesus encounters disbelief in Galilee" (Stock, *Mark*, p. 220). The Pharisees demanded a sign from Jesus. One wonders just how many signs they needed! These people, with their superior intellect and knowledge, should have recognized Christ at once. And yet, they refused to have their eyes opened. Through their stubbornness and rebellion, they remained blind and deaf while others were healed.

The phrase **sign from heaven** may mean that they expected a miracle from heaven, not the earthly miracles Jesus had been performing. If they had just heard about the miraculous multiplication of the bread and fish, perhaps they wanted Jesus to bring down manna from heaven. As Luke records in 16:31, however, those who are set against the Lord will not be convinced even if a person is raised from the dead.

8:12–13. Jesus would not perform signs or miracles on demand. He would not bless unbelief. He could do nothing to convince these people, so he left them to their unbelief and blindness. Barbieri notes that Jesus' rapid departure is a signal of his great indignation for these leaders. There are times when talk is useless (Barbieri, *Mark*, p. 179).

B A Warning (8:14–21)

SUPPORTING IDEA: *Jesus warns the disciples about the Pharisees.*

8:14. In their hurry to get away, the disciples forgot to bring food. One loaf of bread would not be enough to feed all thirteen of them.

8:15. Yeast is generally spoken of in the Bible in a negative way. When used in cooking, a small amount of yeast permeates the dough. Once in the dough, it cannot be removed. Jesus was warning the disciples not to adopt the teachings of the Pharisees or their stubborn hard-heartedness. Without this warning from Jesus, the disciples might have looked up to the Pharisees as very spiritual and pious role models. Perhaps Jesus also wanted to tell them not to accept the prejudiced attitudes of the Pharisees, since they considered themselves superior to unclean sinners and Gentiles.

8:16. The disciples must have felt guilty about leaving their food behind. As soon as Jesus mentioned "leaven," they assumed he was blaming them for their lack of bread.

8:17–18. For Jesus, however, the physical bread was irrelevant. He then asked the disciples a series of questions meant to stir their understanding. When Jesus asked them if their hearts were hard, he was not implying they were as rebellious and stubborn as the Pharisees. The Pharisees were willfully rebellious, while the disciples were simply slow to understand.

8:19–20. Jesus reminded the disciples of the two miraculous feedings of the crowds. He questioned them about what happened, and they responded correctly.

8:21. Jesus wanted his disciples to draw a conclusion from the feedings. How could they worry about not having enough to eat when they had witnessed so many miraculous events? If Jesus can feed over nine thousand people, they must have thought, surely he can supply our basic needs.

C A Two-Stage Miracle (8:22–26)

SUPPORTING IDEA: *Jesus heals a blind man through two important steps.*

8:22. Again, we see the intercession of friends on behalf of a disabled person.

8:23. Jesus led the blind man out of the village because of his concern for him. Cole notes that the village would be busy, noisy, distracting for a man who could not see. Away from these distractions, he could focus on the Jesus whom he could not yet see. This could also be the reason why Jesus used saliva as a healing agent and placed his hands on the man: "Touch means more than sound to a blind man, and only by touch could the Lord's meaning be conveyed. There must be an understanding by him of the Lord's act before that act could become revelation: unexplained miracle, unrelated to God's loving purpose, is too close to magic, and of such we have no instance in the Bible" (Cole, *Mark*, p. 132).

8:24. In response to Jesus' question if he saw anything, the man replied that he saw dimly; he was not yet fully healed. One commentator sees this as a lack of faith on the man's part. But there seems to be no reason to attribute the two stages of this miracle to the man's lack of faith. He apparently had as much faith as did the paralytic whose friends brought him to Jesus.

8:25. Jesus placed his hands on the man again, and his sight was fully restored. The fact that this miracle took place in two stages shows that Jesus' miracles are not formulaic and that healing can be a process. Perhaps Jesus used this miracle to show his disciples that their own "sight" was growing by stages. Because Jesus healed in many different ways, Christians should not try to reproduce the miracles through their own power. This two-stage miracle also shows us that Jesus will not give up on us. He who has begun a good work in us will bring it to completion (Phil. 1:6).

8:26. Jesus told the man not to go into the village. It is possible that Bethsaida was not his home. It is also possible that because Jesus had pronounced judgment on Bethsaida, the people of this village were not to receive the benefit of the healed man's witness.

Ⓓ Peter's Double Image of the Messiah (8:27–33)

SUPPORTING IDEA: *Peter alternately shows great insight and great dullness in response to Jesus' identity and his mission.*

8:27. As Jesus and the disciples traveled to Caesarea Philippi, he questioned them about his identity. Their knowledge of him was growing, their understanding becoming greater. How far had their understanding led them?

8:28–29. As foreshadowed in chapter 6, the disciples recited the list of popular opinions about Jesus. Our knowledge of others' beliefs, however, is never good enough. We must form our own opinions. We must come to Christ for ourselves.

Peter, the spokesperson of the group, replied that Jesus was the Messiah. Matthew gives Peter's fuller response and Jesus' full response to Peter (Matt. 16:17–18). Many scholars believe that Peter dictated the Gospel of Mark to John Mark. If this is indeed Peter's account of these events, it is possible that he did not want the praise of himself recorded here. He wanted only his Savior glorified.

8:30. Jesus told the disciples not to tell anyone about this event. He knew the disciples did not have a full understanding of who the Messiah was or what he would suffer.

8:31. For the first time Jesus spoke plainly about his upcoming passion and death. Note that this prediction came immediately after Peter's confession of him as the Christ. He wanted to emphasize to the disciples that he had not come to establish a political kingdom. His victory would be that of the Suffering Servant in Isaiah 53.

The Messiah must suffer many things. While the crucifixion is the culmination of Jesus' suffering, he suffered other things. He suffered the rejection of his family and the continuous rejection of his teaching and his miracles by the religious leaders. Their attribution of his compassion and good works to the works of the devil was a source of further suffering. Jesus listed three categories of people in this verse: the elders, the chief priests, and teachers of the law. These three groups made up the Sanhedrin. These groups would be the ones that demanded his death.

8:32. Jesus spoke plainly to the disciples. He revealed the full truth about his suffering and death. Peter expressed horror at what Jesus was saying. He allowed his own wishes to cloud the truth of Jesus' words.

8:33. Cole points out in regard to Peter that "no sterner rebuke ever fell on any Pharisee than on this disciple of Christ, this first Christian. . . . The avoidance of the cross had been a temptation faced and overcome by the Lord in the wilderness: and for Peter to suggest it here was to think in human terms, and not in divine terms" (Cole, *Mark,* p. 137).

Jesus' temptation in the wilderness was not the end of Satan's attempts. Satan tried to present another opportunity to Jesus—the opportunity to avoid his painful crucifixion and separation from the Father. Jesus' stern rebuke came on two levels. First, he rebuked Satan. Peter's suggestion represented a very real temptation for Jesus—one that must be rejected forcefully. Second, Jesus rebuked Peter and the disciples. Mark alone records that Jesus looked around at all the disciples. Although Peter was the spokesman for the group, all the disciples agreed with him in his protest of Jesus' statement about his forthcoming death Jesus' condemnation of Peter was meant for all the disciples because they were unwilling to accept a suffering Messiah. Jesus demanded that they accept his mission and his demands for discipleship. While Peter was not "possessed" by Satan, he was used as an instrument of Satan in this instance, even though he seemed to have Jesus' best interests in mind.

E The Process of Growth (8:34–38)

> **SUPPORTING IDEA:** *Jesus tells the listeners what it means to be a true disciple of his.*

8:34. Jesus' next words were not just for the disciples but for everyone in the crowd. After telling his disciples about his impending death, he told everyone about the cost of being a follower of his. The phrase **deny himself** implies that, like Jesus, we must seek God's will and submit our will to his. **Take up his cross** must have been a puzzling, offensive statement to the listeners. They knew what the cross represented. Barbieri notes that when criminals carried their crosses, it showed those who were watching the identity of the one who had authority over the criminal (Barbieri, *Mark,* p. 190). By denying oneself, taking up one's cross and following Jesus, a disciple acknowledges that he is submitting to Jesus' authority.

8:35–37. These statements expand the understanding of verse 34. When people lose their lives by taking up the cross, they find life in Christ. In the same way, trusting in riches will not gain a person eternal life. There is nothing that a person can exchange for his or her soul.

8:38. In verse 31, Jesus spoke of his passion, death, and resurrection. In this verse he speaks of his eventual return in glory. Jesus had full confidence in his triumph over death. After his resurrection, he will judge those who have been **ashamed** of him. He will be ashamed of them as well.

MAIN IDEA REVIEW: *Mark shows us in this chapter that everything is a process. Salvation, healing, the growth of the kingdom often take place in stages.*

III. CONCLUSION

Trust the Process

Almost everything we undertake is a process. Let's say you decide to build a home. You know exactly how you want it to look, right down to the paintings on the wall and the paperweight in your den. You would first hire an architect to draw the plans. But her plans do not look like the image in your head. She says, "Trust the process." Then you hire a contractor to begin building. He digs the foundation, pours the cement. The frame is built. It still does not look like what is in your head. He says, "Trust the process." Eventually you have your home—paintings, paperweights, couches, and chairs.

We understand this process with building homes or building a business enterprise. We even understand it with arguments that build on the previous premise until a conclusion is reached. It is like this with Christianity. Our growth in Christ is a process. The disciples had a little understanding, then they had a little more. Sometimes they were slow to learn.

But Jesus has perfect understanding of where we are in the process of growing as his disciples. It is he who offers us insights through his Holy Spirit. It is he who urges us along, reminding us of what has happened before, showing us what will happen next. It is only through his graciousness that we understand anything of the spiritual life at all. If we deny ourselves and allow him to have authority over us, he will take us to some amazing places and wonderful experiences. Through his authority, we will do great things in the process of building a kingdom.

PRINCIPLES

- Because Jesus had no "outcasts" in his preaching ministry, neither should we as his his followers.
- Spiritual insight does not mean spiritual perfection. Christian growth is a process.
- Confession must always be personal. It is not enough to know what others say about Jesus Christ.

APPLICATIONS

- Utilize your memory of how God has worked in your life in the past to make it through the difficult times.
- Answer Jesus' question, "Who do you say I am?" For further study, read an apologetics book about who Jesus is. Two excellent books are *Mere Christianity* by C. S. Lewis and *More Than a Carpenter* by Josh McDowell.
- Deny yourself daily and submit to Christ's authority over you.

IV. LIFE APPLICATION

Friend of the Outcasts

The girl's parents were separated. The mother, a very large woman, could not work outside the home, so money was tight. The mother stretched the budget as much as she could to give her daughter some material things. But Lisa still went to school in clothes that were too small, too tight, and certainly not in fashion. Lisa herself had a weight problem, and the kids at school made fun of her. They called her names, refused to play with her, and made fun of her clothes. They mocked her mother. Lisa was in danger of blending into insignificance.

Then she met Brenda. Brenda was not super-popular, but she did have a lot of friends. She was not the smartest student in her class, but she was smart enough to be friends with some of the "nerds." Brenda liked Lisa. They had some things in common—like playing with Barbie dolls. Brenda liked going to Lisa's house and sledding down her hill in the winter. They went to Girl Scouts together in elementary school. They tried out together for the talent show.

In middle school, kids who liked Brenda began asking her why Lisa was always hanging around. They did not mind being friends with Brenda, but she would have to give up her friendship with Lisa. Brenda straightened her back, thrust out her chin, and said she would rather have Lisa for a friend than any of them.

Jesus also reached out to the outcasts by touching them and healing them. We as his followers are called to do the same. He even became an outcast himself. Abandoned by his friends, he was subjected to great humiliation as he hung on the cross between two thieves. He was considered a madman, a blasphemer, a criminal, a demon. But there were also those who considered him Lord. They were not ashamed to be numbered with him.

As we follow Jesus, we will also be outcasts at times. We will be thought of as stupid, ignorant, legalistic, and intolerant. But some people will listen to our witness for Christ as we reach out to them. Searching for the life that we have found, they will not be ashamed to be called followers of Jesus.

V. PRAYER

Lord Jesus, I bow to your authority. Send me where you will, ask of me what you will. Because you are the Servant, I am a servant in your service. Help me to reach out to those who are outcasts. Let me show them your love and abiding care for them. Thank you for coming into this world of lonely people to build your kingdom and a fellowship of love. Amen.

VI. DEEPER DISCOVERIES

A. Christ/Messiah (8:29)

When we as Christians think of the word *Messiah,* we think of Jesus Christ. We remember his atonement for us and his resurrection from the dead. The Jews, however, had a very different image of the word. We often read back into the Old Testament the prophecies about Christ. We wonder how many of Jesus' own people could have missed the fact that he was the Messiah.

The word *Messiah* is derived from the Hebrew word *masah,* meaning "to anoint or smear with oil." It means "anointed one," and it referred primarily to the king. Israel knew that it was a select nation, a nation set apart and called by God to be his own people. They expected, and not unreasonably, that they would be blessed. They would be a power among other powers. In order to procure for themselves safety among other nations and to be like other nations, they demanded a king.

God had a king in mind for them (Deut. 17:14–20). He was to be a leader whom God himself had chosen. He would be the "anointed one." The people, however, rushed into crowning a king and chose someone who seemed to have all the qualities they desired. Saul started out well but eventually failed to rely on God.

In time, God raised up a second king—a teen-age shepherd, the youngest in his family. As is God's way, David seemed an unlikely choice at first. But the quality David had—the quality that all leaders need—was that he loved God passionately. Under David's kingship, the nation of Israel entered a time of unparalleled prosperity. Whenever they went out to battle, the Lord went with them and their enemies were conquered.

With David's death (and actually in his later years), the kingdom began to crumble. David's son, Solomon, encouraged the worship of other gods by his own example. With the exception of a couple of bright spots, each successor to the throne was worse than the one before. While hoping for another David, the nation had to keep projecting their hope further and further away. Eventually, the solidity of the nation crumbled and the nation of Israel became the two nations of Israel and Judah. But a house divided against itself cannot stand, and eventually Israel was conquered. It took some time, but eventually Judah also fell to foreign invasion, deportation, and the loss of the land.

In the heart of Jewish people, though, a hope for another David burned. And the prophets promised that an ideal king was coming—one who would be of the Davidic line (Jer. 33; Mic. 5:2). The character of this king and his kingdom was described in Isaiah 9; 11; Jeremiah 22; 23; 30; and Zechariah 9; 12. His coming would signal the end of the age.

The Jews believed that great tribulation would precede the Messiah's coming. This was written about in the apocalyptic literature of the intertestamental period. The Messiah would come as a conqueror. He would destroy all who opposed God, crushing them in battle. He would smash all of Israel's enemies and restore the greatness of the nation. Israel would again enjoy a time of great prosperity that would last forever.

It is easy to see why the disciples were confused and why Peter opposed Jesus' prediction of his suffering. It is also easy to see why Jesus used the title "Son of Man" for himself rather than the more volatile term, "Messiah."

VII. TEACHING OUTLINE

A. INTRODUCTION:

1. Lead Story: Conflict and Resolution
2. Context: Jesus has been ministering in a community mixed with Jews and Gentiles. He performs a miracle for the Gentiles as he had done before for the Jews, authenticating his message to the Gentiles, preparing his disciples for the future kingdom. A blind man is healed in two stages, suggesting that healing is a process and not always instantaneous. After this miracle, Jesus asks his disciples who they think he is. Peter, through the power of the Holy Spirit, announces that Jesus is the Christ.
3. Transition: The mid-point marks a turning point in a play or novel. In this chapter of Mark, Peter's confession of Christ marks the midpoint in Mark's Gospel. From this point on, there will be less emphasis on miracles and more on teaching as the reader is led into contemplation of the final stages of Christ's life.

B. COMMENTARY

1. The Second Feeding (8:1–13)
   a. The people stir Jesus' compassion (8:1–5)

      b. Jesus feeds the four thousand (8:6–10)

      c. The Pharisees ask for a sign (8:11–13)

  2. A Warning (8:14–21)

      a. Yeast (8:14–15)

      b. Trust in Jesus (8:16–21)

  3. A Two-Stage Miracle (8:22–26)

  4. Peter's Double Image of the Messiah (8:27–33)

      a. Peter confesses Jesus as Christ (8:27–30)

      b. Jesus predicts his death and rebukes Peter (8:31–33)

  5. The Process of Growth (8:34–38)

C. CONCLUSION: TRUST THE PROCESS

VIII. ISSUES FOR DISCUSSION

1. How must you deny yourself in order to follow Christ?

2. Discuss the concept of shame. Where do you see this in your own experience?

3. Discuss the yeast of the Pharisees and Herod. How does this apply today? Do you see evidence of this at times in your own life?

4. Do a life-history timeline. At what points did you experience growth in being like Christ? What were some factors in your growth? Where were the low moments in your Christian life? What did you learn from them?

Mark 9

Glory

Quote

"And moving thro' a mirror clear

That hangs before her all the year,

Shadows of the world appear."

Alfred Lord Tennyson

Mark 9

IN A NUTSHELL

The transfiguration of Jesus is the underlying theme of this chapter—the kingdom of God coming with power. In this miracle and the teachings that follow, Jesus reminds the disciples where true power resides. This transforms the disciples' previous understanding of the kingdom and the Messiah. This theme will be continued in chapter 10.

Glory

I. INTRODUCTION

The Lady of Shalott

$\mathcal{T}$ennyson wrote a poem called *The Lady of Shalott*, a tragic story of love and death. The Lady of Shalott is imprisoned on the Isle of Shalott, located in the river flowing down to Camelot. She had been cursed and could not look down from her high tower into Camelot. If she did, she would die.

Through rich language, Tennyson weaves a spell of a woman who can experience the world and all its brightness only through its reflection in a mirror. To look at the actual world means to die. While the Lady of Shalott is happy most of the time, she experiences times of longing to see the world as it is.

One day, handsome Sir Lancelot rode by on his warhorse. His image flashed in the mirror, catching the lady's eye. His beauty was such that she could not resist. She left her mirror and looked down from the window upon Camelot and Sir Lancelot. The curse came upon her, she placed herself in a boat to float past Camelot, and there she died.

We are like the Lady of Shalott. Because of the curse of our fallenness, we can see only reflections. As stated in 1 Corinthians, we see dimly through a glass. And like the Lady of Shalott, we have moments when we say, "I'm sick of shadows." Most of the time we do not think of our shadowed existence. Our lives, filled with busyness, run on auto-pilot. We eat, sleep, go to work, maybe take in a ballgame on the weekend. We do not think about the passing of time, the existence that is a mere shadow on the wall of eternity.

Every now and then, something happens to clear our eyes. A child is born, a parent dies, we face an illness or maybe just another birthday. But we realize that this life is not all there is. For a moment, God pulls back the curtain just a little and we see God, the Creator and sustainer of the universe.

In chapter 9 of Mark, Jesus pulls back the curtain. He allows three men—and us—to glimpse the reality behind the shadows.

II. COMMENTARY

Glory

> **MAIN IDEA:** *The glory of God and, therefore, what is to be the Christian's glory, is revealed. The Christian finds his or her glory in service to God.*

A The Glory of the Son (9:1–13)

SUPPORTING IDEA: *The transfiguration of Jesus reveals his true glory.*

9:1. This verse is actually the ending of chapter 8 rather than the beginning of chapter 9. It sets up the action that follows—one of the most disputed events in the Gospels. **I tell you the truth** is a strong injunction from Jesus to those who are listening to pay close attention. The prophecy in this verse is problematic. What did Jesus refer to when he mentioned the kingdom of God coming with power?

9:2. The phrase **six days** is also mentioned by Matthew. Luke records eight. The eight would be counting the days including Peter's confession and Jesus' transfiguration, while six would be including only the days between these two momentous events. While some commentators believe the mention of six days is Mark's way of noting that this event happened in an historical time and place, it is also possible that the mention of the six days would be a reminder to the reader of the six days of creation. In this case, God's power was being revealed in an undeniable way, as it had been in the days of creation.

Peter, James, and John were chosen as witnesses to the events that follow. Perhaps this was because these three had shown themselves receptive to spiritual truth more than the others. These three had been with Jesus in the earlier miracle of raising Jairus's daughter from the dead.

9:3. R. Alan Cole (*Mark,* p. 210) notes that white was an unusual color in ancient Palestine. It soiled too easily to be of much practical use. Thus, its mention here signifies something unusual. White is the color of purity, most often identified with God's saints.

9:4. The appearance of Moses and Elijah represent the coming together of the Law and the Prophets. Each of these sections of the Old Testament Scriptures had prophesied about the coming of the Messiah. Here was their fulfillment. Furthermore, Elijah was the restorer of all things. "The stress on Elijah's presence at the transfiguration indicates that the fulfillment of 'all things' has arrived" (Lane, quoted in Barbieri, *Mark,* p. 196).

9:5–6. As usual, Peter was the first to speak in this situation. Some people talk when they are nervous, afraid, or embarrassed. Verse 6 suggests that Peter was one of these types. Luke 9:32 records that the transfiguration and surprise visitors awakened the three disciples from sleep. **Shelters** is variously translated as "booths," "tents," and "tabernacles." This suggests that Peter was perhaps ready to celebrate the Feast of Tabernacles. This feast, described in Leviticus 23:42, commemorated the wandering in the wilderness by the Hebrews. It reminded them how God had brought his people out of Egypt and how the people lived in tents or booths in the wilderness. The celebration occurs five days after the Day of Atonement. The two in conjunction were a reminder of humanity's total dependence upon God.

9:7. Peter's suggestion, and indeed Jewish tradition itself, placed the Messiah on the same level with Moses and Elijah. The cloud covered the mountain, and when it was lifted only Jesus was revealed. The voice of God, speaking the same words that were spoken at Jesus' baptism (Matt. 3:17), confirmed that Jesus was on a higher level than the Law and the Prophets—greater than these two highest representatives of everything good in the Jewish religious system.

A cloud was usually identified with God's presence (see Exod. 13:21) and later with Jesus' return in glory. The words regarding Jesus' identity reconfirmed the original message at his baptism, and added an imperative, **Listen to him**. He was the one who carried authority, as they had witnessed in the miracles; therefore, they should listen to him. Listening in this sense involves listening obediently—with one's entire being.

9:8–9. This event could be easily misunderstood. Therefore, Jesus enjoined the three disciples not to tell anyone about what had happened until after his resurrection when it could be proclaimed freely. This may happen to us at times as his followers. We may receive a special insight into Scripture, or the Holy Spirit may move us in new and exciting directions. We may experience a quickening of God's Spirit within us as he prepares us for his work. But God also knows the best timing. Galatians 4:4 reminds us that in the fullness of time, God sent his Son. His timing is perfect.

9:10. This verse may seem puzzling at first. The Jews were familiar with the concept of resurrection, or at least resuscitation, although it was not widely believed. Abraham, ready to do God's command and sacrifice his son, expected Isaac to be raised from the dead (Heb. 11:19), and Elijah raised a widow's son from death (2 Kgs. 4:32–37). So the concept was not foreign to the Jews. The difficulty the disciples had may have arisen from the concept of *Jesus* being raised from the dead. He was the Messiah, and there was no room in their thinking for a suffering, dying Messiah.

9:11. The talk of resurrection may have stirred recollections of Elijah's ministry, leading to the discussion that followed. The fact that they asked the question, though, points to their belief that Jesus was the Messiah. They did not have a clear conception of what the Messiah would accomplish, but it is clear that they believed Jesus to be the Messiah. It was commonly believed among the Jews that Elijah would appear before the Messiah.

9:12–13. Jesus stated that this prophecy had been fulfilled in John the Baptist and that he was rejected. How much worse would the people reject the Son of Man? Most interpreters believe Jesus was referring here to the Suffering Servant song in Isaiah 53. He was still concerned to teach his disciples that the Messiah must suffer and die. The fact that Jesus brought up his death again after referring to it just a few minutes before may point to the disciples' unwillingness to believe what Jesus was saying. But he was determined that they would look at reality and not get lost in theological debate.

B Borrowed Glory (9:14–32)

SUPPORTING IDEA: *Where does glory come from? A failed miracle shows the disciples that glory comes from God.*

9:14. After a mountaintop experience, many Christians hesitate to return to the everyday routine. The disciples felt the same. Peter wanted to remain on the mountaintop with Jesus, Moses, and Elijah. They descended the mountain, however, and were confronted immediately with human needs. Jesus' other disciples were not able to meet the need. They were engaged in a dispute with a group of scribes.

9:15. Some interpreters believe the crowds were **overwhelmed** because Jesus' face shone as did Moses' when he descended the mountain of God. The text, however, gives no indication of this. If this had happened, it would have contradicted Jesus' own words to keep the event secret until after his death and resurrection. The more likely meaning is that Jesus' appearance was sudden and unexpected.

9:16. Jesus' question was meant to draw out the person who needed healing. Before we can be healed, we must admit our need. Some interpreters suggest that Jesus' question was meant to draw attention away from the disciples and to himself. This may be parallel with Jesus' writing on the ground in John 8:6. We don't know what he wrote, but we do know his actions drew attention away from the woman caught in adultery and to himself. It is a snapshot of what Jesus did for all believers on the cross.

9:17–18. The father's intention was to bring his son to be healed by Jesus. Since Jesus was not available, he made his request to the disciples. Because Jesus had previously given the disciples authority in his name, the father's request was not inappropriate. But the disciples were unable to meet this pressing need.

The son is described as mute and deaf (v. 25). The description of convulsions is symptomatic of epilepsy, but the father claimed he was **possessed by a spirit.** This has caused many problems for theologians over the years as they try to decide whether epilepsy is always described as demon possession. A few things can be said in response to this. (1) All sickness is not demon possession. (2) The deafness here is of demonic origin; however, not all instances of deafness are attributed to demons. (3) The seizures were the work of an unclean spirit.

Many people with epilepsy and other severe diseases have been traumatized by well-meaning but misguided people who tried to cast demons out of them. Christians need discernment, compassion, and prayer—something that Jesus pointed out in verse 29. The father's concern for his son was genuine. His graphic detail, recounted possibly by the eyewitness Peter to Mark, shows a brokenness that looked to Jesus for healing.

9:19. Jesus' words are an indication of God's longsuffering patience with his wayward and unbelieving children. They remind us of the failure of the three disciples to understand Jesus' prophecy of his death and resurrection just a little while before. Jesus took immediate action and asked that the boy be brought to him. When we face despair because the task seems too large, we should leave it in God's hands and do the work that needs to be done.

9:20–22. The demon responded violently when it saw Jesus. This is reminiscent of Mark 5:6. Jesus' questioning of the father was meant to bring a confession of need. It may seem a strange question. Why would the father not admit his need? And yet, many parents are blinded to disabilities. Psychologist John White admitted that when his son was born with a club foot, he literally did not see it. Denial can be a strong opponent—perhaps the only thing that can forever block Jesus' healing touch. The Master forced the father to acknowledge that Jesus was his only hope. While the man knew this, he did not know whether this hope was enough. After all, the disciples had been unable to do anything for the son. Perhaps this had shaken his faith somewhat.

9:23–24. Jesus declared that he had the power to heal his son if the man had the faith. **If you can? . . . Everything is possible for him who believes,** he declared. Jesus did not mean that miracles depend on the strength of a person's faith. We must pray always with God's will in mind. The father confessed his belief immediately. It sprang from his heart. But he was aware that he was an imperfect human being; his recent lack of faith proved it. Therefore, he asked Jesus to heal him—the father—first. "Whatever is in me, Lord, that does not believe or want to believe, heal that first." Like removing the log from our own eye, this request was not only appropriate but life-giving.

9:25. Once again, Jesus moved into action before a great crowd could gather. This family had probably been a spectacle for many years; Jesus refused to make them one in this situation. Further, Jesus would not be made the principle participant in a circus. He had often refused to "perform for the crowds" and he did so in this situation by withdrawing. Jesus rebuked the demon and ordered it never to enter the boy again. How encouraging that must have been for the father!

9:26–27. Some interpreters suggest that the boy actually died and that this miracle is reminiscent of the raising of Jairus's daughter in chapter 5. While we cannot be certain that the boy died, this incident gave credibility to Jesus' teaching.

9:28-29. The healing perplexed the disciples. Why had they not been able to perform the miracle? Jesus' answer, **This kind can come out only by prayer,** has been used at times as a magic key to unlock all the closed doors of healing. Some people believe that the strength of the believer's prayer will elicit the desired effect. This, however, is exactly opposite of what Jesus intended.

Jesus had given the disciples authority to cast out demons. Why, then, could they not cast this one out? Because they were relying on their own power. They were relying on the fact that Jesus had given them authority. But he had not given it to them apart from God. They needed to rely on God, to know without a doubt the truth that Jesus later expressed, "Apart from me you can do nothing" (John 15:5).

Some manuscripts add the words "and fasting." There is disagreement among interpreters whether these words should be included or not. For the Jew, fasting was a natural part of prayer and was something that Jesus never condemned. What he condemned was fasting as an external rite, as something to be congratulated, as a sign of advanced spirituality. Fasting, done in the proper spirit, can be a reminder also of dependence upon God and thankfulness for his gifts.

9:30-32. In Hebrew literature, an *inclusio* is a literary device in which two teachings or refrains serve as brackets or bookends to a central teaching or story. We saw in verses 9-10 that Jesus talked about his death and resurrection and that the disciples did not understand his teaching. Then there was this miracle, a reminder of God's power over demonic powers, a reminder of previous miracles, evidence that God can raise someone from the dead, that there is life after death. The *inclusio* is finished in verse 31, where Jesus again predicted his death and the disciples did not understand. This device catches the reader. It says "pay attention." It is the literary equivalent of "he who has ears to hear, let him hear."

Ⓒ The Servant's Glory (9:33-50)

SUPPORTING IDEA: *Through his teachings, Jesus shows the disciples the source and climax of their true glory.*

9:33-34. These verses show how little the disciples understood Jesus and his mission. He has just predicted his violent death at the hands of the authorities, but the disciples argued over who would be the greatest in his kingdom. They were still thinking in terms of their conquering Messiah and the kingdom he would usher in.

Some interpreters believe verses 33-50 are various teachings of Jesus, not necessarily in chronological order. Most of the teachings are repeated in Matthew and Luke in different orders. This may be a case of the Gospel writer arranging material to make his point. In this case, the point is, Where is humanity to find greatness? Three disciples had seen Christ's greatness revealed. Then his glory had been further manifested by a miracle that nine of the disciples could not perform. The circumstances would lead naturally to concern about who would be the greatest.

When Jesus asked the disciples what they had been arguing about among themselves, they remained silent, and the tense indicates that they remained silent for some time. Jesus' probing questions have a way of putting things in proper perspective.

9:35. Jesus did not focus on their arguing about who was the greatest. He spoke frankly, telling them if they wanted to be first, they must be last. The theme of servanthood echoes throughout Mark's Gospel and reaches its greatest expression in chapter 10. Jesus stated again that human values are not necessarily kingdom values. In human institutions, we may fight for status. We may be concerned about being in the right crowd or being seen by powerful people. The old adage, "It's not what you know; it's who you know," has no place in the kingdom of God in the way the world means it.

In another sense, it is *only* who you know that can gain you entrance into God's kingdom. But the image of a humble man or woman falling on his or her knees before God in repentance and asking for pardon and grace is a much different image than that of the businessperson cuddling up next to the person on a higher rung of the ladder.

9:36–37. To illustrate his principle, Jesus placed a child in the midst of them. **Taking him in his arms** (Gr. *enagkalisamenos*) means "to hold in the crook of the arm." It is a picture of reliance, affection, repose. Was it shocking to the disciples to have this child in the midst of them, sitting on the Lord's lap while he taught? It may have been. Children were not viewed favorably in ancient Israel. They were considered among the lowest element in society. Children, even today, have no power. Instead they are needy.

The disciples had been talking about which one was the greatest. After all, they had seen miraculous things, they had been with the Lord, they had performed great deeds. What would this association, this notoriety, give them? We have seen how Jesus treated the sick and outcast; we have seen how he treated women. Now we see his treatment of children.

The Lord's brother James would later write in his epistle that we should not show favoritism in our treatment of people (Jas. 2). Jesus' words here established the principle. Jesus said that the greatest in the kingdom will be the person who serves. With the child, Jesus pointed out that the ones who serve will serve even the least in the kingdom.

Brooks states, "To 'welcome' or 'receive' means 'to be concerned about, to care for, to show kindness to.' To do so in the name of Jesus means to do as he would do, to do so for his sake, to do so as a Christian. To accept the outcasts and oppressed is a way of accepting both God and Jesus. Greatness in the kingdom consists not of position but of ministry" (Brooks, *Mark,* p. 150).

9:38–40. Jesus' lesson continues in these verses. John still wanted to draw lines—to determine clearly who's in and who's out. The child may be in, but this man must surely be out because he was not one of them. In many ancient societies, if exorcists wanted to cast a demon out of someone, they would cast it out in the name of someone stronger. Jesus was making the point that because this man was using his name, he might be a friend and should be treated as such.

Can we reconcile this with Matthew 7:22, "Lord, Lord, did we not prophesy in your name, and in your name drive out demons and perform many miracles"? Jesus provides the answer in the next verse. "Then I will tell them plainly, 'I never knew you. Away from me, you evildoers!'" (7:23). We cannot presume to know who is right and who is wrong. We must leave judgment like this up to Jesus, who knows the heart of every person.

Jesus referred again to service and suggested that an alliance, a bond, is forged when someone serves the Christian because of Christ. We see precious little of that today. Christians are openly persecuted in many parts of the world and subtly persecuted in others. And yet Christians themselves do not practice this form of tolerance. So often we do not treat other people and other denominations as though they belong to Christ.

9:41. In the dry climate of the Middle East, **a cup of water** was a great act of hospitality and kindness. Jesus pointed to service again as he told his disciples that humble acts of service when done because of Christ will be rewarded.

9:42. This verse is a corollary of the one preceding, stated in the negative. If someone does even a small act of kindness, it is noted and rewarded. Likewise, if anyone puts even a tiny stone in the path of a disciple, thereby causing her or him to sin, it will bring judgment. It is unclear to whom **one of these little ones** refers. It could refer to the children Jesus had mentioned earlier, or it could refer to humble believers. Jesus was probably referring to the humble, the weak, the outcast.

Our actions and our words carry significant weight. How many of us have caused someone weaker in faith to doubt or to trust in works rather than in Christ? Some organized religions today insist on law as the means of attaining heaven. And yet, Jesus called this a heavy yoke. Jesus turned the tables and insisted that it would be better for these people to be drowned in the sea by a large stone used to grind grain than to cause even one person to doubt or to sin.

9:43–48. Some early church fathers took verses such as these literally and maimed themselves in order to attain heaven. But this verse is a literary device known as hyperbole, which uses exaggeration to make a point. Jesus was saying that the judgment he had just spoken of was so serious that it would be better to sacrifice yourself than to sin. Do not cause others to sin and do what you have to do to keep from sinning yourself. Sin is so serious that it calls for drastic measures to remove it from our lives.

Is it the hand, foot, or eye that causes one to sin? If you were to cut off your hand, would this remove sin from your life? No. Sin is in our very nature. Only Christ's atoning blood can remove it and change our nature. We must never forget the high price his sacrifice demanded. The word **life** in verses 43 and 45 are parallel with **the kingdom of God** in verse 47. It is not merely human life that Jesus was speaking about here. He was referring instead to eternal life, the life we are granted because of our trust in him.

9:49–50. These verses are difficult because they do not seem to link with the previous verses, except by the word **fire**. Because **salt** is a preservative, verse 49 could refer to the eternality of punishment as does verse 48. This seems an unlikely link, however.

Brooks and Barclay believe that these were separate sayings unconnected to verse 48. In this case, verses 49–50 would have been placed here in order to help people remember them more easily because of the repetitive words.But my position is that these verses do connect with what has just transpired. The link is found in the last part of verse 50: **be at peace with each other.** The disciples had been arguing about who was the greatest. Then they argued about whether this other man was a part of them or not. Jesus had just taught about divisiveness and remembering that anyone who does the work of Christ is a brother or sister. His reminder here acted as an injunction to help the disciples put away divisiveness.

Each sacrifice made in the temple was to be seasoned with salt (see Lev. 2:13). To salt a sacrifice meant to purify it. Jesus had already told his disciples that he would suffer much and be killed. He may have been pointing to the fact that they as his disciples could not expect better treatment, just as modern believers cannot. In being conformed to the image of Christ, we will face the purification of fire and salt—from others in persecution, from ourselves in mortification as we put to death our fleshly desires.

MAIN IDEA REVIEW: *The glory of God and, therefore, what is to be the Christian's glory is revealed. The Christian finds his or her glory in service to God.*

III. CONCLUSION

The Use and Abuse of Power

A coworker used to work at an annual music event in Colorado that sponsored Christian musicians. She eventually quit the job, disillusioned and bitter. So many of the musicians would sing about Jesus Christ and being redeemed, then spend the night with the groupies who hung around after the concerts. Shocked, I asked her if she was certain about this. She was sure.

Being a Christian does not make one immune to the temptations of the world. One of these temptations is to take advantage of power. We can do this in a number of ways. We can seek to be in the presence of powerful people. Sometimes this is manifested in getting to know the pastor, or being sure that all the members of the church staff know who we are. In our culture today—and the Christian subculture is not immune—we see what is called "the cult of the personality." We read only the books recommended by famous people, or listen only to the music that is deemed worthy by a watchdog group. We have given over our minds and wills to the powerful personality. And by invoking their names, we think we borrow some of their power for ourselves. We are like the disciples who think they had power in themselves because they were hanging around with powerful people. Being part of the "in crowd" is a powerful, addictive drug.

Another way we take advantage of power is by abusing the power we have been granted by God. The disciples abused their power by assuming they had power enough within themselves to perform miracles. They forgot where their power originated, thereby losing it when it was most needed.

Jesus' miracles and his teachings in Mark 9 remind us that our power is only a reflection of Christ's power—a shadow compared to the awesome power displayed by the Maker of the universe.

PRINCIPLES

- The Christian life is a balance between mountaintop solitude and valley service.
- Our power to do great things for God comes from God.
- Our commitment to Christ demands that we serve the weak and the outcasts of society as well as the powerful.

APPLICATIONS

- When you are in solitude with God, surrender your "agenda" to him and ask how he would want you to serve.

- Remember that when you are faced with trials, there is a deeper glory and a deeper significance than what we can see in this world.
- Get in the habit of seeing things from an eternal perspective.
- Deal radically with the sin in your life. Begin by confessing your sin to God and then to one other person whom you can trust.

IV. LIFE APPLICATION

The Source of Our Power

Corrie ten Boom's life could have been based entirely on Mark 9. On outward appearances, no one would have thought this quiet girl who cared for her father and ailing sister would be used mightily by God in extraordinary circumstances. Corrie ten Boom, through offering her life to God, became a chief player in the resistance of the Nazis in World War II. Her resistance began when she hid one Jew in her home. Others followed. Soon she had a houseful of Jews, was forging papers to help them cross the border, was lying to conceal a much-needed radio, and was stealing meal coupons to help feed those who were considered outcasts.

When she and her family were captured and put into concentration camps, the jailers did not see a powerful woman whom God had laid his hand on. They saw an old woman weak from undernourishment, naked because her clothes had been taken, dirty because baths had become a luxury, bruised because she was hated. Her true glory was hidden from those without eyes to see.

When Corrie was eventually released from the concentration camp (her sister had died shortly before), she returned to her home and tried to get back into her resistance work. She was to carry release papers into the local prison and give them to the jailer. Not a difficult thing, and yet, she almost made a critical error and was filled with terror the entire time. She wrote, "If I had ever needed proof that I had no boldness or cleverness of my own, I had it now. Whatever bravery or skill I had ever shown were gifts of God—sheer loans from him of the talent needed to do a job. And it was clear, from the absence of such skills now, that this was no longer his work for me" (*The Hiding Place*, 233f.).

Corrie learned, as did the disciples, that the power needed to do God's work comes from God. It is what we pray at the end of the Lord's prayer: "For thine is the kingdom, and the power, and the glory, for ever" (Matt. 6:13, KJV). It is his glory and his power.

V. PRAYER

Our great and glorious God, help us to remember when we go through dark and troubling times that we are seeing only a part of the entire picture. Help us always to seek your glory. Let us remember when we see the outcasts in our society—the weak, the homeless, the suffering—that we may be seeing your face. Grant us your power to do great things or small things for you, realizing that in your kingdom, there are no small things. Amen.

VI. DEEPER DISCOVERIES

A. Transfiguration (9:2–12)

It may be misleading to speak of the transfiguration of Jesus. Transfiguration means to change form, to change the outward appearance. This is probably how the disciples perceived it. But it would be more accurate to note that the disciples' perception changed. Jesus did not change. He was not one thing before the transfiguration and then something different after it. First Corinthians 13:12 says, "Now we see but a poor reflection as in a mirror; then we shall see face to face." Peter, James, and John were given a gift that the rest of the world will not see until Christ returns. It was as though the veil between this world and the next was lowered for a moment so these disciples could see Christ as he really is.

Cole (*Mark*, p. 210) correctly notes that the real transfiguration of Jesus took place at Bethlehem when the God of the universe took on human flesh. On the Mount of Transfiguration, Jesus simply reassumed his original form with Peter, John, and James looking on. "Faith had momentarily passed into sight."

There were two immediate outcomes to the transfiguration. First, it gave assurance to Jesus. Sometimes we think that because Jesus was God, he did not have human emotions. But he *was* human. One reason he may have spent so much time in prayer was because of his desire to make sure of the path he was following. And opposition was tough. Have you ever noticed how temptation gets stronger if you do not give in the first time? His temptations did not stop when Jesus defeated Satan in the desert. Satan used Peter as a tool in Mark 8. Peter was presenting to Jesus a different path. Jesus clearly defeated the temptation here; the transfiguration gave him further assurance that he had chosen correctly.

The transfiguration also gave assurance to the disciples. Jesus' words to them recorded in chapter 8 would have been shocking, wounding words. Was he not the Messiah? What was this death he was talking about? Would he not defeat their enemies and release Israel from Roman rule? The transfiguration assured them that Jesus was God's Son. His appearance with Moses and Elijah would have recalled to the disciples that all the Bible—the Law and the Prophets—point to Christ.

There have been times in my life, points of despair, when I was tempted to give in, to give up. Christ at those times seemed very far away. This must have been how the disciples felt on Black Saturday, the day after Jesus died. But there are experiences I can look back on and say, "But what about this?" They are like the memorial stones of help in the Old Testament. They are "ebenezers" for me to remember what God has done in my life.

The transfiguration may have served the same purpose for the disciples. The crucifixion would have dashed their hopes and sent them spiraling into despair. "But what about this?" These three leaders of the early church could remember that Jesus had been transformed before their eyes, that they had heard the voice of God, that he had spoken to them of being raised from the dead. It gave them comfort in their "dark night of the soul." It can do the same for us.

B. Moses and Elijah (9:4)

Moses was the lawgiver, while Elijah was Israel's greatest prophet. Many similarities exist between these two men and their ministries that foreshadow Christ and his ministry. Both men were central figures in Israel's "miracle-clusters." Although the Bible records many miracles, they were not a daily occurrence. Miracles are miracles precisely because of their unexpected nature. In Israel's history, however, miracles clustered around certain events to validate God's presence in a unique way. Perhaps the three greatest clusters were the miracles surrounding Israel's release from Egypt, the prophetic miracles defeating pagan religions, and the miracles authenticating Jesus' ministry.

Another similarity between the two leaders is that both faced strong political opposition—Moses with Pharaoh and Elijah with Ahab. Jesus, likewise, faced opposition from the Romans and the religious establishment. Pharaoh pursued Moses to the edge of the Red Sea, desiring his death. Ahab and his wife, Jezebel, sought to put Elijah to death after his defeat of the prophets of Baal. We saw earlier in Mark that those in authority plotted to put Jesus to death. But while God provided divine protection for Moses and Elijah, Jesus voluntarily surrendered his life in order to purchase life-giving protection for his followers.

Both leaders appointed a representative to carry on the work after his death. Joshua and Elisha had each sat under their masters' teachings. In today's language, they were "mentored." They had seen God through their masters' eyes. They had witnessed miracles and carried on the work of the miracles. Jesus had twelve close followers who saw his miracles and received authority to perform miracles as well. And those twelve were commissioned to carry on his work, to spread the good news of his atoning sacrifice to the ends of the earth.

Both Moses and Elijah underwent transformation. Moses' face shone when he encountered God in the tent. His face was a reflection of the glory of God. Elijah was transformed when he was caught up into heaven in a fiery chariot. But Jesus was not a mere reflection of God. He was the exact likeness of God in his glory. And his death would transform death for his followers into a thing not to be feared. As a trusting child lets go of a doll to grasp the hand of her father, so believers release their hold on this shadowed life to grasp the hand of the waiting Father.

The appearance of these two men on the Mount of the Transfiguration further validated Jesus' ministry. It was God's word to Israel that Jesus was his beloved Son—above the Law and above the Prophets. God was not denigrating the value of the Law and the Prophets but declaring that life was given only through the Son. We can cling to the law and live by its precepts, even down to tithing a tenth of the dime we find on the sidewalk. We can seek out mysticism and spiritual experiences or voices. We can be experts on biblical prophecy. We can seek life in being a good person. Or we can search the skies for a divine sign. But it is only in becoming a child of God through Jesus Christ that we find the life we have been missing.

C. Elijah and John the Baptist (9:12–13)

Some take Mark 9:12–13 as evidence that the Bible teaches reincarnation. There is no evidence, however, that Jesus believed that John or anyone else was the literal incarnation of Elijah. John was a type or a picture of Elijah. The disciples who heard Jesus make the comparison would have naturally taken it that way.

Similarities exist also between the ministry of these two men. Elijah faced political opposition in his encounters with King Ahab. John the Baptist's opposition was Herod Antipas. Each man spoke out strongly against the evil of these two political powers. But both men's real enemies were the wives of these two leaders: Jezebel and Herodias. Each woman hated the prophet of God and each woman manipulated her husband to have the prophet put to death.

William Barclay notes that every cherished idea of the disciples was being overturned by Jesus. They were looking for Elijah to announce the coming of the Messiah and for the Messiah to bring victory against all their worldly enemies. On the other hand, Jesus "was trying to compel them to see that in fact the herald had been cruelly killed and the Messiah must end on a Cross. They still did not understand, and their failure to understand was due to the cause which always makes men fail to understand—they clung to their way and refused to see God's way. They wished things as they desired them and not as God had ordered them. The error of their thoughts had blinded them to the revelation of God's truth" (Barclay, *Mark*, pp. 213–214.).

D. Hell (9:43,45,47)

The Hebrew for this word literally means Valley of the Son of Hinnom, a valley on the southwest side of Jerusalem. The Greek transliteration of this word in verses 43, 45, and 47 is *gehenna*. The Bible refers to this valley as a place of child sacrifice to the god Molech (Jer. 7:31; 32:35). Ahaz and Manasseh, two wicked kings of Jerusalem, sacrificed sons there (2 Chr. 28:3; 33:6). King Josiah, one of the rare godly kings during the preexilic years, attempted to stop the practice by desecrating the site (2 Kgs. 23:10).

Isaiah notes that it was a place of burning, a place prepared for burning by God (Isa. 30:33). In the intertestamental period, this valley was the garbage and sewage dump of Jerusalem (Brooks, *Mark*, p. 153). Certain apocryphal books make reference to Hinnom as a place of punishment because of the continual presence of fire and worms or maggots on the refuse, which are symbolic of destruction. The imagery used is the same as in Revelation for the lake of fire (Rev. 19:20). It means punishment, eternal separation from God.

The Greek word for "unable to be quenched" is *asbestos*. Many people say the Bible does not teach eternal damnation, believing instead that unbelievers are merely annihilated at death. These verses speak against that. Damnation is for eternity. While we must continually offer the grace of Jesus Christ to unbelievers and outcasts, we must never forget the seriousness of their offenses against God.

The word *hell* with its accompanying imagery is used twelve times in the New Testament, eleven times by Jesus. This signifies the great importance Jesus placed on this teaching. This location in Mark's Gospel, immediately before further opposition from the religious leaders, foreshadows events and teachings in Mark 11, which deal more strongly with Christ's judgment.

VII. TEACHING OUTLINE

A. INTRODUCTION

1. Lead Story: The Lady of Shalott
2. Context: We saw in chapter 8 that Peter gave the clearest indication of who Jesus was when he proclaimed Jesus as the Christ. Jesus predicts his death and then authenticates his teaching with the glorious miracle of the transformation, which allows three disciples to see him as he truly is. The discussions that follow, on Elijah, on John the

Baptist, on authority, on greatness, on sin, all hinge on Christ's glory. Because of who he is, we share in his glory as we share in his service.

3. Transition: Like the Lady of Shalott, we see reality as though we are looking in a mirror. The transfiguration, the crowning miracle before the resurrection, turns us around and allows us to look at reality: If anyone wants to be first, he must be the very last and the servant of all. Jesus' words prepare us for his greatest work: the cross.

B. COMMENTARY

1. The Glory of the Son (9:1–13)
   a. The transfiguration (9:1–8)
   b. Elijah (9:9–13)
2. Borrowed Glory (9:14–32)
   a. The failure of the disciples (9:14–19)
   b. The healing (9:19–27)
   c. Jesus' teaching about the healing (9:28–32)
3. The Servant's Glory (9:33–50)
   a. The servant of all (9:33–37)
   b. Alliances (9:38–41)
   c. Dealing radically with sin (9:42–50)

C. CONCLUSION: THE SOURCE OF OUR POWER

VIII. ISSUES FOR DISCUSSION

1. Read verse 23. What kind of limits do you place on God? Where do you have trouble believing God? What does it mean for you to be able to say, "Help me overcome my unbelief"?
2. What kind of alliances can you think of that illustrate Jesus' point in verse 40?
3. In what ways has God revealed even small parts of himself to you? In what situations can you imagine God asking you not to talk about it until some time later?

Mark 10

Service: A Relational Perspective

I.   **INTRODUCTION**
     An Extension of the Master Servant

II. **COMMENTARY**
     A verse-by-verse explanation of the chapter.

III. **CONCLUSION**
     Greatness in His Service

     An overview of the principles and applications from
     the chapter.

IV. **LIFE APPLICATION**
     First in Service

     Melding the chapter to life.

V.   **PRAYER**
     Tying the chapter to life with God.

VI. **DEEPER DISCOVERIES**
     Historical, geographical, and grammatical enrich-
     ment of the commentary.

VII. **TEACHING OUTLINE**
     Suggested step-by-step group study of the chapter.

VIII. **ISSUES FOR DISCUSSION**
     Zeroing the chapter in on daily life.

Quote

"One of the most revealing snapshots of Francis's approach toward servant leadership is found in one brief sentence in the *Legend of Perugia* that's easy to miss amid all the accounts of the saint's wonderful deeds. But there it is, hidden in a description of Francis's practice of traveling and preaching in churches: 'He brought along a broom to clean the churches.'"

John Michael Talbot

Mark 10

IN A NUTSHELL

Through several situations, Jesus contrasts his teachings with that of the Pharisees. While they believed they were great leaders, Jesus shows his disciples that a great leader is one who serves, even to the point of death.

Service: A Relational Perspective

I. INTRODUCTION

An Extension of the Master Servant

*W*e use the word *service* with several different meanings. We may speak of the worship service, a wedding or funeral service. You can have your car serviced. But service is also a military term. You join the service. In this context, you are placing your rights, your desires, your time at the disposal of your country.

This usage of the word *service* reminds me of the Lipizzan stallions of the Spanish Riding School. These stallions, quartered in Vienna, Austria, perform war dressage movements, called *haute Ècole,* to music. These are difficult movements, and not every horse can perform them. The stallions, bred from Roman cavalry horses, are trained for years in the dressage movements and also in the mid-air leaps.

The rider sits astride the horse and commands him. It looks effortless—a beautiful blend of human and animal, horse and rider. But it is anything but effortless! The rider must be strong, commanding. The stallion has placed himself in the service of the rider/trainer. Each "effortless" movement is the result of this relationship between master and servant. The horse becomes more than a horse in this case. He becomes an extension of the master.

When we offer our lives to God, we join his service. His priorities become our own, his commands our loving duty. In time, our own movements may look effortless as we serve him. In chapter 10 of Mark's Gospel, we find out what God's priorities are and who he commands us to be while we make ourselves available for his service.

II. COMMENTARY

Service: A Relational Perspective

MAIN IDEA: *A great leader, and therefore also the ones who follow Jesus, is one who serves in the midst of relationships with others.*

ⒶThe Relationship Between Spouses (10:1–12)

> **SUPPORTING IDEA:** *Human selfishness is either directly or indirectly the cause of most marital discord and divorce. We can serve our spouses by submitting ourselves to them in love (Eph. 5:21).*

10:1. Jesus then **left that place**—Capernaum, his home base. This corresponds with the statement in Luke 9:51 that Jesus "resolutely set out for Jerusalem." He was leaving a place of comfort and acceptance to go to a place where he knew he would be betrayed and murdered. He would not return to Capernaum again. As Jesus crossed to the eastern side of the Jordan River, he was coming back to the place where John the Baptist was put to death. This region was under the jurisdiction of Herod Antipas. As he traveled, the crowds gathered around him. Jesus was well known here, either from hearsay or from his association with John the Baptist.

10:2. The Pharisees searched for ways to get rid of Jesus. Their motive was not to understand or to learn but to trap Jesus in his own words. The Pharisees might have been hoping that Jesus would condemn Herod Antipas's adultery as John the Baptist had and thus would suffer the same fate. If not that, Jesus' answer to their question would surely offend one of the two schools of thought on divorce. The more conservative school, that of Shammai, stated that the only justifiable ground for divorce was adultery. The school of Hillel taught that any displeasure with a wife—including her cooking or her looks—justified a husband's seeking a divorce.

As William Barclay notes, this was not a disinterested, scholarly topic. Because of the political ramifications with Herod and Herodias and the religious debates, this was a highly charged topic.

10:3. Jesus avoided answering their question directly, showing further that the Pharisees were testing him. When people asked Jesus a question because they wanted to learn or because they did not understand something (see Mark 9:11–12), Jesus did not circumvent the question but answered directly. In this situation, and with questions coming up in later chapters, Jesus turned the question back on the questioner. He asked the masters of the law what the law commanded. It called to their minds that no matter what their motives were in questioning him, Jesus would not go against Moses. In fact, he gave richer meaning to the law.

10:4–5. The Pharisees referred to Deuteronomy 24:1. Jesus, however, stated that this was given because of their hardened hearts. As with much of the law, it was meant to curb behavior already in practice. For instance, with the law known as "an eye for an eye," God was not commanding that an injury be made for every injury received. Instead, he was limiting what amount of retaliation could be sought. The law regarding divorce was similar in that it limited behavior rather than setting precedence. It gave a measure of protection to women from husbands who would leave them for trivial reasons.

10:6. Jesus reminded his listeners that marriage did not come into existence with the law and Moses. It had been instituted at the beginning of creation by God. Marriage should not be entered into lightly or dissolved for trivial reasons.

10:7–8. While God allowed divorce, this was not his original, ideal intention. His intention was the making of new social groups. A man was to leave his family in order to form a new family unit of his own. As strong as the bond between a child and parents is, the bond between a husband and wife is stronger. In fact, Paul used the image of this bond to show the relationship between Christ and his church. They are one flesh.

10:9. The ideal instituted by God in the creation was for a lasting union between a man and a woman. God is the one who separates the couple through death. Barbieri notes that the verb for separate, *chorizeto,* is in the present and literally means "to make it a habit to be separating" (Barbieri *Mark,* p 221). The use of the present tense may indicate a judgment on those who separate lightly, thereby flouting God's ideal of one flesh.

10:10. Again, the disciples needed further instruction, and Jesus complied. Because the disciples truly wanted answers, Jesus answered them more fully. Their questioning showed that Jesus' interpretation of marriage went against what was commonly taught.

10:11–12. Mark's Gospel is often considered to be unfriendly to women. Jesus' statement is a refutation of this myth. The radicalness is in the words **commits adultery against her.** In Jewish society, a woman could commit adultery against her husband. A man could commit adultery against another man by having relations with that man's wife (Deut. 22:13–29). A man could not, however, commit adultery against his wife. Jesus' proclamation raised the status of women.

B The Relationship between Children and the Kingdom of God (10:13–16)

SUPPORTING IDEA: *In order to serve our Lord, we must be like children.*

10:13. Rabbis were known to lay hands on children and bless them. The children in this incident could have been anywhere from infants to twelve-year-olds. The disciples, who were tired and tense with the prospect of going to Jerusalem, were probably trying to protect Jesus' time.

10:14. Note Jesus' anger in this verse. The Greek verb *aganakteo* implies deep, strong feeling. While this is the only use of this verb in Mark's Gospel, the Bible does show Jesus as becoming angry on other occasions (cf. 1:41;

3:5). Those who believe that the God of the Old Testament is an angry God, while Jesus was never anything but meek, miss the richness of the Gospels and the truth that Jesus shared our humanity. Jesus' service, and therefore the service of the disciples, was for such as these children (9:36). This is one more instance where the disciples failed to realize that there are no outcasts or unimportant people in the kingdom.

10:15. Not only were the outcasts as important as others; Jesus also stated that everyone who desires the kingdom must be like these little children. Much has been written about how children act and what Jesus could have been referring to here. We could talk about a child's total dependence and trust—two qualities needed for the kingdom. But Jesus point was, How do children receive gifts? They receive with anticipation. They receive joyfully and thankfully. They receive without believing they did anything to deserve the gift.

This is a picture of how we come to the Father. We know we do not deserve the great gifts he has in store for us, but he loves us and desires to give us good things. Rather than saying, "I won't take your gift until I can earn it," we need to receive the gift of Christ's redemption with joy and thanksgiving. The kingdom belongs to such as these. Therefore, not only are disciples to receive little children (9:36–37); they are to possess childlike qualities themselves.

10:16. In finishing his teaching on children, Jesus took the children in his arms and blessed them. It is a warm image, showing that Jesus practiced what he preached! All who come to Jesus will receive his blessing. In his love and grace, there are no outcasts.

◉ The Believer's Relationship with Money (10:17–31)

SUPPORTING IDEA: *Money is never to be a master over us, nor something that comes between us and God. It is something we offer to the service of our Lord.*

10:17. In Matthew's Gospel, this man is called young (Matt. 19:20), and Luke's Gospel identifies him as a ruler (Luke 18:18). Note that this young ruler ran to Jesus and fell at his feet. In the Middle East, it was undignified for men to run. This man with his youthful passion was throwing his respectability at Jesus' feet.

The term **good** in this context is also unusual. It was not a common practice to call anyone good, leaving the appellation for God alone. Brooks notes further, "The question is also unusual because most Jews would have no doubts about what to do: observe the law. Probably the man had heard about Jesus' teaching that mere obedience to the law was not enough" (Brooks, *Mark*, p. 162). This section follows the previous section naturally, since the man asked what he could do to earn eternal life. Jesus' teaching on the children emphasized that there is nothing one can do to earn it. It is given freely and must be received freely.

10:18. Some interpreters have said that Jesus' response indicated he was disclaiming an identity with God. But we see from Jesus' teachings in other places that Jesus often used questions to draw a statement of faith from a seeker. For example, in Luke 8:45, a woman was healed of a hemorrhage by touching the hem of Jesus' garment. He asked, "Who touched me?" Jesus knew who had touched him, but he wanted her to come forward and acknowledge her faith. It helped restore her to community. Other examples of Jesus using questions to solicit a statement of faith are in Luke 9:20 and Mark 8:29 ("Who do you say I am?"), in Luke 10:36 ("Which of these three do you think was a neighbor to the man who fell into the hands of robbers?"), and John 8:10 ("Has no one condemned you?").

The man called Jesus "good." The Greek word he used is *agathos*, meaning "intrinsically good." This word was not used lightly nor of every good thing. Had the man made the leap that Jesus was indeed God, who was intrinsically good? Was he prepared to lend full weight to his pronouncements? As we see in verse 22, his passion outweighed his commitment.

10:19. Note that Jesus in this verse did not list the commandments dealing with a person's relationship to God. These were internal commandments, not as easily discernible from observing behavior. Perhaps Jesus also knew that this man could not keep the first commandment—to have no other Gods before Yahweh, the supreme God

It is also noteworthy that Jesus mentioned **do not defraud** instead of the tenth commandment, "do not covet." Defrauding someone, however, was listed in the law (cf. Lev. 19:13) and at its heart was covetousness. In this verse and its companion verse (v. 21) is a principle that we see often in Jesus' teachings. It is the same principle as "go the extra mile." The young man had never defrauded anyone, but neither had he gone the extra mile and been generous with his money. This involved the positive application of the law.

10:20. The phrase **since I was a boy** referred to the age of thirteen, the time when he would have become accountable—a son of the commandments. If this list were all the law contained, then it would not be impossible to conform to its demands—difficult, yes, but not impossible. On the commandments that Jesus listed, this man had it made—externally. But had he considered the spirit of the law as Jesus laid it down in Matthew 5–7? Apparently, even he knew there had to be more to it because he did not leave immediately, rejoicing at Jesus' answer. He knew in his heart that he lacked something. Matthew 19:20 records that he asked, "What do I still lack?"

10:21. Mark is the only Gospel writer who records that Jesus **looked at him and loved him.** It gives us a sharp image of a God who loves unconditionally, compassionately. This is the God who asks us to follow him. Some interpreters have taken this verse to mean that poverty is more blessed than riches. But Jesus did not intend this meaning here. He was declaring that nothing must come between a person and devotion to God. Some people may have to give up money. Others may have to abandon a cherished dream. Still others may have to surrender family. But one thing is certain: Jesus' love comes before the command. Whatever he commands us to do is because of his love for us.

Jesus' command to the man to **follow me** came at the time when he was headed for Jerusalem and certain death at the hands of the religious leaders. This echoes Jesus' command to every disciple to take up the cross and follow him (Mark 8:34).

10:22. What a stunning conclusion to this series of verses! Brooks states, "This verse has been described as the saddest in the Bible" (Brooks, *Mark,* p. 163). It is the only instance of someone coming to Jesus with a need and leaving without the need being filled. No matter how much we are loved by God, he will not override our choices.

10:23. The phrase **for the rich** is translated at times as "those who have riches." It means more than having money. It encompasses possessions as well. In our day, it might mean everything that goes with money—cars, furs, jewels, real estate. But even if we do not consider ourselves rich, we still have riches and possessions that often come between us and the Lord.

10:24–26. The disciples' amazement is mentioned twice in this section. In order to understand their amazement, we need to realize the conception they would have had of the wealthy. Money in that day was considered a blessing of God. If a person was righteous, God would bless through wealth and material possessions. This is seen in Genesis with the recounting of the life of Abraham, a man greatly blessed by God. The cause-and-effect relationship between righteousness and wealth is most clearly seen in Job. Job's friends assumed he had lost righteousness with God because he had lost his riches (family was included in the recounting of wealth).

Jesus compared entering the kingdom of God to a camel going through the eye of a needle. This verse has been discussed at length. Many attempts have been made to soften its teaching. Some have said that there is a gate in Jerusalem named "the eye of the needle" and that perhaps Jesus meant this gate. Other interpretations suggest that the word in Greek is not "camel" (*kamelos*) but "rope" (*kamilos*) because the words are very similar. Jesus, however, often used hyperbole (deliberate overstatement) to make his point. This is a good example of such overstatement. But more important is Jesus' teaching. If we try to soften the harshness of this verse, are we guilty of trying to hold on to the riches we have? Are we like the young man who went away sad because he had great wealth?

Who then can be saved? Jesus had declared to his disciples that the most righteous people of that day could not be saved by their own efforts. If this were true, then how would they—poor fishermen—gain entrance? The disciples asked if the best could not be saved, who could?

10:27. Jesus emphasized that gaining treasure in heaven, eternal life, can be accomplished only by God. We come with empty hands. "Discipleship makes all equal; none start with the balance loaded in their favour, when it comes to entry into the kingdom of God. Only the humble, the 'little ones', find entry to the kingdom" (Cole, *Mark*, p. 237). This is something that Jesus has emphasized throughout Mark's Gospel. The needy are healed. The outcasts of society gain entrance to Jesus. When we admit our need, when we admit that we are indeed outcasts, then God performs what was impossible for us—he grants us eternal life and heals us of our sin sicknesses.

10:28. It is natural for us to wonder if our sacrifices have been noticed. Peter, the spokesman of the group and most likely the narrative voice behind this Gospel, reminded Jesus of just how much he and the others had given up to follow him.

10:29–30. If Peter wanted affirmation that the disciples' sacrifices had been noticed, Jesus gave him that reassurance in this verse. There is no material possession that has been left behind that will not be repaid in this life or in the life to come. Many followers of Christ have lost families, but they have found new family members within the body of Christ.

The addition of the word **persecutions** "remove the whole matter from the world of *quid pro quo*. They take away the idea of a material reward for a material sacrifice. They tell us of two things. They speak of the utter honesty of Jesus. He never offered an easy way. He told men straight that to be a Christian is a costly thing. Second, they tell us that Jesus never used a *bribe* to make men follow him. He used a *challenge*" (Barclay, *Mark*, p. 250).

10:31. While many interpreters see this as a warning to Peter against pride in his own sacrifices, it seems to be more than that. Jesus had talked much during his journey to Jerusalem about the reversals in the kingdom. The outcasts are to be sought after and not hindered; the greatest must serve. This verse caps Jesus' teaching on wealth and reiterates his teaching not to judge by externals and surface appearances.

🄳 The Believer's Relationship with Christ (10:32–45)

SUPPORTING IDEA: *As Christians, we have placed ourselves under the leadership of Christ. His purpose must become our purpose.*

10:32. The picture that comes across in this verse is of the disciples lagging behind. They do not want to go with Jesus. They were confused and frightened. Jesus had faced much opposition and they knew they were headed into enemy territory. But Jesus was determined to go, no matter what. The disciples may have been confused about Jesus' absolute insistence on going up to Jerusalem. Two groups were following Jesus—the twelve disciples, whom Jesus pulled aside to give further instructions, and other followers of Jesus who were heading to Jerusalem for the Passover Festival.

10:33–34. Barclay notes that at each prediction of his death, Jesus gives an additional element. "At first (Mark 8:31) it is the bare announcement. At the second time the hint of betrayal is there (Mark 9:31). And now at the third time the jesting, the mocking and the scourging appear. It would seem as if the picture became ever clearer in the mind of Jesus as he became more and more aware of the cost of redemption" (Barclay, *Mark,* p. 252). Furthermore, Jesus would be handed over to the Gentiles. This was the ultimate rejection and humiliation that his own people could lay on him.

At the beginning of Mark's Gospel, we compared Jesus with a hero—a larger-than-life hero. It becomes clear just how heroic he is as we see him headed for Jerusalem, even though he knew what awaited him there.

10:35. The insensitivity of James and John in this verse prefigures the insensitivity of the three disciples in the garden of Gethsemane when they could not stay awake while Jesus was in great agony. It is clear from their words that they did not recognize that Jesus would die; they were expecting him to inherit his kingdom. Some interpreters believe they spoke from faith, because they believed Jesus would die but would overcome through his resurrection. In this case, they wanted to be a part of his kingdom when he came back victoriously. This interpretation does not fit with the rest of Mark's Gospel or with the general disbelief of the disciples.

In Matthew 20:20, Salome, the mother of John and James, is reported as being the one who approached Jesus. "Salome was the sister of Jesus' mother. . . . In making this request, she apparently hoped to take advantage of this relationship" (Dowling, Foster, Marshall, Root, *Mark,* p. 97). Whether the request was made by Salome at her sons' instigation, or by John and James at their mother's initiative, the fact remains that it was a request born of selfish motives.

10:36–37. Jesus, however, did not rebuke them, but invited them to tell him the desires of their hearts. They were asking for seats of high honor, ruling positions. Although they believed that Jesus would eventually conquer, they misunderstood what kind of kingdom Jesus had come to establish through his suffering and death. To balance this, however, we must remember that James and John loved Jesus and were loyal to him. Although they misunderstood his words, at least they promised they would be with him.

10:38. Again, Jesus did not rebuke them, perhaps because he knew of their love for him. But Jesus asked them if they were prepared to suffer as he would suffer. Jesus asked them, as he asks all disciples, to count the cost (cf. Luke 14:27–33). In the Old Testament, "the cup" signified divine judgment on sin. By "his cup," Jesus was probably referring to the divine judgment poured out on him on behalf of all humanity. This phrase further points out the disciples' lack of understanding.

10:39–40. Whether or not they knew what they agreed to, Jesus told James and John they would share his sufferings. James was martyred when he was beheaded by Herod Agrippa I (Acts 12:2), thus becoming the first apostle to be martyred. Although tradition says that John was the only apostle not to be martyred, he was persecuted for Christ and eventually died in exile on the island of Patmos. Jesus' reply that their request was not his to grant shows his reverent submission to his Father. In all matters, he submitted to his Father's will.

10:41. Mark's statement about the other disciples that they **became indignant** is an obvious understatement. Their anger and resentment was probably not because of their concern for the Lord. They were probably thinking of their own positions. How did the other disciples hear about this incident? Did James and John tell the others? Were they overheard? Did Salome brag to others in the group that her sons would receive special privilege? While all these may be possible, the Bible does not specify how they knew.

10:42–44. Jesus called the disciples together. They had been with many other people, but Jesus pulled them away to teach them, as he had done so often in the past. This act reminded them that they were to live in unity. His words underscored the need for this. A good example of Gentile lordship can be found in Daniel 4. King Nebuchadnezzar believed that his kingship gave him the right to claim the status of God: "Is not this the great Babylon I have built as the royal residence, by my mighty power and for the glory of my majesty?" (v. 30). God took away his authority and he lived as an animal, "until you acknowledge that the Most High is sovereign over the kingdoms of men and gives them to anyone he wishes" (v. 25).

This is why God did not want King David to take a census (2 Sam. 24:1–17). God wanted his ruler, the shepherd placed over the sheep, to put his trust in God, not in the number of warriors. Such things are characteristic of unbelievers. At the time of Jesus, Gentile lords (such as the Caesars) loved to equate themselves with gods. They placed their likenesses on coins to remind people of their self-proclaimed divinity. They did not rule their subjects with benevolence, but they required them to bow down and worship them. Do not be like these Gentiles, Jesus told his disciples. He repeated essentially what he had been saying for the last two chapters of Mark: To be great, you must serve.

10:45. In this verse, Jesus delivered the stunning summary of all his teaching on servanthood in the Gospel of Mark. He gave the disciples the supreme example of servanthood: himself. And they had seen him serve.

They had seen him touch the unclean. They had seen him heal the multitudes. They had seen him feed thousands. Before it was over, they would see him wash the grime from their feet. They had seen the only one who truly deserved to be called "Lord" place himself in humble service to others.

If we remember where Jesus came from, we can see how absurd this must have sounded to them. Jesus had ten thousand angels at his disposal. He was the Creator of everything that exists. He was in eternal fellowship with the Father and the Holy Spirit. He shared their glory and splendor. And yet he gave it all up and was born in a stable to a poor teenager in order to draw all people to God. "*Even*. This adverb hits hard," Enos Dowling declared. "When we are moved to complain as our pride is wounded over failed ambition or service that did not receive much praise from our fellows, we need to spend some time contemplating this adverb *even*. Who are we to complain?" (Dowling, *Mark*, p. 100).

And to give his life as a ransom for many. Brooks states, "Implicit in this statement is a bold challenge reminiscent of other sayings of Jesus: those who readily accept Jesus' ransom ought also accept his example of service" (Brooks, *Mark*, p. 171). Barbieri also closely links ransom and service. "It appears that John ultimately understood the Lord's intention, for in later years he said, 'We know by this, that He laid down His life for us; and we ought to lay down our lives for the brethren' (1 John 3:16)" (Barbieri, *Mark*, p. 239). The ones who wanted the superior positions in his kingdom came to understand Jesus' conception of greatness.

Ⅰ The Believer's Relationship with Others (10:46–52)

SUPPORTING IDEA: *As servants of Christ, we must bring others to knowledge of Christ.*

10:46. The Bible does not state how much time passed between what had transpired above and this story of the healing of Bartimaeus. Jesus and his disciples came to Jericho. At this time, there were two Jerichos, one an ancient city and the other a newer one built by Herod the Great. Jericho was situated between the Jordan River and Jerusalem. The road leading from Jericho would have been well traveled by pilgrims heading to Jerusalem for the Passover Festival. It would have been an ideal place for begging. Mark names the beggar as Bartimaeus, suggesting that he may have been known in the community to which Mark was writing.

10:47. Bartimaeus called out **Son of David**—a clear messianic title. This title is not used often in Mark (who preferred the "Son of Man designation"). This could be, however, because Mark wrote to a largely Gentile audience. Bartimaeus was expressing faith in the one he knew could help him—the expected Messiah—and he begged for mercy.

10:48. Some people tried to stop Bartimaeus from seeking Jesus. Could it have been Jesus' determined stride that made them think he had no time for the blind beggar? "In comparison with the destiny of a nation, the fate of one blind beggar must have seemed unimportant" (Dowling, *Mark*, p. 100). But Bartimaeus did not let the crowds deter him, and he shouted all the more for Jesus to have mercy on him.

10:49. The followers of Jesus were not aware that more than the destiny of a nation awaited Jesus at Jerusalem. The destiny of the world hung in the balance. And yet, Jesus paused and called the blind beggar to him. We often think in terms of sacrificing the one for the many. In the kingdom of God, however, even the one is sought out and blessed. Once Jesus' will was known, the crowd hurried to help Bartimaeus find his way to Jesus. We as Christians know the will of our Lord and should likewise hurry to bring others to his side.

10:50. The garment mentioned, a *himation* or outer garment, must have been priceless to Bartimaeus. It was something that not a lot of beggars owned, and yet he cast it away. "The blind man recognized that in this particular matter, his cloak could become a hindrance; it might trip him as he hurried toward his Benefactor . . . with rare abandon he made absolutely sure the hindrance was removed before it had the chance to do damage. He had some sight after all, but it emanated from his soul and not his eyes" (Powell, *Mark's Superb Gospel*, p. 281). Compare Bartimaeus's devotion in casting away his cloak with the rich young ruler, who could not bring himself to cast away anything he owned to gain what he wanted.

10:51. Jesus first asked Bartimaeus what he wanted. We may think this an absurd question. Couldn't Jesus see that the man was blind? And yet, Jesus wanted him to admit to a need. After all, Bartimaeus could have been asking alms from Jesus. Bartimaeus called Jesus **Rabbi** (other translations use the stronger *rabboni*). Either word means "teacher" or "master," a title of deep respect. Bartimaeus did not hesitate to tell Jesus what he wanted: his sight.

10:52. As Jesus did with the woman with the hemorrhage, he pronounced that Bartimaeus's faith had healed him. The word *seso,* meaning "healed," carries the connotation of "saved." Brooks notes, "Mark probably intended a double meaning. The man was healed physically and saved spiritually. The latter is implied by the fact that he began to follow Jesus. The statement certainly means that Bartimaeus joined with the other pilgrims in accompanying Jesus on the road to Jerusalem . . . but again it is likely that Mark intended a double reference. 'Following Jesus on the way' is a technical term for discipleship. That Bartimaeus's name was remembered and recorded probably means that he did become a disciple" (Brooks, *Mark*, p. 174).

MAIN IDEA REVIEW: *A great leader is one who serves in the midst of relationships with others.*

III. CONCLUSION

Greatness in His Service

Francis of Assisi was dedicated to serving God. In the cross he saw an example of how Christians should live. The horizontal beam of the cross represented how God came down to earth. The vertical beam represented God's love for all humanity, reaching out to the ends of the earth. He saw love and Christianity as service to humanity. He gave to the poor and hugged lepers and sacrificed in order to give to others.

John Michael Talbot, a musician and a Franciscan monk, wrote, "The truth that we incarnate Jesus when we serve others destroys the common distinction between 'spiritual' work (praying, preaching, teaching) and other kinds of service (nursing the sick, feeding the hungry). It means that when members of our community help provide clothing to poor people in our area, God is mystically there in our midst, smiling upon tht simple act of charity" (Talbot, *The Lessons of St. Francis,* p. 198).

St. Francis was right. We come closer to Jesus when we serve. As Jesus said to his disciples, anyone who wants to be great in the kingdom of God must be a servant.

PRINCIPLES

- If anything comes between us and the Lord, we must cast it aside.
- We must not hinder anyone from coming to Christ because of our words or actions.
- In service to Christ we will find our true greatness, our true wealth.
- In submitting ourselves to others, we serve Christ.

APPLICATIONS

- At least once a month, do some kind of service in your church. Clean a room, dust, volunteer in the nursery, do some minor repairs.
- Take inventory of the things that stand in the way of discipleship.
- Be persistent in your pursuit of Jesus.

IV. LIFE APPLICATION

First in Service

Why do we call our worship times "service"? What is the Sunday service, or the worship service? Who is being served? Oftentimes, it is service to ourselves. We come to see our friends or to be seen by others. We come perhaps to make business contacts. We come because it is our obligation to come. But our perspective should be to serve God and others. We come to the Sunday service to receive training so we can go out and serve. Here we learn about needs that we can meet. Or we come to worship service to offer our praises to God.

I will never forget the time I walked in to my church on a Friday afternoon to drop some things off. The associate pastor was on the stair landing with rubber gloves and a pail of hot, soapy water washing the walls. I wondered if perhaps our regular custodian had the day off. No, he replied. He had just noticed the last time he walked up the stairs that the wall was looking a little dirty, so he had taken the opportunity to wash it.

I do not know why we should be so surprised at the service of such leaders. After all, Jesus on the night before he died served his friends by washing the dust from their feet. And the word *servant-leadership* is certainly a buzz word in Christian circles today. Perhaps the surprise comes from the fact that it is not what comes naturally; it is not the "American" way. The truly great person is the one who does not do his own cooking or her own driving. He has cooks, butlers, chauffeurs, nannies, or maids to serve him. We tend to think the greater a person is, the more servants he or she will have!

Jesus turned this human idea (and it is not a twentieth-century invention!) on its ear. His teaching was that the greater a person is, the greater his or her service will be. The person who gives the most is the greatest.

V. PRAYER

Lord, we find it a hard saying that the greatest must serve. We want instead to be served. It is hard to look at things from your perspective and not the world's. And yet, with you is eternal life. Help us to seek out ways to serve and to place ourselves always at your command. Urge us to seek you as persistently and as joyfully as Bartimaeus did, and to follow as loyally. Amen.

VI. DEEPER DISCOVERIES

A. Divorce (10:2–12)

The Pharisees were masters of the Jewish law. God gave humanity the law in order to set a fence around behavior. The Pharisees could take certain laws and tighten the boundaries until the meaning of the original law was lost. For example, hundreds of manmade rules obscured the Sabbath's true purpose. In other cases, the Pharisees could loosen the boundaries until the law lost its original intent. Such was the case with marriage and divorce.

The Jews of Jesus' day agreed that divorce was lawful, but not all agreed on the proper grounds for divorce. The rabbinical schools of Hillel and Shammai were sharply divided on the issue. The original law is found in Deuteronomy 24:1, "If a man marries a woman who becomes displeasing to him because he finds something indecent about her, and he writes her a certificate of divorce . . ." The debate was over the interpretation of the word *indecent*.

B. Serve/Servant/Slave (10:35–41)

The Greek word for servant is *diakonos,* and it means a household servant. We get the English word *deacon* from this word (cf. 1 Tim. 3:8; Rom. 16:1). The word is also used of someone under another person's authority. The English word *slave* is the Greek word *doulos,* meaning a common bond slave. Slaves were acquired in a number of ways. They could be taken from their households as prisoners of war. Parents sometimes sold their children into slavery. If people could not pay their debts, they sometimes sold themselves into slavery to cover these debts.

Hebrew law governed the treatment of slaves and allowed for them to buy back their freedom. Relatives were also allowed to pay the price to buy someone back. In the Jewish year of Jubilee, property reverted to its original owners and slaves were set free. Slaves were also considered to be part of the family. They were permitted to celebrate the feasts and, if Hebrew, to rest on the Sabbath. Because the Jews had been slaves, treated cruelly, in Egypt, the Lord constantly reminded them to treat others with kindness and justice.

While slaves were treated fairly by the Hebrews—certainly more fairly than slaves were treated in early American history—the fact remains that slaves were not their own masters. They could not go or act as they pleased but were at the disposal of their masters.

This offers a picture of what the Christian's relationship is to be to Christ. Every person is in slavery to either God or the devil. Selling a person's soul to the devil is a popular theme in fiction. In reality, a person's soul does not need to be sold to the devil because he owns it already. The non-Christian is a slave to Satan, a slave to sin and to death. Only through Christ's work of redemption is a person freed from Satan's realm. The Christian becomes the slave of Christ. He is our master, and our lives are at his disposal.

C. Ransom (10:45)

When we hear the word *ransom,* we typically think of a kidnapping and a sum of money demanded. When that amount of money is paid to the kidnappers, they free the hostage. Jesus' use of the word in verse 45 raises the questions of what is meant by *ransom* and to whom is the ransom paid. The Greek word for ransom is *lutron,* which occurs only here and in the parallel passage in Matthew 20:28. This word is closely linked with the concept of slavery. It referred to buying the freedom of a slave, but in the Old Testament it also referred to redeeming oneself or one's property (cf. Lev. 25:26, 51; Exod. 21:30; Num. 18:15) (Brooks, *Mark,* 171). Jesus himself paid the ransom price—his own blood.

Peter, whom most believe was Mark's key source, reminds us, "For you know that it was not with perishable things such as silver or gold that you were redeemed [ransomed] from the empty way of life handed down to you from your forefathers, but with the precious blood of Christ, a lamb without blemish or defect" (1 Pet. 1:18–19).

But to whom was the ransom paid? In the early church, Origen first suggested that Satan had been paid the ransom, since our souls belong to him. When Christ redeemed us, we were freed from sin and death as citizens of Satan's realm. A reading of C. S. Lewis's wonderful book *The Lion, the Witch and the Wardrobe* seems at first to confirm this theory. In this book, the witch is demanding to kill one of the children because he is a traitor. "You know that every traitor belongs to me as my lawful prey and that for every treachery I have a right to a kill" (Lewis, p. 114).

Aslan, the Christlike lion, does not dispute the witch but seems to make a deal with her. Later, after he has been humiliated and killed, he is raised from the dead. Aslan explains, "Though the Witch knew the Deep Magic, there is a magic deeper still which she did not know. Her knowledge goes back only to the dawn of Time. But if she could have looked a little further back, into the stillness and the darkness before Time dawned, she would have read there a different incantation. She would have known that when a willing victim who had committed no treachery was killed in a traitor's stead, the Table [the Law] would crack and Death itself would start working backwards (Lewis, p. 132).

At first reading, this seems to support the theory that a ransom was paid to the devil. This, however, gives Satan equal power with God—a belief that does not have biblical warrant. But the witch herself in Lewis' story tells us to whom the ransom was paid. Right before she reminds Aslan of her rights regarding traitors, she says, "You at least know the magic which the Emperor put into Narnia at the very beginning" (Lewis, p. 114). It is the Emperor, God himself, the Creator of all, who is owed the ransom.

When God established the law, it specified the death penalty for disobedience. His holiness could not demand less. A sacrifice was needed to atone for the sins of humanity. The law set forth what kinds of sins demanded what kind of sacrifice. The problem was that these sacrifices needed to be offered continually (Heb. 10). A sacrifice was needed that would be for all time, a once-for-all ransom. What was needed was a man, because it was man who had sinned. But this man would have to be blameless. Only one who was God could satisfy the requirements of a holy God. Jesus Christ satisfied all parts of the law perfectly (Heb. 10:14). His ransom price was offered and accepted; our redemption was complete.

VII. TEACHING OUTLINE

A. INTRODUCTION

1. Lead Story: An Extension of the Master Servant
2. Context: Jesus is on the road to Jerusalem. His encounters with the Pharisees will increase. This time with his disciples gives him a chance to teach them about service.
3. Transition: Like Lippizan stallions, we must offer ourselves to God. We have placed ourselves in his service. He is our great commander.

B. COMMENTARY

1. The Relationship between Spouses (10:1–12)
   a. The question of divorce (10:1–2)
   b. Moses (10:3–5)
   c. Marriage and creation (10:6–9)
   d. Jesus teaches his disciples further (10:10–12)
2. The Relationship between Childen and the Kingdom of God (10:13–16)
3. The Believer's Relationship with Money (10:17–31)
   a. Inheriting eternal life (10:17–20)
   b. Not enough (10:21–23)
   c. The impossibility of man's efforts (10:24–27)
   d. "We have left everything" (10:28–31)
4. The Believer's Relationship with Christ (10:32–45)
   a. Jesus predicts his death (10:32–34)
   b. Two brothers' request (10:35–37)
   c. Jesus' cup (10:38–40)
   d. Teaching on being a servant (10:41–45)
5. The Believer's Relationship with Others (10:46–52)
   a. Bartimaeus (10:46–48)
   b. Jesus summons Bartimaeus (10:49)
   c. Bartimaeus casts everything aside to be with Jesus (10:50–52)

C. CONCLUSION: FIRST IN SERVICE

VIII. ISSUES FOR DISCUSSION

1. In what ways can you serve others?
2. What hinders you from a relationship with Christ? How can you throw it away?
3. How can you remove this hindrance?
4. How can you make money a servant instead of a master?

Mark 11

Found Wanting

Quote

"He has sounded forth the trumpet

that shall never call retreat,

He is sifting out the hearts of men

before his judgment seat.

O be swift my soul to answer him,

be jubilant my feet!"

Julia Ward Howe

Mark 11

IN A NUTSHELL

Jesus enters Jerusalem. He is hailed as king by the people. He clears the temple of those who use it for commerce, thus setting in motion the final conflicts with the religious leaders.

Found Wanting

I. INTRODUCTION

Judgment Day

*I*t happened when I was a teenager. I was going to spend the night at a friend's house. His parents were going out of town for a wedding and would not be back until the next day. Wow, what luck, we thought. Maybe we should have a few friends over, not really a party, just a few friends. Well, the few friends turned into a lot of friends and eventually turned into friends of friends of friends. I do not know who brought out the cigarettes, but quickly the room was filled with smoke, music louder than we intended, and certainly more of the opposite sex than we bargained for.

We spent the next two hours trying to get people out of the house, trying to get people to use ashtrays instead of the furniture, and trying to clean onion dip and ground-up potato chips out of the carpet. All of it was unsuccessful. And then it got worse. Headlights in the driveway. My friend's parents had experienced car trouble, rented another car, and skipped the wedding. Judgment day had come very quickly for two teenagers.

Chapter 11 of Mark hints at the same impending doom. The king is coming into his kingdom, and his authority takes on a sharper tone.

II. COMMENTARY

Found Wanting

> **MAIN IDEA:** *We think of the triumphal entry of Jesus into Jerusalem as the beginning of holy week, the beginning of the end of his earthly life. And yet, it is also the beginning of judgment. Those who will not accept Jesus as Lord and king will be judged by him.*

A The True King (11:1–11)

> **SUPPORTING IDEA:** *Jesus presents himself in public as a king.*

11:1. This verse introduces a new section in Jesus' ministry as he entered Jerusalem. This introduces what is typically called the passion week, beginning with his triumphal entry into Jerusalem on Palm Sunday and ending with his resurrection on Easter Sunday. Six of Mark's sixteen chapters deal with this last week. This shows the importance of these events in Jesus' life. Jesus went through the village Bethany on the eastern slope of the Mount of

Olives, two miles east of Jerusalem. Bethphage is less well-known but near Bethany.

11:2–3. Most interpreters think the city Jesus sent the disciples to was Bethphage because it was closer to Jerusalem. Some commentators take this verse as evidence of Jesus' omniscience. Others believe that Jesus had prearranged receiving the colt on one of his other trips to Jerusalem. The text does not indicate which view is correct, but neither does damage to the text or to the character of Jesus.

Jesus gave instructions that if anyone asked what they were doing, the disciples were to reply that **the Lord needs it**. The word *Lord* (Gr. *kyrios*) could mean "Lord" or simply "master." It is the first time in Mark's Gospel that Jesus referred to himself as Lord. While he could have meant simply "master" or "sir," he probably meant Lord in our fullest interpretation of the word. The messianic secret which is so prevalent in Mark's Gospel is slowly being revealed. Jesus has spoken to his disciples of his messiahship, identity, death, and resurrection. It would not be out of keeping with this gradual revelation for him to further reveal himself here.

11:4–6. The fact that a great number of details are given here may point to Peter as one of the two disciples sent on this errand. The situation happened as Jesus warned them, and they repeated Jesus' words to the questioners. While a few interpreters think the words had a powerful effect on the listeners—enough for them to relinquish their possession of the colt—the text does not support this. It seems more likely that the owners would have heard of Jesus. Perhaps they knew him personally and they realized he was an honest man, if not a prophet. They could be sure of having the colt returned.

11:7–8. Cloaks were laid on the colt to serve as a rough saddle. The cloaks thrown on the ground along with the branches served as recognition of royalty. Cole sees in this a lavish expression of love similar to that offered to Jesus by Mary (Cole, *Mark*, p. 248). Barclay, on the other hand, believes this to be further evidence of a people who willfully misunderstood Jesus' words and actions (Barclay, *Mark*, p. 266). I think both can be satisfied by the account. There was lavishness in their love, even though their love had not reached full potential. At this moment, they did love him with all their hearts and desired to honor him as king. But Barclay is right—they misunderstood what kind of a king he was.

11:9–10. These two verses make it clear what the crowds were expecting. **Hosanna** means literally "save now." It was an acclamation of praise to one who had the power the save. The same word is used in Psalm 118:25, where it is translated, "O LORD, save us." This psalm is a thanksgiving psalm. Interpretations vary as to what it referred to. It may have referred to deliverance from Egypt, or it could have celebrated release from captivity and the rebuilt temple. In either case, it celebrated deliverance from captivity. It was an appropriate psalm for Jesus, who came to deliver humanity from captivity to sin and death.

The reference to David's kingdom is a clear messianic title. The crowds were acknowledging that Jesus was heir to David's throne. **He who comes** was another euphemism for the Messiah. The crowds expected Jesus to establish his kingdom immediately.

11:11. True to Mark's Gospel, the triumphant entry into Jerusalem is a bit more somber here than that recorded in Matthew. The Gospel of Matthew states that the city was stirred, and Luke says that the crowd was singing joyfully. But Mark records that when these events were finished, he went to the temple, had a look around, and then went back to Bethany, most likely to the home of Martha, Mary, and Lazarus. This verse shows Jesus as thoughtful, deliberate. This thoughtful pause here and the actions that follow remind us of a prophecy of judgment in Daniel: "You have been weighed on the scales and found wanting" (5:27). The guilty verdict was in; the sentence would be carried out the next day.

Ⓑ True Worship and True Fruit (11:12–22)

SUPPORTING IDEA: *With a dramatic metaphor and an accompanying action, Jesus declares what he will judge.*

11:12–13. As we saw in chapter 9 of Mark's Gospel, in Hebrew literature, an *inclusio* is a literary device where two teachings or refrains are wrapped around a central teaching or story. The material that is bracketed between these literary bookends is important teaching. This is not a true *inclusio*, since the words are not the same. But the cursing of the fig tree and Peter's notice of the withered fig tree bracket material that further explains Jesus' actions in the temple. These are troublesome verses. Without the bracketed material about the temple, Jesus would seem to be sulking at not finding something to eat. The bracketed material, however, gives meaning to this enacted parable. Enacted parables were common to prophets in the Old Testament (see Jer. 19).

Trees in Jerusalem get leafy in March (and remain so for approximately nine months) but they do not produce fruit until June. If such was the case, how could Jesus expect fruit from the tree? Some have suggested that he acted in anger, but the account contains no words of anger. Others suggest that this was a miracle inserted at a later time and thus is not truly a part of Mark. This solution, however, causes more problems than it solves. Why would the later church put in a miracle that would cast Jesus in a dubious light?

Perhaps the best interpretation is that Jesus in his omniscience saw that the tree would never produce fruit, so he used the occasion to teach the disciples. The tree, which looked so promising because it was full of leaves, was fruitless. Notice that Mark called attention to the fact that it was not the season for figs. This signals that this was a symbolic action.

11:14. Mark made sure that the reader knew that all the disciples heard Jesus pronounce judgment upon the fig tree. They understood the symbolism. The fig tree had long been a symbol of Israel's peace and security (cf. Mic. 4:4; Zech. 3:10). Jesus' curse upon it meant that Israel "would not again be the primary instrument of accomplishing God's purpose" (Brooks, *Mark*, p. 182).

11:15. Jesus had seen the buying and selling going on in the temple the night before, so his actions here are deliberate and well thought out—not a random act of violence, as some have suggested (Lightfoot). Matthew and Luke also record the clearing of the temple at this time. John places this event at the beginning of Jesus' ministry. It is possible that there were two separate cleansings of the temple by Jesus. In his *Harmony of the Gospels*, A. T. Robertson places one cleansing at the beginning and the other three years later when the earlier incident may have been forgotten. Other interpreters believe there was only one clearing of the temple because of the way it incited the religious establishment. They suggest that it happened in the last week of Jesus' ministry and that John placed it earlier in his Gospel for theological significance.

11:16. The word translated "merchandise" actually means any type of utensil. Dowling notes: "The temple area, covering much of the eastern half of the city, furnished a formidable barrier to those who wished to take short-cuts across the city. The temple meant nothing to them except that it was in the way of their speedy travel. Jesus demanded that these worldly persons carry their possessions around the temple rather than through it. They were to regard the temple as holy and dedicated to the worship of God rather than a mere convenience and means of profit" (Dowling, *Mark*, p. 105).

11:17. Notice the phrase, **as he taught them**. After throwing out the merchants and overturning their tables, Jesus the rabbi would have explained his actions to his disciples. Jesus quoted from Isaiah 56:7 and Jeremiah 7:11. The rest of the passage in Jeremiah prophecies God's destruction of Solomon's temple. The hearers most certainly noted this and the veiled threat it implied. It is no wonder that the rulers **feared him**.

Jesus' mention of **a house of prayer for all nations** signifies that he had in mind the Gentiles. They had been pushed out of the outer court of the temple area by the proliferation of merchandise. Gentiles were allowed to worship in the temple, although only in its outer circle. "With the conversion of the court of the Gentiles into a bazaar with all its noise and commotion and stench, they were deprived of the only place in the temple where they could worship. By clearing out the traders Jesus literally *and symbolically* provided a place for Gentiles in the temple of God" (Brooks, *Mark,* p. 186).

Brooks goes on to note that **den of robbers** does not mean a place of dishonest dealings, although it may have been that. This phrase probably referred to a refuge for unjust persons. The Jews of the day felt secure in God's acceptance because of their rituals and laws. They were like a tree in full foliage that bore no fruit.

11:18. Brooks makes this interesting observation about this verse: "Although the Jews despised Herod, they gloried in the temple he built for them. It was virtually synonymous with Judaism itself. Although the notion proved to be false, it was believed there could be no Judaism without it. Therefore for Jesus to expel Jews from the temple was looked upon as expelling them from the presence and favor of God" (Brooks, *Mark,* p. 184). The chief priests knew, as did the rulers, that Jesus was claiming an authority higher than theirs. They feared him because the crowd loved him and believed him to be the Messiah.

11:19. It would not have been safe for Jesus to remain in the city with the all the plots against his life. They probably returned each night to Bethany, where Jesus could spend time with friends.

11:20–21. Peter's astonishment at the withered fig tree was not because Jesus had worked the miracle. After all, he had seen dead people revived by Jesus. His astonishment arose from the fact that the miracle took place so quickly. There may also have been a note of horror that Jerusalem's judgment would come soon—as indeed it did in A.D. 70. Mark's mention of the tree being withered from the roots up points to its total destruction.

Jesus' parable is clear. The religious system of the day had plenty of leaves but no fruit. Its surface piety was seen in tithes and prayers and fasts (cf. Matt. 5–7), in the ritual purity that kept out women, lepers, blind beggars, and those possessed by demons. The foliage of the religious leaders offered much promise but no fulfillment. As the figless tree could not satisfy Jesus' appetite, so the religious system could not satisfy the spiritual hunger of the people.

11:22. The Bible translations have this verse as the beginning of a new paragraph and a new section on the teaching of prayer. But this verse is actually a response to Peter and should finish the scene of the withered fig tree. Brooks links this verse more closely with the following teaching on prayer. "Mark evidently was saying, 'Despite the cursing of the fig tree (i.e., Israel), continue to trust in God' because faith and prayer and not the temple are now the way to God" (Brooks, *Mark,* p. 182).

The disciples understood Jesus' metaphor and knew that the temple would be destroyed some day. Peter's fear would have been a natural reaction to the loss of a way of life, no matter how burdensome. This is reminiscent of Habakkuk 2:4. Habakkuk learned that God would punish Israel by using the invasion of the Babylonians. He was horrified but testifies, "The righteous will live by his faith."

True Prayer (11:23–26)

> **SUPPORTING IDEA:** *Jesus had spoken of the temple as a house of prayer. He briefly discusses prayer and the faith that gives rise to prayer.*

11:23–24. Barclay notes that this saying is in Matthew and Luke, although in different contexts (Barclay, *Mark,* p. 275). This is probably because Jesus taught on prayer more than once. Jesus was using hyperbole as he did in 10:25. He did not intend for Christians to try to move literal mountains. But he did expect us to believe that our prayers can overcome great difficulties. We must have faith when we pray. But our faith is not in the strength of our prayers, nor in the size of our faith.

11:25. This is not Jesus' only teaching on prayer. We know that Christians are to pray within God's will, as taught in the Lord's prayer (Matt. 6:10). John states this clearly. "This is the confidence we have in approaching God: that if we ask anything according to his will, he hears us. And if we know that he hears us—whatever we ask—we know that we have what we asked of him" (1 John 5:14–15). God's will is a prerequisite of the prayer of faith. We know that God's will is for us to forgive as we have been forgiven. If we cannot forgive, then we are not praying in God's will.

Commit Yourselves (11:27–33)

> **SUPPORTING IDEA:** *The king has arrived and has shown that true worship will take place somewhere other than the temple. Therefore, Jesus calls listeners to commit themselves to him.*

11:27. The chief priests, the teachers of the law (or scribes), and the elders made up the Sanhedrin, although this would have been a delegation and not the entire body. The chief priests had charge of the temple by the regulation of Old Testament law. It may seem imprudent for Jesus to go into the temple after clearing the merchants from it. But the Sanhedrin was probably afraid of what the crowds would do if they made an attempt on his life at this point. However, they did have the courage to approach him.

11:28. Jesus was not a priest, a Pharisee, or an elder. By what authority, they demanded, had he done these things? The phrase **these things** probably refers to the things they had just seen—the clearing of the temple and the triumphal entry. They wanted him to say that he had no authority, that he had acted on his own. James R. Edwards sees in the question an echo of 2:7: "Who can forgive sins but God alone?" (quoted in Barbieri, *Mark,* p. 259).

11:29. The question Jesus asked them in return was not meant as an evasion. His counter question was a typical practice of rabbis. He told them he would not answer their question until his question had been answered. Even with his counter question, Jesus showed he had a higher authority than those who were questioning him.

11:30. Jesus' question brought up the issue of John the Baptist. The Sanhedrin certainly remembered John's fiery sermons and his insistence that Jesus was the Son of God, the Messiah. The link answered the leaders' question about Jesus' identity and authority. But he wanted a response from them. The phrase **Tell me!** is an imperative not found in the other Gospels. It demanded a response, some kind of commitment—one way or the other—from the leaders.

11:31–32. The leaders were in a verbal trap, and they knew it immediately. If they answered **from heaven,** meaning John's authority came from God, then they would be condemned by the people for not listening to John regarding repentance as well as Jesus' identification as the Messiah. On the other hand, to say that his authority was not from God was to risk the wrath of the people. The verb for **discussed** means they discussed Jesus' question among themselves for some time.

According to verse 18, the Sanhedrin feared Jesus. Here, Mark states that they feared the people. They had no faith—only fear—and their fear must have given rise to all their decisions.

11:33. In the end, they said the only thing they could say without commitment: **We don't know.** They were like the Laodiceans in Revelations 3:16—lukewarm, neither cold nor hot, playing it safe. Jesus knew their hearts, so he refused to answer their question. "If they are not willing to risk themselves, what difference will it make what Jesus says? . . . For timid and cautious men who are unwilling to take the risk involved in either answer, the only possible response is, 'Who knows?' But then, what is there left for Jesus to say? We do not know the Christ and then commit ourselves to him. Commitment is the one and only way by which we may know the Christ" (Bell, *The Way of the Wolf,* p. 103).

MAIN IDEA REVIEW: *We think of the triumphal entry as the beginning of holy week, the beginning of the end of Jesus' earthly life. And yet, it is also the beginning of judgment. Those who will not accept Jesus as Lord and king are doomed to be judged by him.*

III. CONCLUSION

Judging by Externals

Bill Hybels, pastor at Willow Creek Church in Illinois, wrote a book some years back entitled *Who You Are When No One's Looking* (InterVarsity Press, 1989). The gist of the book and the title is that Christians should be people of integrity. Do you tithe once a month and then squirm the other three weeks because it looks like you are not giving anything when the plate goes by? Do you curse at someone for cutting you off in traffic, and then feel chagrined when they turn into your church parking lot? Do you condemn certain television programs when you are talking with your friends and then watch them yourself when you are alone?

A friend of mine who has been struggling with God recounted a recent experience to me. Although she had not been to church in about three months, she decided to go because she knew she needed to get back in regular worship. A woman she did not know came up to her at church and commented on her dress. She said it was nice to see someone honor God by dressing up for church. At least she was not like "that man"—and she pointed at a young man who had on shorts. "I was staggered," my friend said. "The woman had no idea where my heart had been. And she had no idea where that man's heart was." The woman was judging people by externals.

It is very easy for Christians, like the Pharisees, to judge relationships based on externals. We even judge ourselves by such external criteria—keeping track of our daily devotions, our praying, tithing, fasting, and reading the Bible. We judge our own relationship with God based on our performance.

But Jesus reminds us in this chapter of what really matters. Unless our performance springs from faith, life, and relationship, it is like a tree that yields no fruit.

PRINCIPLES

- Impressive religious performance does not mean our lives are right with God.
- When life looks bleak and frightening, faith in God sustains us.
- No matter what barriers confront us, we can overcome them through prayer.
- Our first priority in prayer is forgiveness—to receive it for ourselves and to grant it to others.
- Commitment to Jesus removes all barriers to God.

APPLICATIONS

- Keep short accounts; forgive those who have wronged you.
- Do not be guilty of making God too small. Dream big things for God.
- Purge your life of the external things that keep you from a true relationship with God.
- Do not be lukewarm. Declare your commitment to Christ with boldness.

IV. LIFE APPLICATION

Playing to Win

The football rivalry between Cherry Creek High School and Thomas Jefferson High School in Colorado has been going on for a long time. Some time ago, the two schools battled for the state championship. Thomas Jefferson was leading in the fourth quarter and it looked like they might upset Cherry Creek, who was seven points behind. Then Cherry Creek scored a touchdown, bringing them within one point of tying the game. The coach faced a tough decision. Should he play it safe and go for the one-point PAT and then try to win the game in overtime, or should he risk everything and go for the two-point conversion to win?

He went for the two-point conversion. It failed, time ran out, and Thomas Jefferson won the coveted championship. Asked later about the decision, the coach stated that if he had it to do over, he would make the same choice. He said he did not believe in "playing it safe" or playing for the tie. Always play to win.

This is the call of Jesus in our lives. He does not call us to play it safe, and there are no ties in life. You win or you lose. You live or you die. Martin Bell writes that there is deeper question that the Sanhedrin, the religious leaders of the day, needed to face and that question is what difference will the answer make: "What risks are they prepared to take? Is this question really one of final seriousness for them? How ready are they to commit themselves before God? . . . To live is to decide, to risk being wrong, to bet your life. Life itself is inextricably bound to decision making. It is not enough to be interested in this man, or fascinated by him or drawn to him. . . . It is not enough to be frightened, cautious, and bewildered spectators. Curiosity about the Christ Event in history is not enough. Either we stand ready to commit our deaths to him or we don't" (Bell, *The Way of the Wolf,* pp. 104–105).

His judgment is at hand. Our response to him is at hand. "O be swift my soul to answer him, be jubilant my feet!"

V. PRAYER

Lord Jesus, You are Lord. You order the universe and you step into our lives. I recognize your authority over my life. Cause even my small acts done for you to produce everlasting fruit. Help me to overcome fear and to live life fully, deliberately, making choices, taking chances, because it is all for your glory. Amen.

VI. DEEPER DISCOVERIES

A. Colt (11:2)

Although a colt can mean the young of any animal, Matthew's account indicates that it was a donkey (Matt. 21:2) and says that the mother was brought as well.

The fact that the animal was never ridden symbolizes that it was to be used for a religious purpose. Numbers 19:2 and Deuteronomy 21:3 mention unyoked animals to be used by the Lord or his priests. First Samuel 6 records the return of the ark of the covenant by the Philistines to the Israelites. They used two newly calved and unyoked cows to return the sacred ark. Animals not accustomed to the yoke or to a rider would not be easily ridden. Jesus' ease in riding this particular colt shows his command over the animal kingdom.

Jesus' coming into Jerusalem on the donkey was a symbolic act. Barclay points out that when the Israelites of old would not listen to the words of a prophet, the prophet would perform a drama (Barclay, *Mark*, p. 264). Jesus had predicted his death several times, and each time the disciples refused to understand. Jesus' action here provided them a picture of what he had been trying to say. The symbolism is a fulfillment of Zechariah 9:9: "See, your king comes to you, righteous and having salvation, gentle and riding on a donkey, on a colt, the foal of a donkey."

Jesus was the king, but he came in peace. He would not attack or overthrow Rome. "In Palestine the ass was not a despised beast, but a noble one. When a king went to war he rode on a horse, when he came in peace he rode on an ass" (Barclay, *Mark*, p. 264).

He did not attack Rome; he attacked the religious establishment because they focused on rules and regulations rather than a personal relationship with God. He did not overthrow Israel's political enemies; he overthrew the tables in the temple because they were dishonoring to God. He came in peace, but it was the peace of a sacrificial lamb. Through his sacrifice, he would conquer humanity's greatest enemy—death.

B. Temple (11:15–17)

Originally, God was worshiped in the wilderness tabernacle, described in Exodus 25–31. This tabernacle was portable. When the Lord gave David rest from his enemies, David wanted to replace the tabernacle with a permanent structure, the temple. David's son and successor, Solomon, was given the task of building the temple. Over time, there were three different temples on this same site in Jerusalem. The last of these was called Herod's temple. This was the temple that existed in Jesus' day. In fact, Herod's temple was still under construction during the time of Jesus' death and resurrection.

At the time of Jesus, the temple was divided into several sections. The first section, the outer ring, was called the court of the Gentiles. Gentiles could come and worship God here, but they could not go further. This is where the merchants whom Jesus drove out were buying and selling. They were blocking the area, and the Gentiles had no place to worship. The next court was the court of women. Then came the court of the Israelites and finally the court of the priests. The Jews thought that holiness proceeded from outside to inside the temple. The more holy you were, the deeper inside the temple you were allowed.

The inner court of the temple was further divided into two rooms: the holy place and the Holy of Holies. A curtain separated the two. On the Day of Atonement, the high priest entered the Holy of Holies to offer a blood sacrifice for the people. When Jesus died, the curtain separating the Holy of Holies from the Holy Place split in two. This symbolized what Jesus spoke of in this chapter: His house would be a place of prayer and mercy for all nations, for all people.

Merchants found easy and eager buyers for sacrificial animals. As Barclay notes, "A sacrificial victim had to be without blemish. Doves could be bought cheaply enough outside, but the temple inspectors would be sure to find something wrong with them, and worshipers were advised to buy them at the temple stalls." The price for these animals when bought inside the temple was extravagant.

A temple tax was also collected at Passover. This tax equaled approximately two days wages and had to be paid at the temple. But it could not be paid in ordinary coin; it had to be paid in temple shekels. The priests charged a fee for exchanging the coins into shekels. Further, if the person needed change back, he was charged extra for this service. It was a heavy expense for a pilgrim coming to the temple to worship God! The temple was a sign of kingship. In chapter 11 of Mark, we see the king entering his kingdom. He had the right to clear the temple because it was his temple. He was the king.

However, the primary vocation of the temple and its priests was holiness. God had called his people to be "set apart," to be holy because he was holy. The temple was to be the place where God's people came to be cleansed, to offer thanksgiving, to be God's people. The temple was also a sign of God's continuing presence with his people. In the New Testament, Paul developed the theme of God's presence by calling Christians "the temple of the living God." The Gospel of John calls Jesus Christ the temple, as the embodiment of God, the word made flesh (John 1:14). In fact, the word *tabernacle* means "dwelling." The Gospel of John stated that the word became flesh and "tabernacled" among us (see John 1:14). It is significant that the temple was where people received atonement for their sins and were cleansed.

C. Prayer (11:17)

Prayer is the simplest thing a Christian can do and yet the most difficult subject to write about. At its simplest, prayer is communicating with God. It is how we make contact with God and how he communicates with us.

Prayer takes many forms throughout Scripture. It can be merely a request for sustenance or a curse on enemies. It is praise to God and pleading for renewal. It is confession and remembrance. It is thanksgiving to God for what he has given—and forgiven. It is a request for guidance and a plea for mercy. There is only one thing that prayer is not: an attempt to manipulate God. Often we think that if we pray hard enough or long enough or have enough faith, God will act. We treat God as though he is a cosmic candy machine; if we plug in enough quarters, he will give us the candy bar.

A student at seminary once prayed that if he received six hundred dollars (enough at that time to pay the tuition for one class), he would continue on with his education. If he did not receive it, he would know that the Lord's answer was no. He received three hundred dollars. This student said that the lesson to him was clear: Prayer is a relationship, not a series of conditions.

Cole notes regarding the cursing of the fig tree: "This is a reminder to us that prayer is not simply asking God for the pleasant things which we may desire, but an earnest yearning for, and entering into, the will of God, for ourselves and others, whether it is sweet or bitter. This was the prayer of Jesus in Gethsemane, and such prayers will always be answered by God" (Cole, *Mark*, p. 255).

VII. TEACHING OUTLINE

A. INTRODUCTION

1. Lead Story: Judgment Day
2. Context: Jesus resolutely set his face to go to Jerusalem. The predictions of his death have increased. In this chapter, Jesus arrives in Jerusalem and pronounces judgment on the religious leaders of Israel.

3. Transition: It might sound like a cliche, but eventually the piper must be paid, the cat comes home. Judgment is as sure as mercy. It awaits those who will not avail themselves of Jesus' mercy.

B. COMMENTARY
1. The True King (11:1–11)
    a. Jesus requests a colt (11:1–6)
    b. The triumphal entry into Jerusalem (11:7–10)
    c. Jesus looks at the temple (11:11)
2. True Worship and True Fruit (11:12–22)
    a. Jesus curses a fig tree (11:12–14)
    b. Jesus purges the temple (11:15–19)
    c. The dead fig tree (11:20–22)
3. True Prayer (11:23–26)
4. Commit Yourselves! (11:27–33)
    a. The Sanhedrin questions Jesus' authority (11:27–28)
    b. Jesus' counter question (11:29–30)
    c. "We don't know" (11:31–32)
    d. Jesus refuses to answer (11:33)

C. CONCLUSION: PLAYING TO WIN

VIII. ISSUES FOR DISCUSSION

1. How do we keep people from coming to God by our actions (cf. Mark 11:15)?
2. Since you are now the temple of God, what things do you do that defile the temple or dishonor God? How can you make your body a holy place?
3. What things or people do you need to forgive? Why do you think this is such a hard teaching?

Mark 12

❦

Final Questions

"*I* know now, Lord, why you utter no answer. You are yourself the answer. Before your face questions die away. What other answer would suffice?"

C .   S .   L e w i s

Mark 12

IN A NUTSHELL

As the theme of judgment continues, hostility grows toward Jesus. Jesus is tested by various political and religious groups. When they cannot trap him, they stop asking questions, looking for other ways to put him to death.

Final Questions

I. INTRODUCTION

Stop the Questions

A lot can be learned by the questions people ask. Two physics students wanted to go to a party in a town fifty miles away, even though they had a major physics test first thing the following day. The only way they could go to the party was to spend the night there and return late the next day, too late for the test.

"That's okay," one student said. "We'll tell the professor we had a flat tire. He can't punish us for having a flat tire."

The other agreed, so they went to the party and had a wonderful time. When they returned, they told the professor they had had a flat tire and they asked if they could take a make-up test. The professor agreed.

The next day, as they took their seats for the make-up test, the professor handed out a sheet of paper. "There are only two questions on this test, one on each side of the paper," he said. "Question one is worth 10 percent, and question two is worth 90 percent. Take your time, answer the questions fully and completely. This final will make up 50 percent of your grade."

Both students read the first question: "Who came up with the theory of relativity?" Both students smiled. "Albert Einstein," they wrote. What an easy test, they thought as they flipped to the back side of the sheet.

Question 2 was, "Which tire was flat?"

In Mark chapter 12 opposition to Jesus grows to monumental proportions. This chapter contains a few more questions put to Jesus by the religious establishment of the day in an attempt to trap him. Failing this, they abandon this course of action. They ask him no more questions until his trial.

II. COMMENTARY

Final Questions

MAIN IDEA: *Various political and religious groups try to trap Jesus with questions. Jesus, however, has the final question—and the final say.*

ⒶA Parable of Judgment (12:1–12)

SUPPORTING IDEA: *Continuing the discussion of authority in chapter 11, Jesus tells a parable proclaiming his authority to pronounce judgment.*

12:1. This parable continues the discussion in Mark 11:27–33. Jesus was speaking this parable to the chief priests, the scribes, and the elders. Although it was a parable, it was meant to elucidate truth, not veil it, as some of his parables did. It is clear from the reaction in verse 12 that the leaders knew exactly what Jesus was saying. This parable also contains more allegorical elements than other parables, where one idea is central. Many of the allusions in this parable would have been familiar to the Israelites, and certainly to the leaders, because of their symbolism in much Old Testament prophecy (see particularly Isa. 5:1–7).

A man would have been understood to be God because **he planted a vineyard,** which symbolized Israel. While the medieval church interpreted this strictly as an allegory and assigned symbols to the wall, the pit, and the watchtower, it is more likely that these are fictional details, added to enrich the story. Rather than being symbols of something, they show that the landowner cared deeply about his vineyard and went to some lengths to make sure it was protected. The wall protected it from wild animals, the pit is where the fruit was processed, the watchtower protected it from thieves.

The renting of the vineyard to tenants was not unusual at this time. They would have lived in the watchtower and offered protection to the vineyard. In this parable with allegorical elements, the tenant farmers represented the religious leaders whom God had sent to serve the nation of Israel.

12:2–5. When the owner sent a servant (or slave) to the vineyard, the tenants beat him severely. The servant was to collect some of the fruit for the owner. The servants symbolize the prophets, who were sent repeatedly to Israel to call the nation back to holiness in their role as a separate and holy people for God. Note that the treatment of the prophets grows worse throughout the story. The first servant was beaten. The next was hit on the head and treated shamefully. The next was killed.

12:6. The phrase, **son, whom he loved,** gives the sense of an only son, a beloved son. Words similar to these were used by God of Jesus at his baptism (Mark 1:11). Only the foolish would not respect the son of the owner. As Cole points out, there is finality in the act of sending the son. God could do no more. If the leaders would not respect the son, why should he send more prophets? The time for judgment had arrived. How they treated the son would determine their judgment.

12:7. At the sight of the son, the farmers may have mistakenly believed the father, the owner, to be dead. Hence their plot to kill the son. An "ownerless" piece of property could be claimed by anyone. To read these words is to feel the sorrow of God and yet how just his judgment! "It was not through their failure to recognize the Son that they killed him; that would have been pardonable. It was, as in the parable, precisely because they recognized him for who he was . . . We reject the claims of Christ not because we misunderstand them, but because we understand them only too well" (Cole, *Mark*, p. 259).

12:8. The tenants carried out their heinous plot, killing the son and throwing his body out of the vineyard. Not burying a body was a sign of disgrace. Although Jesus was buried by those who loved him, he was humiliated and disgraced by being mocked, stripped of clothing, and hung on a cross like a common criminal.

12:9. In the parallel passage in Matthew 21, the listeners themselves pronounce judgment. In Mark, the words come from Jesus' lips. **To others** is a direct pronouncement that the blessings of God have come to the Gentiles. Because Mark's Gospel was written for a Gentile audience, he may have wanted to make it clear that God's blessings came from Jesus. Whether or not the pronouncement came from Jesus or from his listeners, the point is plain: judgment is inevitable and is deserved.

12:10–11. Notice the phrase, **haven't you read this scripture?** Of course they had. They were scribes, they were religious leaders, they were the learned people of their day. Jesus' words echo Mark 4:12: "They may be ever seeing but never perceiving, and ever hearing but never understanding." The quotation in this verse is from Psalm 118:22, the same psalm that had been quoted upon Jesus' entry into Jerusalem. With this quote, linked as it is with the messianic titles bestowed upon him on his triumphal entry, and with the unmistakable claim of identity in the parable, Jesus answered the question the leaders had originally posed to him in 11:28, "By whose authority?"

12:12. The Sanhedrin did not miss the message of the parable. They recognized that Jesus had claimed divinity for himself, that he had prophesied destruction against them and their elaborate system, and that God's blessings would come upon the hated Gentiles. But again, their fear of the people, with whom Jesus was popular, kept them from taking action at this point.

B The Question of Government (12:13–17)

SUPPORTING IDEA: *This political question tries to trap Jesus between loyalty to God and loyalty to Rome.*

12:13. Cole notes that a game of "cat and mouse" begins with this verse. When the Pharisees asked Jesus about his authority, he placed them in a position where any answer they gave involved danger. They would try now to do the same to him in order to trap him into blasphemy or treason. The Herodians and Pharisees were strange bedfellows. The Herodians were loyal to Herod, who was unscrupulous and wicked. The Herodians were more interested in political alliances, and they had little patience with religion. The Pharisees, on the other hand, were intensely religious. But Jesus, their common enemy, brought them together.

12:14. They came to Jesus and flattered him with words. Everything they said was true, but commitment to him was far from their hearts. **You pay no attention to who they are** is a reference to Jesus' lack of favoritism—a quality that must have been lacking in that day.

Their question regarding taxes may seem simple to us who struggle with income tax forms every April 15. Why would they try to trap Jesus with this question? This tax was one denarius a year, approximately one day's wages of a common laborer, so it was not an excessive amount. The tax, however, was instituted by Rome in A.D. 6 when Israel's king was deposed. For a freedom-loving people, the tax represented "foreign domination and because it had to be paid with a coin that bore an image of the emperor" (Brooks, *Mark,* p. 192). The Israelites held strongly to the second commandment that prohibited the making of graven images. The coin, with its image of Tiberius, would have been particularly repulsive to them.

12:15. The questioners thought they had Jesus trapped. If he answered, "don't pay," he could be accused of treason. If he said "pay," it might incite the crowds against him. And for men who had been afraid of the crowds, this was a significant step. Jesus knew their hypocrisy, and he knew they were testing him.

12:16. Jesus asked a question of the questioners that demanded a response. With the answer, the questioners answered their own question.

12:17. Jesus' answer proclaimed that people have an obligation to the state (cf. Rom. 13:1–7), but also an obligation to God. Because Caesar's image was on the coin, it belonged to him and could be returned to him. However, certain things are not owed to Caesar but to God: our souls, our worship.

Dowling observes, "They were paying for value received: law and order, military protection from marauders, good roads and harbors, freedom of travel, all the sturdy building for which Rome was famous. They were not to render to Caesar the things that belong to God; but where form of worship was being permitted, they were to render to Caesar the things that were Caesar's" (Dowling, *Mark,* p. 112). As Barclay puts it, "No man can honourably receive all the benefits which living in a state confers upon him and then opt out of all the responsibilities of citizenship" (Barclay, *Mark,* p. 287).

🄲 The Question of Marriage (12:18–27)

> **SUPPORTING IDEA:** *This theological question tries to trap Jesus between two religious groups.*

12:18. Not much is known about the Sadducees. They were inclined to trust what they could see, so they denied supernaturalism, including resurrection, angels, and demons. They were wealthy aristocrats, more than willing to align themselves with the prevailing political climate to protect their status. They held strongly to the Pentateuch, less so to the Prophets and the Writings. After the destruction of the temple in A.D. 70, the Sadducees died out. It is possible that by attacking Jesus they were hoping to attack the beliefs of the Pharisees and the common people.

12:19. The Sadducees brought to Jesus the "levirate" law, found in Deuteronomy 25:5. If a man died without an heir, his brother was to marry his widow. The first son would be named with the man's name in order to keep his line intact and his property within the family.

12:20–22. This may have been a true story, or it may have been a retelling from the apocryphal book of Tobit. Mark does not say, and the point is made without knowing for sure where the story comes from. Brooks notes that the Sadducees "falsely presumed that Jesus held the same materialistic doctrine of resurrection as did many Pharisees. This doctrine held that defects in the physical body and various earthly relationships would be carried over into future life" (Brooks, *Mark*, p. 195).

12:23. The question was meant to cast Jesus in a bad light. The question, for those not believing in the resurrection, was absurd. For those who did believe in the resurrection, it was meant to show how impossible such a situation would be.

12:24. Jesus declared that they had misunderstood the Scriptures and the power of God. If they had understood the power of God, they would have realized that God could raise a person from the dead. They would have realized also that the afterlife is more than just a continuation of the life on earth.

12:25. This is a difficult verse, and it has caused people much consternation. Some have taken this to mean that the spouse a person has when he dies is the spouse he will have in heaven. This interpretation, however, carries too much of this world into the next one. Some interpreters have taken the reference to angels in heaven to mean that humans will spend all their time worshipping God, such as the angels do, and will not have time for earthly relationships. Other interpreters believe the sexual relationship will be done away with, because its original creation was for procreation, for populating the earth. In heaven, such repopulating will not be necessary.

The truth is that the Bible has little teaching about the nature of heaven, except that we will have glorified bodies, we will enjoy God, and we will worship and serve him forever. Whatever earthly relationships we enjoy now will be transformed. We will continue to enjoy these relationships in heaven, we do not know the exact nature of these relationships.

12:26–27. Jesus took the Sadducees into further teaching, and he taught them from the only part of Scripture they respected—the Pentateuch, or the first five books of the Bible. **The account of the bush** refers to the time when

God spoke to Moses (Exod. 3:6). God said, "I am the God of your father, the God of Abraham, the God of Isaac, and the God of Jacob." If death were truly an obliteration, as the Sadducees believed, would not God have referred to himself as "I *was* the God"? Lane observes, "If God has assumed the task of protecting the patriarchs from misfortune during the course of their life, but fails to deliver them from that supreme misfortune . . . his protection is of little value" (Lane, quoted in Barbieri, *Mark,* p. 273).

Jesus' final words to the Sadducees rebuked their meager understanding of the Bible. As believers, we must seek to understand the full meaning of his Word.

Ⅾ The Important Question (12:28–34)

SUPPORTING IDEA: *An honest seeker receives a straightforward answer and Jesus' commendation.*

12:28. Some interpreters believe this scribe was a representative sent by the Pharisees. The Pharisees must have been pleased with Jesus' answer to the Sadducees. Did they send this scribe to Jesus to question him further? But notice that the Pharisees were anything but friendly to Jesus, and this scribe seems to be sincere. He was the only scribe who received a commendation from Jesus. It is more likely that he heard the discussion with the Sadducees, and possibly the Pharisees, and was impressed with Jesus' answers.

His question was honest and straightforward. There were lively discussions on which law was the most important and which teacher could summarize the entire body of law in one commandment.

12:29–31. Jesus quoted first from the Shema in Deuteronomy 6:4–5. This describes a man or woman's relationship with God: **with all your heart . . . soul . . . mind . . . strength.** Jesus emphasized that love for God should consume our entire being. It encompasses everything that we are, everything that God created us to be. We are to love him with our minds, our emotions, and our will.

The scribe did not ask for the second greatest commandment, but Jesus gave it anyway, quoting from Leviticus 19:18. By giving this commandment, he showed that the two could not be separated. If we love God with all our being, then we will love our neighbor as well. Following this question in Luke 10:29, Jesus went on to define one's neighbor, using the parable of the good Samaritan. Jesus declared to the Jewish people that the neighbors they were to love as themselves included their hated enemies, including the Gentiles.

12:32–33. The scribe not only affirmed what Jesus said; he restated it in such a way as to indicate that he understood the difference between the letter and the spirit of the law.

12:34. Jesus commended the scribe, and this is the only commendation of a scribe in Mark's Gospel. This reminds us that groups as a whole are never bad. There are always individuals within those groups who are open to the gospel and to God's movement in their lives. The words, **You are not far from the kingdom of God,** were meant to encourage the scribe to continue down this path he had described. It may be the equivalent of Jesus' "Follow me." Whether or not the man did is not recorded.

No one dared ask him any more questions. After this encounter, Jesus was not tested again with trick questions by his enemies. From our perspective, he had passed every test. From their point of view, he had failed every test, but they had failed to trap him. Barbieri has an interesting note on why the Pharisees and scribes did not question him any longer: "Jesus' opponents realized they had come close to losing one of their own [the questioning scribe], and, before they lost anyone else, they backed away and stopped asking" (Barbieri, *Mark,* p. 277). Jesus will not turn away any person who seeks him with sincerity.

E The Real Question (12:35–37)

> **SUPPORTING IDEA:** *Jesus turns the tables and asks the teachers of the law a question.*

12:35. The teachers of the law taught that the Messiah was to come from the line of David. This raises the question, Was Jesus trying to deny this in his encounter in this passage? No, Jesus was trying to elevate their conception of the Messiah. The Messiah was surely more than the physical seed of David—more than the earthly conqueror they were expecting.

12:36–37. Jesus quoted from Psalm 110. The Jews considered this a psalm of David and a messianic psalm. David was considered the highest authority on earth by the Jews. How, then, could he refer to his descendant as "my Lord"? Was David saying that there was an authority higher than him? The answer, of course, was that David recognized that his sovereignty was of the earth. But the sovereignty of the Messiah, who would be from his lineage, was of God. The crowd was delighted with Jesus' teaching. They recognized that Jesus taught with authority. He did not fear the crowds or the teachers, which was more than could be said for his opponents.

F True Spirituality (12:38–44)

> **SUPPORTING IDEA:** *Jesus contrasts the hypocritical teachers of the law with a woman who demonstrates true spirituality.*

12:38–39. These verses are perhaps the closest thing to Matthew's Sermon on the Mount in Mark's Gospel. Jesus compared empty religious trappings with true spirituality. Beware, he said, of those who put on a religious show. The scribes, most of whom were Pharisees, walked around in long, white robes. This set them apart from the common people. They liked to be greeted in the marketplace, as everyone recognized their title and their profession. The important seats in the sanctuary were the seats at the front where they could be seen by everyone. They also made sure they were seated next to the host at the place of honor at a banquet. This reminds us of Jesus' admonition to James and John that the place of honor was reserved for those who served.

12:40. But it was not just the religious trappings that Jesus condemned. Their attitude was bad enough, but they also acted out their attitudes of superiority by oppressing other people. Because of their great knowledge of the law, they should have acted with compassion toward widows as they knew God did.

Notice Jesus' mention of the lengthy prayers of the Pharisees and the teachers of the law. Most interpreters feel their prayers are closely linked with their actions toward widows. Perhaps their prayers were efforts to cover up their treacherous dealings with the widows. "It is precisely because they pray, that their condemnation will be the more terrible, more than that of a rogue who robs outright without pretence of prayer or religion. . . . Greater knowledge and greater opportunities only bring greater responsibility, which can, if rejected, bring greater condemnation" (Cole, *Mark,* p. 271).

12:41–42. Jesus contrasted the greed of the scribes with one on whom they preyed—a poor widow. The temple treasury was located in the court of women. Here Jesus sat to watch the people as they put in their offerings. He did not condemn the people who put in large amounts of money. Jesus' intent was to show the disciples what true sacrifice is.

12:43–44. The woman did not call attention to herself. She was elevated by Jesus for all time. Perhaps it was one such as she who would sit on Jesus' right or left. Although poor, she gave all she had. God does not look on the amount of money a person gives, but on the attitude with which it is given and on how much the person keeps back. Because the widow put in all she had, she had to trust God for her life. This may actually be an answer to Peter's implied question in 10:28: "We have left everything to follow you!" Those who give sacrificially will not be forgotten by God. With this illustration, Jesus ended his public ministry.

> **MAIN IDEA REVIEW:** *Various political and religious groups try to trap Jesus with questions. Jesus, however, has the final question—and the final say.*

III. CONCLUSION

The Purpose of Questions

Questions can be used to accomplish many different purposes. Socrates used questions to help people search for truth. Some people ask questions that they already know the answer to. Parents are famous for this use of questions. "Do you have anything to tell me?" really means, "I know what you have been doing and, boy, are you in trouble!" "What are you doing?" often meant, "Stop whatever it is you are doing." Satan, who is recorded as asking the first question, used this strategy. "Did God really say?" he asked, but he knew what God had said.

Questions can be an effective way to get people to think. Questions are used to learn what other people are like. Friends and lovers ask questions to discover the qualities of their friend or beloved.

The questions the Pharisees and the teachers of the law asked Jesus revealed what kind of people they were: conniving and deceitful. They wanted to trap Jesus with their questions and his words. Jesus' question revealed what kind of man he was. He drew people out with his questions. As seen in his encounter with those in need, he continually asked, "What would you have me do for you?" He used questions such as "Who am I? Who is the Messiah?" to bring his disciples to a clear understanding of his identity and of their relationship with him.

PRINCIPLES

- Believers have an obligation to the state as well as to God.
- Christ's love compels us to love others as we love ourselves, even those who are outcasts in our society.
- God sees our actions even when people do not.
- To give sacrificially is better than to give large sums without a willing spirit.

APPLICATIONS

- How much money would you give to the church if it were not tax-deductible?
- Love God with all your mind by studying his Word and learning about him.
- Love God with all your heart by allowing him to open up wounded emotions.
- Love God with all your soul and strength by making yourself available to him and his work.

IV. LIFE APPLICATION

The Answer to Our Question

A sign on a friend's wall lists "important things kids have taught us." Some are humorous: "If you are drawing a horse and someone says it looks like a dog, call it a dog" or "Bang on the door until someone opens it." Others are generally good principles for a happy life: "Ask for sprinkles on everything." One good principle in this list is, "Ask *why* until you understand."

Have you ever noticed that kids always ask *why?* Sometimes their questions have easy answers: "Why can't I eat that candy bar before dinner?" Other questions have no answer: "Why did God create cockroaches?" Some questions are heartbreaking in the asking and give adults cause to also ask why: "Why did God make that little boy blind?"

Kids have a curiosity and a liveliness that demands answers. It is not such a bad thing to ask *why* until we understand. We need to have this same kind of curiosity about life and faith. There is nothing wrong with questioning God when this questioning comes from a sincere and honest desire to know God and his ways.

A man at a local church was struggling with his faith. He did not know if he believed any more or why he should. One of his struggles was over why there is so much sin in the world and why God does not seem to do anything about it. He went to someone in his church, but that person told him to "just believe." But that was precisely what he could not do. He needed answers.

There are times in our lives when we need answers. At times, God's answer to us will be, "Peace, child, trust me with this." And at those times, God gives us grace to trust and to wait for a fuller answer. At other times, God is simply waiting for us to ask. In the final analysis, he is our answer—the only answer we need.

V. PRAYER

God, help us to know what questions to ask. Sometimes your word seems so hard, like in the story of the tenants. And yet, how righteous you are! Remove the blinders from our eyes. Help us to understand, to act rightly, to question out of a desire to know you more deeply. Amen.

VI. DEEPER DISCOVERIES

A. The greatest commandment (12:28–34)

The scribes had listed 613 separate commandments, some of greater importance than others, but all binding. Of these, 365 were negative and 248 were positive. As one Christian comedian put it, "If you do the do's, you will not have time to do the don'ts!"

Shema is the Hebrew word for "hear," and it comes from the first word of Deuteronomy 6:4: "Hear, O Israel." Conscientious Jews said this prayer every morning and every evening. It was carried in the phylacteries, small leather boxes which Jews wore on their foreheads and wrists when they prayed (Deut. 6:8). These boxes were also affixed to the door of Jewish homes so that family members were reminded of God and prayed this prayer upon entering or leaving the house.

Perhaps more than any verse in the Old Testament, the Shema summarized who the Jews were. Since they lived among pagan nations, the temptation to polytheism was strong. The Shema reinforced who their God was: "The Lord is one." The Jews' monotheism kept them separate from the other nations. Although they were lax at times and were influenced by other religions, they never denied their monotheism—God is one and he alone is supreme. Jesus' recitation of the verse reminded his listeners that God is one. By claiming to be God, he was not establishing a polytheistic religion. He and God are one.

"You shall love your neighbor as yourself" is from Leviticus 19:18. The Jews understood this verse as "treating your fellow Jew the way you would want to be treated." Jesus expanded its definition (in Luke 10) to include even those people we hate—our enemies. Barclay notes, "It is always easy to let ritual take the place of love. It is always easy to let worship become a matter of the Church building instead of a matter of the whole life. The priest and the Levite could pass by the wounded traveler because they were eager to get on with the ritual of the temple. This scribe had risen beyond his contemporaries and that is why he found himself in sympathy with Jesus" (Barclay, *Mark*, p. 296).

B. The tax (12:13–17)

The Jewish people were divided over the use of coinage in Jesus' day. The use of a certain coin implied they were obligated to that institution, that they had to obey the laws represented by the coin.

The taxes levied upon the Jews by the Roman government were represented by the coin in this passage. Most people took these taxes calmly enough, viewing them as a necessity of living under foreign rule. Judas the Galilean (cf. Acts 5:37), however, revolted, declaring that taxation was no better than slavery. While Judas' rebellion was squelched, his vision was not. It is possible that the Zealot party grew out of his rebellion. In any case, the tax, which the Zealots steadfastly refused to pay, was levied on all Jewish citizens.

The image on the denarius that Jesus examined would have been of the Roman emperor Tiberius. It carried the inscription, "Tiberius Caesar Augustus, son of the divine Augustus." On the other side Caesar was shown sitting on a throne, robed as a high priest.

Barclay notes that people held to three principles in regard to coinage (Barclay, *Mark,* p. 286). First, coinage was a sign of power. When someone conquered a nation, he issued a coin. It suggested money, authority, kingship, and power. Second, a king's reign went as far as his money. Third, because of the king's image on a coin, it was considered the king's property. We still see these principles in operation today. For instance, it is illegal to destroy money because it belongs to the state, although we carry it in our pockets. By using the coin, even today, we agree to abide by the laws of the state; we recognize a political power over us.

VII. TEACHING OUTLINE

A. INTRODUCTION

1. Lead Story: Stop the Questions
2. Context: Jesus has just purged the temple and pronounced judgment on the religious temple system. The rulers have asked him by whose authority he is doing these things. While he does not answer them directly at first, the opening parable in this chapter answers the question clearly.

   The Sanhedrin then tries to trap Jesus with various questions, but he answers them all. Finally, he asks them a question about the Messiah, further showing them that he is the Messiah.
3. Transition: Questions are important. Knowing the answers to the right questions can mean the difference between passing and failing. All of us must come to a point of answering certain questions about our faith. And when Jesus asks questions of us, we must know how to answer.

B. COMMENTARY

1. A Parable of Judgment (12:1–12)
   a. Treatment of the servants (12:1–5)
   b. Treatment of the son (12:6–8)
   c. Judgment (12:9–12)
2. The Question of Government (12:13–17)
   a. The trap (12:13–15a)
   b. The answer (12:15b–17)
3. The Question of Marriage (12:18–27)

a. The trap (12:18–23)
b. The answer (12:24–27)
4. The Important Question (12:28–34)
   a. A sincere seeker's question (12:28)
   b. The answer (12:29–31)
   c. Response (12:32–33)
   d. Jesus' commendation (12:34)
5. The Real Question (12:35–37)
6. True Spirituality (12:38–44)
   a. Beware the scribes (12:38–40)
   b. Be like the widow (12:41–44)

C. CONCLUSION: THE PURPOSE OF QUESTIONS

VIII. ISSUES FOR DISCUSSION

1. What role do you think government plays in religion? Do you think Jesus' statement supports or opposes the separation of church and state?
2. How do you link the two greatest commandments in your daily life?
3. Jesus condemned the scribes in 12:38–40. Do you see this attitude in the church today? Do you see it at times in yourself? How can you correct the situation?

Mark 13

Looking and Living

Mark 13

I N   A   N U T S H E L L

*T*his chapter is particularly important because of the insights and instructions Jesus gives to his disciples. These instructions not only impact those listening but those who will become believers in the future.

It is clear that the main purpose of these instructions is not merely to satisfy the curiosity of his disciples concerning the future but also to give practical, ethical teachings on how to handle the future. Jesus was preparing his disciples—and beyond them the church—to live and witness in a hostile world.

Mark uses this material to demonstrate to his Roman readers that Jesus is not only a sacrificial servant but also the powerful Lord of history.

Finally, we find a shift back and forth between an immediate and remote future, especially in verses 5–23. Some of the events seem to have a dual fulfillment—particularly the destruction of Jerusalem. The first destruction happened in A.D. 70, and the other will occur in the end times.

Looking and Living

I. INTRODUCTION

Alfred Nobel

*A*lfred Nobel was a Swedish chemist who made a fortune by inventing dynamite and other powerful explosives used for weapons. Years later when Nobel's brother died, a newspaper accidentally printed an obituary for Alfred instead. He was described as a man who became rich by enabling people to kill one another in unprecedented quantities. Shaken by this assessment, Nobel resolved to use his fortune to honor accomplishments that benefited humanity. Thus, he created the Nobel Peace Prize, among others.

Alfred Nobel, in essence, had a sneak preview into how he would be remembered if he were to die that day. One might say he got a glimpse of the future today. As a result of his seeing his own obituary, Alfred Nobel was able to make some key changes in his life. Similarly, Jesus has given us a glimpse of the future. How will this information change our lives? How will we live life differently? Mark 13 points out that the best thing we can do is to follow Jesus' instructions concerning the future and live by the Boy Scout motto, "Be Prepared."

II. COMMENTARY

Looking and Living

> **MAIN IDEA:** *Jesus prepares his people, both present and future believers, for the end times.*

A The Beginning of the End (13:1–4)

> **SUPPORTING IDEA:** *Jesus begins the preparation of his disciples for the end times.*

13:1. On a recent trip to Alaska, our group had an opportunity to see a glacier up close from a small plane. It was so massive and blue. The blueness came from the severe cold. The glacier stretched for miles. We were amazed. So were the disciples when it came to the massiveness of the temple.

The temple was considered one of the great wonders of the Roman world. It had been under construction for forty-six years and was just nearing its completion. It was located on a spectacular site on Mt. Moriah. The Jewish historian Josephus wrote: "The exterior of the building wanted nothing that could astound either mind or eye. For, being covered on all sides with massive plates of gold, the sun was no sooner up than it radiated so fiery a flash that persons straining to look at it were compelled to avert their eyes, as from the solar rays. To approaching strangers it appeared from a distance like a snow clad mountain; for all that was not overlaid with gold was of purest white."

Some of the foundation stones of the temple were forty feet long by twelve feet high by eighteen feet wide. These stones were also pure white in appearance. This may have been what prompted one of the disciples to say, **Look Teacher! What massive stones!** The courtyard of the temple had been greatly enlarged (to about four hundred by five hundred yards) in order to accommodate the large throngs of Jews who came to Jerusalem for the festivals. The temple complex covered approximately one-sixth of the area of the city of Jerusalem.

13:2. Instead of carrying on a polite conversation about the greatness of the temple with the disciples, Jesus shocked them. He said, **Not one stone here will be left on another; every one will be thrown down.** Imagine the incredible power and devastation it would take for such a prophecy to come true. Jesus' prophecy did come true when the Roman general Titus first conquered Jerusalem. He ordered that the temple be preserved, but it was gutted by fire. So completely was the temple and the accompanying buildings destroyed that only parts of the Wailing Wall remained.

13:3. Four of the disciples were riveted by such a prophesy concerning the destruction of the temple. Peter, James, and John formed the inner circle of Jesus' disciples. Andrew, being Peter's brother, got to be a part of this "private" time as well with the master. Jesus began his teaching about the future on the Mount of Olives. Rising 150 feet above Jerusalem, the mountain offered a dramatic view of the temple. The prophet Zechariah had prophesied that the Lord would return upon the Mount of Olives (Zech. 14).

13:4. The disciples asked two key questions that introduce this chapter: (1) **Tell us, when will these things happen?** (2) **And what will be the sign that they are all about to be fulfilled?** These questions have been asked over and over again across the centuries by followers of Christ. Every generation has had inklings that Jesus would return during their time because of certain signs or spectacular events of their day. Jesus eventually answered the disciples' questions but not in the way they expected. There is a double perspective to Christ's answers. Some of the events described were to be fulfilled in the destruction of Jerusalem in A.D. 70 and some were to be fulfilled during the time of tribulation before his second coming. Yet, throughout Jesus' discourse he was more concerned to prepare them for the trials that lay ahead than to give them dates and signs.

ⓑ Get Ready (13:5–8)

> **SUPPORTING IDEA:** *Jesus prepares his people, both present and future, for the end times by warning them about false saviors and false signs.*

13:5. A more detailed account of what Jesus said to the disciples can be found in the parallel passages in Matthew 24–25 and Luke 21. For instance, Luke's emphasis with the Olivet Discourse centers on the fall of Jerusalem and the captivity of the Jews and domination of the city by the Gentiles. Mark emphasizes the danger to faith that will arise in the time that follows Jesus' crucifixion and resurrection. In fact, Jesus started by saying, **Watch out that no one deceives you.** At least three times Jesus warned his disciples to "watch out" or "be on your guard" (vv. 5,23,33). In other words, "Do not be caught napping. Live life in alertness and awareness."

13:6. Jesus began to answer the disciples' questions by pointing out certain "non-signs." These are signs that have deceived people throughout time. The first of the non-signs Jesus pointed out are claims of others to be the returning Messiah. Jesus taught that popular religious leaders will claim to be the Messiah and have solutions for the problems of life. Jesus warned his disciples not to be deceived by these imposters.

Over eight hundred people lost their lives by following the command to drink poisoned Kool-Aid from Jim Jones, in Jonestown, Guyana. Many people were killed in a fire that destroyed their compound in Waco, Texas, because of following David Koresh, who claimed he was the Messiah. Finally, over thirty suicides took place in Los Angeles, California, among a group called Heaven's Gate because they followed a leader who claimed to know when God was returning. These people were barren in their souls. Their thirst for meaning and purpose caused them to follow these so-called Messiahs. Jesus warned us not to be deceived by such false prophets as these.

13:7–8. Jesus also warned the disciples not to be deceived by political conflicts (**wars and rumors of wars; nation will arise against nation, and kingdom against kingdom**). Mark's Roman readers had enjoyed a measure of peace for many years, but this would eventually come to an end. Even though the fall of such a great kingdom as the Roman Empire would be catastrophic, it did not mean the end was near. Also, natural disasters such as **earthquakes** and **famines** would not indicate the end times. Jesus warned us of the dangers of making these types of events benchmarks for the end times.

Notice his statements, **these are the beginning of birth pains** (v. 8) and **the end is still to come** (v. 7). These seem to refer back to the signs just described in verses 7–8 as a beginning point and not the end. Just as labor increases for a mother when it is time for her child to be born, these signs are only the beginning point of the labor period before the return of Christ. Jesus wanted to prepare his people to be ready to face a turbulent world with confidence in the midst of suffering. Mark wanted to assure his Roman readers that the appearance of wars and persecution were a part of God's overall plan. Also, in Jewish thought the messianic kingdom would emerge after a period of intense suffering. The word **beginning** suggests many more sufferings would come. So do not be deceived, Jesus declared. Be ready.

Do Not Be Discouraged (13:9–13)

SUPPPORTING IDEA: *Jesus prepares his people for the end times by encouraging them to remain steadfast in the midst of persecution.*

13:9. Jesus wanted to prepare his people for the suffering they would encounter on two levels. They would suffer publicly. Persecution for believers (**flogged in the synagogues**) would begin in the local Jewish courts (**local councils**) but would move to the higher courts where governors and kings would be involved. Yet, the purpose of such persecution was that his followers might be **witnesses** of the good news of Jesus Christ. Persecution would result in proclamation.

13:10. Jesus declared that **the gospel must first be preached to all nations.** The word **first** probably means "before the end." This suggests that when the gospel has penetrated a nation to the extent that it comes to the attention of the governing authorities—who will demand an accounting from those who preach the gospel—then the gospel has been given as a testimony to that nation. The primary goal of Christ's disciples is to preach the gospel to all nations (Matt. 28:19–20). Jesus emphasized to the disciples the need to preach the gospel to all nations before the end times. This was more important than looking for signs about the end times. In other words, "get busy."

13:11. Jesus wanted the disciples to know that even as they were hauled into court and cross-examined by authorities, they would not be alone. He promised them that in those situations the **Holy Spirit** would be their supernatural resource. The Holy Spirit would reveal to them, on the spot, the appropriate words to speak (cf. Jer. 1:9; Acts 6:10; 7:55).

13:12–13. Jesus then warned the disciples of the severity of the persecution they would face. They would face not only public humiliation but private persecution as well from their own families. The phrase, **brother will betray brother to death,** shows the persecution a believer could receive from his or her own family. Those who became followers of Christ and were part of a family that still practiced orthodox Judaism would be cast out of the family and considered as dead.

The Roman Empire also considered anyone who did not declare Caesar as Lord to be a traitor who was worthy of death. Both Jews and Gentile who trusted Christ could expect persecution from their own families for their faith. Yet, this hatred would not be limited to relatives, but **all men will hate you because of me.** If we identify with Christ, we can expect persecution, even from those we love the most.

The phrase, **but he who stands firm to the end will be saved,** does not imply a doctrine of salvation by works. Jesus was emphasizing that genuine faith is revealed through the trials and tests that a person endures. As one man said, "Hammering hardens steel . . . but crushes putty." Those who have genuine faith in Christ will not give up their faith under such intense persecution. This section with its warnings and encouragement was especially important for the church to hear, since great suffering and persecution would come upon the followers of Jesus. Some of these verses occur in Matthew (10:17–22) and Luke (12:11–12; 12–17).

D You Can Run . . . But You Cannot Hide (13:14–23)

SUPPORTING IDEA: *Jesus prepares his people for the end times by instructing them about the abomination that will cause desolation and desertion.*

13:14a. This is probably one of the most difficult verses in Mark's Gospel, if not the New Testament. Much speculation has centered around the meaning of the phrase, **the abomination that causes desolation.** This key phrase seems to be derived from the Book of Daniel (9:27; 11:31; 12:11). The word *abomination* suggests something that is offensive to God, while *desolation* implies that the temple will be left deserted. In other words, those who come to worship in the temple will no longer occupy it but vacate it because of this abomination.

The fulfillment of Daniel's prophecy (Dan. 11:31) about the "abomination that causes desolation" is attributed to the Syrian ruler Antiochus IV Epiphanes.In 167 B.C. he desecrated the altar of burnt offering in the Jewish temple by sacrificing a pig and pouring swine's blood on the altar. No Jewish worshiper would enter the temple because pigs were considered vile and unclean. Yet, Jesus used the same phrase as Daniel. He made it clear that the fulfillment of this prophecy was not restricted to the events mentioned above. Interpreters disagree about what Jesus meant. Some believe he was referring to events that surrounded the fall of Jerusalem in A.D. 70. The Romans, after conquering the city, entered the temple with their military flags and set them up as objects of worship (cf. Luke 21:20).

Yet, there seems to be more to Jesus' statement. He could have had in mind a prophecy that would be fulfilled in the ends times by the Antichrist (cf. Matt. 24:29–30; 2 Thess. 2:3–10). Perhaps the best solution is to understand the "abomination that causes desolation" as having a multiple fulfillment in (1) the Maccabean period when Antiochus IV desecrated the temple, (2) the events of A.D. 70, and (3) the end times.

13:14b–16. The warning, **then let those who are in Judea flee to the mountains,** fits the context of the approach of the Roman army before the fall of Jerusalem in A.D. 70. No one would be able to flee from the judgment of God during the end times, so the more immediate fall of Jerusalem in A.D. 70 seems to be what Jesus was referring to.

There are two key admonitions in these verses. First, **no one on the roof of his house** was to go inside to get any belongings. The roofs of Palestinian houses were flat, and they were often used as places of prayer. In order to get to the roof, a person had to go up an outside staircase. Jesus was showing the urgency of the moment by instructing people on the roofs not to entertain any idea of going into the house to get belongings. Once they were down the staircase, they must keep on going. Jesus used hyperbole (a deliberate over-statement for effect) to make his point: "Time is of the essence."

Second, **no one in the field** was to return to the house for his or her outer garment. The outer garment was used at night to keep a person warm; in the daytime it was taken off to allow freedom of movement while working. Even though the outer garment would act as a blanket to keep a person warm at night, Jesus instructed people that they should not go back to the house to get it. They should head for the mountains immediately. In other words, crisis takes precedence over comfort.

13:17–18. Jesus emphasized the winter season would be an especially hard time for those attempting to flee, since the cold and rain-swollen streams would present great hazards. The phrase, **pregnant women and nursing mothers,** indicates that women who were pregnant or with small babies would have a hard time getting away because of their condition. Being able to cover ground quickly was of the utmost importance. These warnings were especially appropriate because of what actually happened when Jerusalem was destroyed by the Romans.

13:19–20. These verses probably shift to the end times. The catastrophic and cataclysmic language seems to look forward to the Great Tribulation that would precede the end times. Mark uses language derived from Daniel's description of the last days (Dan. 12:1; cf. Jer. 30:7). Revelation 14–19 gives further details about the judgment and wrath that God would pour out during the end times. Mark's statement about the **elect** refers to God's people. God will remember mercy in the midst of judgment because of his people.

13:21–23. Jesus finished this section as he began it—by warning against false christs. A major crisis, such as the fall of Jerusalem and the end times, would produce many false messengers who would claim to be the returning Messiah. Jesus pointed out that they would have supernatural power that enabled them to **perform signs and miracles.** Yet, they would not be able to deceive God's people because God would protect his people. He emphasized that believers should **be on your guard.** No matter how compelling these false messengers might be in their words and deed, we must not believe or obey their admonitions.

E The King Is Coming (13:24–27)

> **SUPPORTING IDEA:** *Jesus prepares his people for the end times by describing his triumphal return as the Son of Man.*

13:24–25. Jesus wanted to give his people hope in the midst of incredible persecution and pain, especially during the tribulation of the end times. He did so by describing his return as the conquering king of the cosmos. The phrase **in those days** is an Old Testament expression referring to the end times (cf. Jer. 3:16,18; 31:29; 33:15–16; Joel 3:1) When Jesus returns, there will be spectacular celestial phenomenon and cosmic disturbances that the world has never seen such as **the sun will be darkened, and the moon will not give its light.** The imagery and language is similar to the Old Testament descriptions of the "Day of the Lord"—another phrase for the end times in the Old Testament (Isa. 13:9–10; 24:23; 34:4; Ezek. 32:7–8; Joel 2:10;30–31). Judgment will certainly come. As Haddon Robinson said, "God may not pay at the end of every month . . . but God pays." Judgment and rescue of his elect will happen.

13:26–27. The return of Jesus will not be seen by just a few people, as was true of his entrance into the world when he was born in a manger. This time **men will see the Son of Man coming in clouds with great power and glory.** The reference here is to Daniel 7:13. This is the first time Jesus definitely connected the title "Son of Man" with the Daniel prophesy (cf. Mark 14:62).

All of humankind will see the Son of Man as the ruler of this universe. His major concern will be to gather his people together so they might share in this time of triumph. The phrase, **gather his elect from the four winds, from the ends of the earth to the ends of the heavens,** has a dual meaning. Not only will he send his angels to gather his people from the ends of the earth but apparently those in the heavens who have gone on before will also be with him to celebrate his triumph.

F Signs of the Time (13:28–31)

> **SUPPORTING IDEA:** *Jesus prepares his people for the end times by instilling hope in the midst of horror.*

13:28. After showing the infinite power of God, Jesus wanted to make certain truths personal. He did so by ending this chapter with two key illustrations. The first illustration centered around the fig tree. In Palestine most trees remained green throughout the year, with the exception of the fig tree.

During the fall the fig tree would lose its leaves. In the spring the sap would fill the branches and the tree would begin the process of putting forth its leaves. This meant that summer was not far away. Jesus did not want his disciples to despair about the persecution they would face. Jesus was showing that just as he promised there would be persecution, deliverance would follow through his return as the Son of Man.

13:29. The phrase, **these things**, could refer to the events surrounding the fall of Jerusalem in A.D. 70 or to the events immediately preceding the end of the age. This phrase could relate to the phrase, "all these things," in verse 30. This also could be a dual reference for both the near prophesy of the fall of Jerusalem and the coming end times. If this is the case, then Jesus was referring to the events most likely to affect the believers at that time, which would be the fall of Jerusalem in A.D. 70. But he may have been referring as well to the end times.

The next phrase, **it is near**, may also be translated as "he is near." Again, a dual interpretation of this phrase is possible. For instance, if verses 28–31 are taken to refer primarily to the events surrounding the fall of Jerusalem, then the *it* would be linked to the "abomination that causes desolation" (v. 14)—to the fall of Jerusalem itself. If, on the other hand, verses 28–31 are descriptive of the end times, the "he is near" would fit, indicating the near return of Christ. Both interpretations are possible. Jesus may have been referring to both the near future and the distant future.

13:30. The phrase, **I tell you the truth**, calls attention to what Jesus was about to say: **This generation will certainly not pass away until all these things have happened.** The understanding of this verse hinges on two phrases: **this generation** and **all these things.** There are several ways to understand the phrase, "this generation." It could be applied to humankind in general, Israel, or Christians in general and unbelievers. In this case, " all these things" could refer to the events described in verses 5–23.

At the same time, however, the incarnation, crucifixion, resurrection, ascension, and return of Christ all seem to go together. God's desire is that everyone repent. He could be holding back the last stage of the coming of the end times (cf. 2 Pet. 3:9–10). This understanding of "all these things" would make "this generation" mean that the return of Christ is at hand for every generation.

13:31. Jesus was clear that his word is absolute. Literally, **heaven and earth will pass away.** There will be a new heaven and a new earth, but Jesus' words will last forever. They are certain. His words will be authenticated by the fall of Jerusalem in A.D. 70 and culminated in the fulfillment of the end times.

G Pay Attention (13:32–37)

SUPPORTING IDEA: *Jesus prepares his people for the end times by exhorting them to be ready for his return.*

13:32. Jesus was serious about his followers being vigilant during the time before his return. He emphasized the need to pay attention four times in six verses: be alert (v. 33), therefore keep watch (v. 35), do not let him find you sleeping (v. 36), and watch (v. 37).

The phrase, **that day**, refers to his return after the great tribulation. Even though certain signs have been given about that day, no one knows, **not even the angels in heaven, nor the Son, but only the Father.** Even Jesus does not know. This shows clearly his humanity. Jesus purposely laid aside the exercise of his deity—in this case his ability to know all things past, present, and future—as a consequence of his human existence. Jesus answered one of the key questions of the disciples, "When will these things happen?" Jesus declared that he did not know and they should not worry about it. Even at Jesus' ascension, he clearly said to the disciples that it was not for them "to know the times or dates the Father has set by his own authority" (Acts 1:7).

13:33–36. The emphasis of this parable is a stern exhortation to **be on guard** because Christ could come back at any time. This parable has some of the features of the parable of the talents (Matt. 25:14–30) and the parable of the pounds (Luke 19:12–27). Like a doorkeeper who must watch because he does not know when the owner will return, they also must be on guard. The four times—**evening, or at midnight, or when the rooster crows, or at dawn**—were the four watches of the night used by the Romans. A constant vigil must be kept because he could arrive **suddenly.**

13:37. Jesus ended this discourse the way he began it—with an exhortation to **watch.** He emphasized this for **everyone** as well as the disciples. All believers in every age must watch. Jesus exhorted all believers not only to keep watch for his return but also to watch out so nobody would deceive them and rob the house. Temptations and pressures would come, causing troubles and despair. His followers were to watch out for these things as well. Do not let anything derail you from your task of preaching the gospel and remaining steadfast, he encouraged. Maranatha—come quickly, Lord Jesus.

MAIN IDEA REVIEW: *Jesus prepares his people, both present and future believers, for the end times.*

III. CONCLUSION

The True Beam

After landing at the Los Angeles airport, the pilot made an unusual announcement: "This landing was made without any human help." A concerned passenger, on the way out of the plane, asked the pilot what he meant by "no human help." The pilot explained that there was a laser beam coming from the control tower. This "true beam," as they called it, had the ability to connect to the onboard computer of the airplane. As the plane approached the runway, the control tower directed the pilot by saying, "O.K., twenty degrees to the right—now ten degrees to the left. You are now connected to the true beam." Once the place was in the proper position and connected to the true beam, the computer took over and brought them in safely for a perfect landing. The key was to be connected to the true beam.

Jesus declared in Mark 13 that we should not get distracted by timelines and events concerning his coming. His orders were for us to stay connected to the "true beam," Jesus Christ. If Jesus is in control of our main computer—our heart—then we will not miss him when he comes. Stay focused on the "True Beam."

PRINCIPLES

- Believers can rely upon the Holy Spirit's sustaining power in the midst of persecution and problems.
- Believers can have absolute confidence in the certainty of God's Word.
- Believers are commissioned by God to preach the gospel, especially in light of Christ's imminent return.
- Believers are to live life consciously and not complacently

APPLICATIONS

- Pray for the Lord to help you live life consciously each day. Ask him to help you be willing to witness for him while we are waiting for his return.
- Expect misunderstanding and even persecution from those you love because of your faith in Christ. Take comfort in the fact that even our Lord went through similar experiences.
- The Bible tells us to "number our days" (Ps. 90:12). Let's say the average life span of a person is seventy-five years old. If you are 45 years old, you would subtract your age from 75 and then multiply the difference by 365 days (75 − 45 = 30 years; 30 x 365 =

10,950 days). In light of the number of days and the imminent return of Christ, thank God for each day he has given you to live for him.

IV. LIFE APPLICATION

Running for Our Lives

Cradling his rifle in the crook of his arm, a hunter was following an old logging road nearly overgrown by the forest in the wilds of Oregon. It was nearly evening, and he was just thinking about returning to camp when a noise exploded in the brush nearby. Before he had a chance to lift his rifle, a small blur of brown and white came shooting up the road straight for him.

The hunter said, "It all happened so fast, I hardly had time to think. I looked down and there was a little brown cottontail—utterly spent— crowded up against my legs between my boots. The little thing was trembling all over, but it just sat there and didn't budge." Wild rabbits are frightened of people, and it's unusual to see one—let alone have one sit at your feet.

While the hunter was puzzling over this, another player entered the scene. Down the road—maybe twenty yards away—a weasel burst out of the brush. When it saw the man—and its intended prey sitting at his feet—it froze in its tracks, its mouth panting and eyes glowing red.

It dawned on the hunter that he had stepped into a little life-and-death drama of the forest. The cottontail, exhausted by the chase, was only moments from death. The man was its last hope of refuge. Forgetting its natural fear and caution, the little animal instinctively crowded up against him for protection from the sharp teeth of its relentless enemy.

The hunter did not disappoint the little cottontail. Raising his rifle, he shot into the ground just underneath the weasel. It leaped into the air and rocketed back into the forest. For a while the little rabbit did not stir. It just sat there, huddled at the man's feet in the gathering twilight. "Where did it go, little one?" the hunter asked. "I do not think he will be bothering you for a while. Looks like you're off the hook tonight." Soon the rabbit hopped away from its protector into the forest.

That rabbit had an uncertain future. It was running for its life, and it just happened to "luck out" by finding refuge in one who was greater than its enemy. Sometimes we also feel like we are running for our lives. The predators of our past—trouble, worry, fear, and uncertainty of the future—can wear us down to the point where we feel like the weasel is going to win. But the Bible says, "Call upon me in the day of trouble and I will deliver you and you shall glorify me." No matter how rocky and uncertain life may seem, we are promised a bright future. Jeremiah 29:11 says, "For I know the thoughts that I think toward you. Thoughts of peace and not of calamity, to give you a future and a hope."

No matter how troublesome life may become and how uncertain our future may seem, run to your protector and huddle at his feet. He stands with his arms wide open. In Mark 13 Jesus warns us about the future but does not want us worrying about the future or even trying to figure it out. Jesus, in his humanity said, "I do not know when these things will occur." His focus was not on figuring out the future but on remaining faithful to his mission. How can we do this? By staying close to the Father. We also must focus daily upon him.

V. PRAYER

There are times, Lord, when I find myself worrying and stressing out about my future. I do not want to live my life fretfully but faithfully. Help me to "huddle at your feet" when I begin to be eaten up by the weasel of doubt. Let me remember that this is not my home—I am just passing through. May I live each day as a gift from your hand and know that I have a future and a hope because I have you. Amen.

VI. DEEPER DISCOVERIES

A. Watch; be on guard; be alert (13:5,9,23,33)

Waiting to be interviewed for a job as a Morse code operator, a group of applicants paid little attention to the sound of the dots and dashes that began coming over the loud speaker. Suddenly, one of the applicants rushed into the employer's office. Soon he returned smiling. "I got the job," he exclaimed.

"How did you get ahead of us?" the other applicants asked.

"You might have been considered if you had not been so busy talking that you did not hear the manager's coded message," he replied. The message said, "'The man I need must always be on alert. The first one who interprets this and comes directly to my private office will be hired.'"

Jesus warns us repeatedly in Mark 13 of the need to stay "tuned in" to him. If we do that, we will not miss how he is working in our lives today. We will be ready when he returns for us in the future.

B. He who stands firm to the end will be saved (13:13)

Will Campbell tells the story of an Anabaptist woman who lived in Antwerp, Belgium. She had been arrested a few days earlier for proclaiming the gospel of Christ as she understood it from her personal reading of the Scriptures as well as from study with others of like faith. She underwent the inquisition of the religious leaders of that day for heresy. She was also tortured by the civil authorities. Yet, she would not buckle under the pressure. After six months, she had not promised to stop preaching the word. So the authorities did what they thought they had to do: They sentenced her to death on October 5, 1573. Included in the sentence was a stipulation to the executioner that her tongue be screwed to the roof of her mouth so she could not testify along the way as they took her to be burned at the stake.

That day her teenage son, Adriaen, took his youngest brother, three-year-old Hans Mattheus, and they stood near the stake so her children might be near her at the moment of death. Three other men and a woman were to die that day for the same offense—unauthorized preaching of the gospel. When the flames were lit, Adriaen fainted. He could not witness the horror of his mother being burned at the stake. But when it was all over and the ashes had cooled, he sifted through them until he found the screw that had silenced his mother's tongue. It would not silence his as he also preached the gospel.

This woman, in the midst of great persecution and even death, clearly illustrates the meaning of the phrase, "he who stands firm to the end will be saved." The word *saved* literally means "will reveal they are saved." Our trials and troubles reveal the genuineness of our faith. In fact, it is through our suffering that the gospel displays its keeping power in our life. Second Corinthians 4:7–9 says, "We have this treasure [the gospel] in jars of clay [us] to show that this all surpassing power is from God and not from us. We are hard pressed on every side, but not crushed; perplexed, but not in despair; persecuted, but not abandoned; struck down, but not destroyed."

C. The abomination that causes desolation (13:14)

This key phrase is used also in Matthew 24:15. It is a quote from the Book of Daniel (11:31; 12:11). Daniel's translation reads, "The abomination that makes desolate." Daniel prophesied that the temple would be used for a despicable purpose at some time in the future. As a result, God's people would no longer worship there. There would be such great contempt and revulsion for what took place at the temple that the people of God would no longer come to worship there. The temple would actually become "desolate."

According to the verses in the Gospel, a similar misuse of the temple would take place in the future. This would show that a time of great persecution and tribulation would be coming to Judea. Some interpreters believe Daniel's prophecy was fulfilled in 165 B.C. when Antiochus the IV, Greek ruler of Syria, polluted the Jewish temple in Jerusalem by sacrificing a pig on the holy altar. This would be an abomination to the Jewish worshipers because a pig was considered unclean and the worst type of abomination. It is also believed that this prophesy was fulfilled when the Romans ransacked the Jewish temple in A.D. 70.

But in another sense, the prophecy of Daniel has not been fulfilled completely. Some interpreters insist that the abomination of desolation refers to the idolatrous image or the "man of sin" who will take over God's place in the temple and make people bow down and worship him (2 Thess. 2:3–4). This would be considered the final act of sacrilege that marks the beginning of the end time.

VII. TEACHING OUTLINE

A. INTRODUCTION

1. Lead Story: Alfred Nobel
2. Context: Jesus has just left the temple after teaching a series of lessons that offends the religious leaders. Jesus knows that this is his last time to leave the temple alive, before his crucifixion, burial and resurrection. Perhaps to break the tension, one of the disciples comments on the glory of the temple, pointing out the massiveness of the stones and the buildings surrounding the temple. If anything was stable and permanent, it would most certainly be the temple and its courts.

   Jesus then prophesies that not one stone will be left upon another. Four of the disciples are so taken aback by this prophecy of Jesus that they pull him aside privately on the Mount of Olives to ask two key questions. When will these events happen and what will be the signs tipping us off?
3. Transition: In chapter 13 Jesus answers these two key questions of the disciples about the "end times." We will see that Jesus is not so much concerned about *when* these events will happen as to *what* we are doing as his people to preach the gospel in the meantime. Among the nineteen commands in this chapter, the one command that stands out most is, "Watch." As the Boy Scout motto declares, "Be Prepared." We just never know when Jesus might show up.

B. COMMENTARY

1. The Beginning of the End (13:1–4)
2. Get Ready (13:5–8)
3. Do Not Be Discouraged (13:9–13)
4. You Can Run . . . but You Cannot Hide (13:14–23)
5. The King Is Coming (13:24–27)
6. Signs of the Time (13:28–31)
7. Pay Attention (13:32–37)

C. CONCLUSION: THE TRUE BEAM

VIII. ISSUES FOR DISCUSSION

1. Define "end times." Why do so many people concentrate on the return of Christ? What can happen if we spend too much time trying to predict Christ's return?

2. Name some "false cults" or people who have claimed to be Christ or are getting ready for Christ's return. What were people's perception of them? Did it help the cause of Christ?

3. Have you ever been persecuted for your faith in Christ? If so, what was it like? Does being a steadfast Christian cause conflict within your family? If so, how?

4. Should we expect public persecution for being a Christian? If so, what would this persecution look like?

5. How does the imminent return of Christ impact the way we go about living life? Our relationships? The way we do evangelism?

Mark 14

Prelude to the Passion

I. INTRODUCTION
The Principle of Love

II. COMMENTARY
A verse-by-verse explanation of the chapter.

III. CONCLUSION
The Rejected Cornerstone

An overview of the principles and applications from the chapter.

IV. LIFE APPLICATION
Life Is Not Fair

Melding the chapter to life.

V. PRAYER
Tying the chapter to life with God.

VI. DEEPER DISCOVERIES
Historical, geographical, and grammatical enrichment of the commentary.

VII. TEACHING OUTLINE
Suggested step-by-step group study of the chapter.

VIII. ISSUES FOR DISCUSSION
Zeroing the chapter in on daily life.

"Is death the last sleep? No, it is the last and final awakening."

Sir Walter Scott

Mark 14

IN A NUTSHELL

Chapters 14–16 of Mark are known as the passion and resurrection narratives. Out of 661 verses in the book, 128 are devoted to the passion and resurrection of Jesus. A total of 242 verses are devoted to Jesus' last week (from the triumphal entry to the resurrection). Over half of the Gospel of Mark is devoted to the last week of Christ's life. These events—the suffering, death, burial, and resurrection—are the core of the Christian faith. Mark wants his Roman readers to understand that they have a future and a hope no matter how severe the suffering they may encounter for their faith.

Chapter 14 concentrates on the theme of Christ's suffering, which is highlighted by Judas's betrayal, Peter's denial (Judas, Peter, and all of the disciples), as well as the mockery and injustice he suffers in the trials before the Sanhedrin and Pilate.

Prelude to the Passion

I. INTRODUCTION

The Principle of Love

Author and business leader Fred Smith writes: "One of my treasured memories comes from a doughnut shop in Grand Saline, Texas. A young farm couple was sitting at the table next to mine. He was wearing overalls and she a gingham dress. After finishing their doughnuts, he got up to pay the bill, and I noticed she did not get up to follow him.

"But then he came back and stood in front of her. She put her arms around his neck, and he lifted her up, revealing that she was wearing a full-body brace. He lifted her out of her chair and backed out the front door to the pick-up truck, with her hanging from his neck. As he gently put her into the truck, everyone in the shop watched. No one said anything until a waitress remarked, almost reverently, 'He took his vows seriously.'"

For better and for worse, this man was going to honor his commitment, no matter how burdensome or inconvenient. He did what he did because a core principle operated in his life: the principle of love. There are many such stories of people making great sacrifices because of their love for others.

In Mark 14 we see the incredible love that Jesus has for us. Jesus was about to enter the most agonizing time of his ministry. He would be betrayed into the hands of his enemies by one of his own disciples; be forsaken by all of his other disciples; agonize at the thought of being separated from his own Father in bearing the sins of all mankind; be rejected and denied by one of his closest friends; and face the cruel injustice of his enemies. Why? Love. As hard as it is to understand or comprehend, Jesus "so loved the world" that he was committed to giving up his life for us. As you read Mark 14, see the power of committed love.

II. COMMENTARY

Prelude to the Passion

MAIN IDEA: *Jesus, the sacrificial servant, experiences severe suffering at the hands of his friends and foes.*

Betrayal and Blessing (14:1–11)

SUPPORTING IDEA: *Jesus experiences blessing in the midst of betrayal.*

14:1–2. The religious leaders could not stand it any longer. They wanted to get rid of Jesus, so they began to hatch a plan to accomplish their goal. Timing was critical. **Now the Passover and the Feast of Unleavened Bread were only two days away.** The Passover was the annual Jewish festival or feast celebrating the time when the angel of the Lord passed over the homes of the Hebrews on the night when all the firstborn of the Egyptians died (Exod. 12:13,23,27). A lamb was to be sacrificed and eaten to commemorate this event. These lambs had to be slain on the fourteenth of Nissan (March/April), and the meal was to be eaten that evening between sundown and midnight. According to Jewish time, that would be the fifteenth of Nissan, since the Jewish day began at sundown.

The Feast of Unleavened Bread followed this Passover meal, and it lasted for seven days (Exod. 12:15–20; 23:15; 34:18; Deut. 16:1–8). The Last Supper was probably the celebration of the Passover, and it took place on a Thursday night. The decision to do away with Jesus probably began the night before the Passover celebration, a Wednesday.

The religious leaders realized there would be thousands of people in Jerusalem from all over the world to attend this time of celebration. They knew it would be risky to go after Jesus during this time: **or the people may riot.** The crowd would be highly excitable during this time, and they could not be sure of controlling and persuading the people to be on their side. So the religious leaders decided to wait until the feast was over. Yet, God had other plans; and this part of their plan did not work out. Verse 11 indicates that the religious leaders gained some unexpected help from one of Jesus' own friends, Judas. This may have convinced them to move ahead with their plan during the celebration of the Passover.

14:3. Between the accounts of the plan to arrest Jesus, Mark contrasts the betrayal and treachery of Judas and the religious leaders with the love and devotion of Mary. The Gospels of Mark and Matthew do not report this woman's name, but the Gospel of John tells us it was Mary of Bethany, the sister of Martha and Lazarus (John 11:1–2). Mary is mentioned three times in the Gospels; each time she is at the feet of Jesus (Luke 10:38–42; John 11:31–32; 12:1–8). Mary loved Jesus.

Mary was at the home of **Simon the Leper** in the village of Bethany. Simon may have been healed by Jesus. Perhaps they were celebrating his healing. The **expensive perfume, made of pure nard** came from the root of a plant that grew chiefly in India. Mary broke the neck of the white jar and began to pour this sweet-smelling perfume over Jesus' head.

14:4–5. The phrase, **some of those present were saying indignantly to one another,** seems to describe the disciples (Matt. 26:8). Yet, Judas, who was the treasurer for the disciples, may have been the most vocal (John 12:4–5). His value system, as we shall see later, centered on money. The more he had, the happier he was, since he served as the group's treasurer.

The phrase, **it could have been sold for a year's wages,** shows the incredible extravagance of this sacrifice by Mary. The critics of Mary's extravagant expression said the perfume **could have been sold** and **the money given to the poor.** Giving gifts to the poor on the eve of Passover was customary for the Jews. More importantly, it shows the insensitivity of the disciples in comparison to the great love Mary had for Jesus. Mary shows that Jesus deserves our best. The more we love Jesus, the more we will show it by what we offer to him.

14:6–9. Jesus defended Mary's actions by saying, **Leave her alone . . . Why are you bothering her? . . .She has done a beautiful thing to me.** Jesus received Mary's gift for what it was—an unselfish act of love and devotion. Jesus pointed out to Mary's critics that he would not be with them much longer. In this context, Mary's expressing of affection toward him was quite appropriate. The opportunity to help the poor would always exist. Jesus cared for the poor. This is evident in such passages as Matthew 5:3; 6:2–4; Luke 6:20,36–38; 21:1–4. Yet, this was a very special occasion. It is so important for us to give flowers to those whom we love while they can appreciate them.

The phrase, **she poured perfume on my body beforehand to prepare for my burial,** was a reminder of Jesus to his followers about his upcoming crucifixion and burial. The motivation for Mary's act was love and devotion. But Jesus interpreted her act of sacrifice as a fitting preparation for his death and burial.

14:10–11. In the midst of such an expression of love by Mary, there was great hatred and jealousy by another follower of Jesus—Judas. **Then Judas Iscariot, one of the Twelve, went to the chief priests to betray Jesus to them.** Judas was on the "inside" with Jesus. He traveled with him and was one of his chosen disciples. Yet, Judas's action shows that just to know a lot about Jesus does not save a person. There must be a response of faith and love.

The religious leaders were **delighted to hear this.** They now had an "inside man" who could pick the right time to hand Jesus over to them. Now they could avoid a riot by the people during the Passover and Feast of Unleavened Bread. They sealed the deal by giving Judas what he loved most—money. Matthew 26:15 spells out the amount—thirty silver coins. This also was the fulfillment of a prophecy about the Messiah in Zechariah

11:12–13. Judas did not know it, but he was fulfilling Scripture by his act of betrayal.

B Betrayal and the Lord's Supper (14:12–26)

SUPPORTING IDEA: *Jesus announces his betrayal by a friend while instituting the Lord's Supper.*

14:12. The phrase, **on the first day of the Feast of Unleavened Bread, when it was customary to sacrifice the Passover lamb,** shows that the Jews observed the Passover feast as part of the eighth-day celebration of the Feast of Unleavened Bread. The day of the week was Thursday. The Passover was to be celebrated in Jerusalem. Preparations needed to be made for the feast, since Jesus and his disciples were in Bethany and the meal needed to be eaten by midnight.

14:13–16. Jesus sent two of the disciples (Peter and John, according to Luke 22:8) to make the preparations for the Passover observance. They would know where to go to prepare for the Passover because they would meet **a man carrying a jar of water.** Women, not men, usually carried water jars. This man would lead them to a house where there would be a **guest room.** According to Jewish custom, if a person in Jerusalem had a room available, he was to lend it to any pilgrims who needed a place to celebrate the feast. It appears that Jesus had already made arrangements with this man. The room had all that was necessary for Jesus and the disciples to celebrate this "last supper' together. It would be up to Peter and John to prepare the food.

The food consisted of roasted lamb, unleavened bread, and the dish of bitter herbs (Exod. 12:8–20). The lamb reminded the Jews of the blood that was applied to the doorposts of their homes to keep the angel of death from slaying their firstborn. The bread was unleavened to remind them of the haste in which they left Egypt (Exod. 12:39). The bitter herbs spoke of their suffering as Pharaoh's slaves. The drinking of wine was added later to the ceremony.

14:17. Jesus and the other disciples apparently spent the day in Bethany while Peter and John prepared the feast. Bethany is a suburb of Jerusalem, only a couple of miles away. After they had made the preparations, Peter and John probably went to get Jesus and the disciples so they could celebrate the Passover feast. The Jewish day began at sundown, so it was Thursday night when they gathered at the room in Jerusalem.

14:18. While they were eating the Passover meal, Jesus declared, **one of you will betray me—one who is eating with me.** To break bread with someone was to enter into a pact of friendship and mutual trust. It would be an act of incredible treachery to break bread and then to betray your host. Not only was it someone who was breaking bread with Jesus—but it was one of his own friends who had been with him for more than two years. This would have seemed unbelievable to the disciples. They did not know that Judas had already made arrangements to betray Jesus.

14:19. The disciples must have felt like they had been punched in the stomach. The phrase, **they were saddened,** shows incredible grief and pain at the thought that one of them could be Jesus' betrayer. One by one, including Judas, they asked, **Surely, not I?** This question seems almost rhetorical in that each one was hoping to hear, "No, not you." All of the disciples, except Judas, were honestly seeking an answer because of their fear. Judas asked in order to maintain his cover-up as the inside man for the religious leaders. If he had not asked, he might have made the others suspicious.

14:20. Jesus made it clear that his betrayer was in the room eating with him. Now Jesus gave another detail by saying, **it is . . . one who dips bread into the bowl with me** (dipping a piece of unleavened bread in the Passover sauce). Each disciple had dipped a piece of bread in the bowl while eating with Jesus, so the specifics of "who" exactly was Jesus' betrayer was not revealed. Yet, Jesus emphasized that the person who betrayed him had enjoyed a close relationship with him.

14:21. While Judas betrayed Jesus for his own selfish reasons, behind his action was a divine purpose. The upcoming events concerning the Son of Man (Jesus) were not chance occurrences. The Scriptures were being fulfilled (Isa. 53) Yet, the phrase, **but woe to that man who betrays the Son of Man,** shows he was responsible for his decision and its consequences in betraying Jesus.

14:22. Jesus **took bread, gave thanks and broke it, . . . saying "Take it, this is my body."** Jesus took the unleavened bread they were eating, divided it, and gave it to the disciples. The bread represented Jesus' body.

14:23–24. The phrase, **then he took the cup,** referred to the wine they were drinking with the meal. Jesus gave **thanks.** The word *thanks* means "Eucharist" in the Greek language.

Jesus expanded on the meaning of the cup by saying, **This is my blood of the covenant, which is poured out for many.** On the cross, Jesus would fulfill the old covenant and establish a new covenant. The animal sacrifices of the old covenant were carried out repeatedly. The new covenant was accomplished, once and for all, by the sacrifice of Jesus Christ on the cross (Heb. 9–10). The new covenant would take away sin and cleanse the heart and conscience of the believer. Salvation no longer would come by Old Testament avenues but by faith in Jesus Christ as our Savior. The prophet Jeremiah prophesied of such a day (Jer. 31:31–34). This day was about to happen.

14:25–26. From this verse we get the phrase "Last Supper" or "Lord's Supper." This was Jesus' last supper or feast of celebration until **that day**

when I drink it [the wine] anew in the kingdom of God. Jesus pointed out to his disciples that there was a future and a hope. He was facing incredible suffering, persecution, and rejection, but he would be victorious when he rose from the grave. This victory would be complete when he celebrated with a new redeemed community in the kingdom of God (Rev. 3:20–21; 19:6–9). They ended the meal, as was customary, by singing Psalms 115–118, the traditional Passover hymn.

Ⓒ Running Scared (14:27–31)

SUPPORTING IDEA: *Jesus predicts that his disciples will abandon him in the midst of his suffering.*

14:27. After the "Last Supper," Jesus and his disciples headed toward the Mount of Olives. Their hearts were heavy. Not only were the disciples about to lose their Lord, but one of them would betray him into the hands of his enemies. Jesus predicted that all of the disciples would forsake him when it came to crunch time. The phrase **fall away** does not mean that the disciples would lose their faith in Jesus but that their courage in following him during the upcoming intense events would fail them. They would forsake him.

The phrase, **I will strike the shepherd, and the sheep will be scattered,** is a quote from Zechariah 13:7. When the Shepherd—Jesus—was struck down by God on the cross, the sheep—the disciples—would forsake him physically and emotionally. They would refuse to identify with him because of their fear of reprisal by the Jewish religious leaders. This prediction by Jesus came true. The disciples did forsake Jesus during his trials and crucifixion.

14:28. Paul Harvey, a famous radio personality, often gives one part of a story before he goes to commercial. When he comes back, he says, "And now . . . the rest of the story." Jesus wanted to make sure the disciples heard the rest of the story. **But after I have risen, I will go ahead of you into Galilee.** Jesus was saying that death might be real but it was not final. Notice these two keys. He will be "raised." There is hope. The resurrection is a certainty. Also, they would still be his disciples, even though they would forsake him. He would meet them in Galilee. The work would go on . . . with them.

14:29–31. Peter could not take it any longer. Everyone else might lose their courage—but not him. Imagine telling God that he was wrong. Essentially, that is what foot-in-the-mouth Peter did. Even our best intentions do not always prove to be enough. Jesus was even more emphatic concerning Peter's personal denial of him. The phrase, **I tell you the truth,** meant, "Not only will you deny me, but it will happen this very night." Jesus further declared that in spite of hearing a rooster crow twice as a warning, there would be no stopping Peter's denying Jesus as his Lord.

Peter was in denial. No way was this going to happen. Peter was just as emphatic in his belief that he would not deny Christ: **Even if I have to die with you, I will never disown you.** Peter had no idea how weak he was spiritually and physically. His enthusiastic attitude must have been infectious; the other disciples were equally adamant that they would not deny Jesus.

D Father . . . Please (14:32–42)

SUPPORTING IDEA: *Jesus faces his fear of his upcoming suffering by praying for strength to do his father's will.*

14:32. Jesus was one hundred percent God and one hundred percent man. Mark reveals for us the complete humanity of Christ as he faced the most severe testing of his faith. The Garden of Gethsemane (Heb. "oil press") was one of Jesus' favorite spots (Luke 22:39; John 18:12). He often went there with his disciples to be alone. Gethsemane was part of an olive orchard at the foot of the Mount of Olives. This garden was possibly the plot of land where an olive press extracted oil from the olives. Symbolically, Jesus would now be pressed hard concerning the fulfillment of his mission as the "sacrifice" for our sins.

14:33. When facing a crisis, most of us want moral support from others. Jesus was no different. Leaving the rest of the disciples behind, Jesus took with him the three disciples closest to him—**Peter, James and John.** They had been with Jesus on the Mount of Transfiguration (9:2), and they had accompanied him to the home of Jairus (5:37). They had been with Jesus during the best of times and now during the worst of times. True friendship operates in this fashion.

The words **distressed** and **troubled** describe the intense emotional, psychological, and spiritual suffering that Jesus was experiencing. Jesus knew what was about to happen to him on the cross. Not only would he suffer great physical agony but he would bear all of the sins of the world—past, present, and future. He would become the sin bearer; he would be forsaken by his own Father.

14:34. Jesus' command to **keep watch** could have two meanings. Perhaps he was telling his disciples to "be on the lookout for those who are coming to arrest me" or "pray for me while I am praying."

14:35. How would you feel if you knew you had to jump the Grand Canyon in your own strength with two people on your shoulders and your success determined the survival of all mankind. Overwhelmed, impossible, too much. This is how Jesus felt. He was about to bear the penalty for the sins of all mankind. God would pour all of his judgment against humanity on Christ. Jesus **fell to the ground** because of this overwhelming task. He lay prone on the ground praying to his Father because of this heavy responsibility.

14:36. Here the Son wanted the comfort of his Father. The word **Abba** is the Aramaic word that means "Papa" or "Daddy." The Jews did not use this word in addressing God because they felt it was disrespectful. But Jesus as the unique Son of God was on the most intimate terms with his Father. Jesus knew that his Father could do anything, and he asked that he **take this cup from me.**

In the Old Testament, the cup is referred to symbolically as punishment and judgment (Isa. 51:17; Jer. 25:15–29; Rev. 14:10). In this case, it refers to Jesus' death on the cross. Jesus showed us the clear purpose of prayer in the phrase, **yet not what I will, but what you will.** Prayer is not to get God to change his mind. Prayer is to align our desires and will to God's desires and will. Jesus willingly placed his desires in submission to his Father's will.

14:37–38. This seems to be a simple request—"keep watch." But the disciples could not do it. Jesus, upon returning from the garden, found his disciples sleeping. They were tired. The time would have been around midnight or later, and it had been a long, emotion-filled day. Jesus singled out Peter, who claimed he would be there for Jesus. Yet, Jesus pointed out that Peter could not even watch **for one hour.** Jesus once again exhorted the disciples to **watch and pray.** Then Jesus added, **that you will not fall into temptation.** The formula for conquering temptation is to stay alert and to pray. Jesus shows that no matter how willing we are to do the right thing in our spirit, our human body is **weak** (in this case the disciples inability to stay awake).

14:39–40. Jesus once again cried out to his Father. Upon returning he found the disciples **sleeping, because their eyes were heavy.** Jesus confronted them, but they had no excuses. They were probably embarrassed and ashamed. For once, Peter could not think of anything to say. They must have been tired!

14:41. After Jesus went to pray for the third time, he returned to find the disciples asleep again. The phrase, **are you still sleeping and resting?** shows the hurt Jesus must have felt. His word **enough** could be interpreted as "time for sleeping is over" or "the account is closed." In other words, "It is time to go to the cross and finish my mission." Both could fit because Jesus said, **The hour has come. Look, the Son of Man is betrayed into the hands of sinners.** The **sinners** were the people who would bring about his death.

14:42. The word **rise** indicates the disciples were still asleep on the ground. Jesus told them to get on their feet. Then Jesus faced his fear head on by greeting the person who was about to betray him—Judas. Mark knew that his Roman readers would themselves face persecution for their faith. Jesus' formula to "watch and pray" would help these Roman Christians face their own fears when confronted with the possibility of their own deaths through persecution.

E The Kiss of Death (14:43–52)

SUPPORTING IDEA: *Jesus responds to the betrayal of his friend to his foes.*

14:43. The phrase, **Judas, one of the Twelve,** emphasizes the closeness of the one who betrayed Jesus. The **crowd** that had come to arrest Jesus was not just a mob of common people. It consisted of the religious leaders (**the chief priests, the teachers of the law, and the elders**) as well as a detachment of soldiers and some official attendants of the Sanhedrin (John 18:3). They came armed with swords and clubs, obviously ready for a fight.

14:44–46. Judas had arranged with the group a signal by which he would identify Jesus—a **kiss.** Rabbis were customarily greeted by their disciples with a kiss. Since it was very late at night and rather dark, the arresting group would need this sign from Judas to arrest the right person. They planned to lead him away under guard so there would be no chance of escape. Judas had designed the plan so there would be no foul-ups.

14:47. The Gospel of John tells us that the person who wielded this sword was Peter. The servant, whose ear Peter cut off, was named Malchus (John 18:10). Peter was probably trying to imitate a Roman soldier in striking his foe. The Roman soldier would raise his sword and then aim for the middle of the head. Peter, not being a professional, missed and hit the servant's ear. Jesus' rebuke to Peter (Matt. 26:52) and the restoration of the ear (Luke 22:51) are not recorded by Mark.

14:48–50. Jesus, through the use of his questions, showed the evil intent of his enemies in their arrest. Jesus pointed out that **every day** they had opportunities to **capture** him while he was **teaching in the temple courts.** He also had not committed any crime like robbery. Yet, they arrested him outside of the city and at night. Why? Because they feared the people's reaction to Jesus' arrest, and they knew they had no legitimate grounds against him. The arrest was officially sanctioned by the Sanhedrin. Jesus also pointed out that their actions were part of a plan to fulfill a higher purpose. What they were doing fulfilled Scripture (Isa. 53:12; Zech. 13:7). At this point all the disciples fled.

14:51–52. This event is recorded only in Mark's Gospel. The **young man** is not identified. Possibly it was Mark himself. Maybe Mark wanted to assure his Roman readers that he also witnessed some of these events as well. Usually men wore an undergarment, like a woman's slip, but this man only wore the outer garment. The word **linen** indicates it was an expensive material, probably the type worn by the rich. The young man **fled naked.** Jesus was now totally forsaken by his closest followers and friends.

F The Beginning of the End (14:53–65)

SUPPORTING IDEA: *Jesus suffers injustice and mockery from his foes. Jesus went through a series of six trials. Three religious trials took place before the Jewish religious leaders, and three civil trials were conducted before civil authorities.*

14:53. According to the Gospel of John, Jesus was first led away to the former high priest Annas for a preliminary hearing (John 18:12–14,19–23). Then Jesus was taken for a second trial before Caiaphas, the current high priest with the Sanhedrin (the chief priests and the elders). The Sanhedrin was made up of seventy members. All may not have been at this trial, but there certainly was enough for a quorum. This must have been a large room to accommodate so many people. To ensure secrecy, it was held at the high priest's house rather than in a public hall where the Sanhedrin usually met.

14:54. Mark shows the good intentions of Peter. In Peter's feeble way, he was trying to stay close to Jesus. Peter may have followed **at a distance**, but he did follow. Peter went into **the courtyard of the high priest**. According to the Gospel of John, Peter was not alone in his following of Jesus. Another disciple, possibly John himself, was also there (John 18:15–16). The reason why Peter **warmed himself at the fire** was because this was springtime and the nights get rather cool at this time in Jerusalem. These two disciples could not actually witness Jesus' trial, but they were close enough to hear about the proceedings.

14:55–56. The unfairness of the trial is underlined in these two verses. If ever a trial was rigged—this was it. The religious leaders did not seem to have any problems finding false witnesses, even though it was early in the morning. These witnesses were the best money could buy. But according to Old Testament law (Num. 35:30; Deut. 17:6; 19:15), two witnesses had to agree in their testimony before a criminal could be condemned to death. The testimony of these false witnesses was inconsistent, so it was disqualified.

14:57–59. Finally, the religious leaders thought they had a charge that would stick. Two people had heard Jesus say, **I will destroy this man-made temple and in three days will build another, not made by man.** Yet, even here the witnesses could not agree on what Jesus had actually said.

14:60–61. Finally, having failed to get consistent witnesses, the high priest himself chose to interrogate Jesus. The high priest was hoping to bait Jesus into giving an answer to the accusations made against him and thereby to trap him. Jesus had kept silent up to this point. Probably in an act of desperation, the high priest went for the jugular. He needed a charge of blasphemy, which was a capital crime. So he asked Jesus, **Are you the Christ, the Son of the Blessed One?** Literally, "Are you the Messiah, the Son of God?"

14:62. Jesus replied without hesitation, **I am.** Jesus up to this point had not claimed publicly to be the Messiah. He did not want to be identified with the false perceptions of the Messiah that existed among the Jews. But this was the right time to make public such a claim.

Jesus then elaborated by combining two key verses from the Old Testament about the Son of Man (Ps. 110:1; Dan. 7:13). Jesus was saying that he was in ultimate control (**sitting at the right hand of the Mighty One**) and he would return to earth to set up his kingdom (**coming on the clouds of heaven**). He declared that he would rise again after his crucifixion and that he would have full authority as well as the power to bring ultimate judgment (Rev. 1:7).

14:63–64. This was what the religious leaders had been waiting for. The high priest **tore his clothes** at this statement, which was considered blasphemous. **Blasphemy** was any statement or act that reviled the name of God or affronted his majesty (Lev. 24:10–23; Mark 2:7, John 5:18). All of the members of the Sanhedrin concurred with Caiaphas's judgment of blasphemy against Jesus and **condemned him as worthy of death.**

14:65. The incredible hatred and anger against Jesus is seen in this verse. Spitting and hitting was the traditional Jewish way of showing rejection and anger (Num. 12:14; Deut. 25:9; Job 30:10). They mocked Jesus by asking him to **prophesy**—to say who was hitting him while he was blindfolded. He was then turned over to the guards.

I've Never Met the Man (14:66–72)

> **SUPPORTING IDEA:** *Jesus suffers the ultimate rejection from one of his closest friends.*

14:66–68. While Jesus was being railroaded by the Sanhedrin, Peter was outside in the courtyard waiting to see what would happen to Jesus. Peter loved Jesus—or he would not have been there. Yet, even his love for Jesus could not overcome his fear of being identified with him. While Peter was warming himself at the fire, one of the high priest's servant girls identified Peter with Jesus. She said rather sarcastically, **You also were with that Nazarene, Jesus.** Peter feigned ignorance by declaring, **I don't know or understand what you're talking about.** He then retreated to the porch for fear of being arrested himself. Yet, he still stayed close by.

14:69–70. Apparently this servant girl was not convinced that Peter did not know Jesus. She followed him out to the porch and publicly stated to those standing around, **This fellow is one of them.** The second time Peter denied any association with Jesus. Now the heat was really on because those standing around got suspicious and said, **Surely you are one of them, for you**

are a Galilean. This was like saying, "Jesus is from the South and you have a southern accent too, so you must be one of his followers."

14:71–72. Now Peter was in a dilemma. Would he say he knew Jesus and risk possible persecution himself or would he deny Jesus? The pressure was too great, and Peter **began to call down curses on himself**. In essence, Peter was saying, "May God curse me if I know Jesus. I do not know him."

After Peter's third denial, **the rooster crowed**. Luke 22:61 says Jesus looked at Peter when this occurred. The words of Jesus, **Before the rooster crows twice you will disown me three times**, along with the look from Jesus must have awakened Peter to what he had just done. The grief and shame of denying his Lord caused him to burst into tears, literally sobbing in deep regret for what he had done.

We must not be too hard on Peter. If an apostle could deny Christ, so can we. Mark wanted the church to take heed, pray, and be on guard because their faith would also be tested. The good news is that God always opens a way for repentance, forgiveness, and restoration to God's service. Just ask Peter.

> **MAIN IDEA REVIEW:** *Jesus, the sacrificial servant, is betrayed by Judas and begins a series of trials at the hands of his enemies.*

III. CONCLUSION

The Rejected Cornerstone

The Jews had a legend based on a statement of the psalmist. According to the legend, when the Temple of Solomon was being built, the masons sent from the quarry a stone different in size and shape from all the other stones. Looking at it, the builders said, "There is no place for this stone. There must be some mistake." So they rolled it over the cliff into the Valley of Kidron below the temple area. As time went on (the temple was seven years in building), they were ready for the chief cornerstone. When they asked for it, the workers at the quarry replied, "We sent it to you long ago."

One of the workmen said, "I remember it now. There was a stone altogether different from the rest, and we thought there was no place for it and rolled it down to the valley below." Men were sent down into the valley to find the stone. When they brought it up, it fitted perfectly into its place—the headstone of the corner.

Jesus said in Matthew 21:42 to the religious leaders of the day, "Have you never read in the Scriptures: 'The stone the builders rejected has become the capstone; the Lord has done this, and it is marvelous in our eyes'?"

Jesus is the chief cornerstone who was rejected. Mark 14 shows the pain and rejection Jesus faced not only from the religious leaders but from his own disciples as well. Yet, in spite of this rejection, he will become the foundation and chief cornerstone of the church. He is rejected now but will eventually rule and reign over those who rejected him.

PRINCIPLES

- What believers experience is not the result of circumstance but a wise and good distribution from our loving Father's hand.
- Every believer can "do something" to bring glory and honor to Jesus.
- Believers can be sustained through the "Gethsemanes" of life by prayer.
- Believers will face mistreatment, misunderstanding, and betrayal, even when there is no basis for such treatment.
- Every follower of Jesus has a future and a hope because of the new covenant based on Jesus' shed blood and the promise of his return.

APPLICATIONS

- Pray for protection when feeling exhausted or weak.
- Recognize your weakness, and avoid situations where you are likely to fall.
- Do something "special" for someone you love.
- Set apart a special place to pray.
- Do not be afraid to tell the Lord your deepest fears and frustrations.

IV. LIFE APPLICATION

Life Is Not Fair

Ten maxims or observations about how to live life are called "The World's Rules." For instance, one of the rules states, "Unconditional love is for babies . . . after that you are on your own." Or how about "P.O.B.Q. Actually, P.O.B.M.Q." Translation: "Plan on Being Quoted. Actually, Plan on Being Misquoted." These are just some of the rules. Rule number one is: "Life is not fair." This is a phrase we hear quite often, but fairness has a lot to do with perspective. Usually when people say, "Life is not fair," they mean they are not getting what they want or they are being forced to do something they do not want to do.

Actually, life is not fair. If anyone would say "Amen" to this, it would be a Christian. Life certainly was not fair in Jesus' case. One of his closest friends betrayed him. The "chief priests, the teachers of the law, and the elders" made up the Sanhedrin, the supreme religious and legal court in Judea. Yet, instead of giving Jesus a fair hearing, they plotted to seize Jesus secretly and to drag him off to an illegal trial (vv. 43,53). The same court tried to manufacture evidence against Jesus (v. 55). When Jesus affirmed his deity, he was condemned, even though the law called for a full day between conviction and sentencing in capital cases. There was nothing fair about the trial and conviction of Jesus.

Jesus came to earth and did only good. He taught of God's love for us. But he was beaten and mocked by his enemies. When we feel that life is unfair, let us remember our Lord and what he endured. Yet, there is good news. The apostle Peter, who saw all of this happen to our Lord, said later, "If you suffer for doing good and you endure it, this is commendable before God. To this you were called, because Christ suffered for you, leaving you an example, that you should follow in his steps" (1 Pet. 2:20–21). Suffering for doing the right thing may not be fair . . . but it will be a blessing. There is an audience of One who sees and knows it all. He keeps good records and rewards accordingly.

V. PRAYER

Dear Lord, help me not to be a whiner. Help me, when I am tempted to complain and grumble about how life is not fair, to remember that to "follow you" means life will not be fair. It was not with you. May I respond to my difficulties and trials in life with your grace, knowing that you will sustain me just like you did your Son. I thank you that when all I have left is you, you are enough. Amen.

VI. DEEPER DISCOVERIES

A. Passover (14:12,16)

The Passover feast was instituted when the Jews were slaves in Egypt. The last plague upon Egypt was the most devastating. The death angel was to kill the firstborn sons of all of the Egyptians. The Jews, in order to avoid the fate of the Egyptians, were directed to sprinkle the blood of an unblemished lamb on the archway as well as the two sides of the doors into their homes. God promised that the angel of death would "pass over" the door and not kill their firstborn sons.

The Jewish people obeyed and ate their meal of the slain lamb under the shelter of the blood. They were commanded to keep the Passover feast as a yearly memorial of what God had done to release them from their slavery in Egypt (Exod. 12:3–28; Lev. 23:4–8).

The Passover meal may have followed an order something like this:

1. When all the participants were reclining on their cushions, the head of the feast gave thanks, and they drank the first cup of the wine diluted with water.
2. All washed their hands.
3. The participants were served the roasted Passover lamb as well as unleavened bread (no yeast, which meant it would be flat in appearance), bitter herbs, and a dish of thick sauce into which the lamb and bread would be dipped.
4. They all dipped a portion of the bitter herbs into the sauce and ate it.
5. The children were taught the meaning of the Passover.
6. The head of the feast might then say, "This is the Passover which we eat, because the Lord passed over the houses of our Fathers in Egypt." Then holding up the bitter herbs, he might say, "These are the bitter herbs that we eat in remembrance that the Egyptians made the lives of our Fathers bitter when in Egypt." He might then speak of the unleavened bread and repeat Psalms 113–114, concluding with a prayer. Everyone would then drink the second cup of wine.
7. The person presiding over the feast would then break a loaf of unleavened bread and give thanks.
8. The participants would then eat some of the lamb.
9. They would take a piece of bread and some of the bitter herbs, dip them in the sauce, and eat them.
10. They would then drink the third cup of wine called "the cup of blessing."
11. Finally, the participants would sing Psalms 115–118. A fourth cup of wine would conclude the feast.

Connected with the Passover Feast was the Feast of Unleavened Bread. This feast was celebrated for seven days. On the first day and the seventh day, no work was to be performed. The Passover is symbolic of Christ's death on the cross as our Passover lamb to deliver us from slavery to sin.

B. Last Supper (14:22–25)

There are four accounts of the Last Supper or Lord's Supper in the New Testament (Matt. 26:26–29; Mark 14:22–25; Luke 22:14–20; 1 Cor. 11:23–26). There are slight differences in each of these accounts. Luke and Paul introduce the words "in remembrance of me." Matthew and Mark have "this is my blood of the covenant" instead of "this cup is the new covenant in my blood." The Gospel accounts highlight the pledge by Jesus to abstain from drinking of the wine until the kingdom has come. Paul says, "Whenever you eat . . . and drink . . . you proclaim the Lord's death until he comes."

The Gospel accounts indicate that the supper was a Passover meal eaten on the Passover night. But according to John, Jesus was slain on the cross when the Passover lambs were slain in the temple. There may have been two different calendars for calculating the feast date, each followed by a rival group. Some interpreters suggest that Jesus deliberately ate the Passover meal earlier than the official date. Others suggest that the meal was a farewell festive meal of a type common among friends, or a Jewish Kiddush—a simple meal of preparation either for a Sabbath or a festival.

C. Sanhedrin (14:55)

The word *Sanhedrin* is a Greek word meaning "a council." The term was used by the rabbis for the supreme council and court of the Jews in Jerusalem, consisting of seventy-one members, and for the lesser tribunals of twenty-three members. In the New Testament, the Sanhedrin was a body dominated by the high priest and aristocratic Sadducees.

D. Blasphemy (14:64)

In Greek society, to blaspheme was to use abusive words to destroy another person's reputation. In Judaism the object of such blasphemy was always God. The penalty of such a sin was death (Lev. 24:11–23). To commit blasphemy is to speak abusively of God, to discredit his word, or to diminish his majesty (e.g., 1 Tim. 6:1; Titus 2:5; Rev. 16:11,21). Jesus was accused of blasphemy, and this charge called for his death. Stephen, the first martyr of the church, and the apostle Paul also were so accused. The most heinous sin of all, according to Mark 3:29, is blasphemy against the Holy Spirit.

VII. TEACHING OUTLINE

A. INTRODUCTION

1. Lead Story: The Principle of Love
2. Context: Our Lord in Mark 14 embarks on the most intense time of suffering he will ever face. Not only will he be at the merciless torture of the religious leaders who hate him; he will also suffer betrayal, denial, and rejection from his closest friends.
3. Transition: As we look at chapter 14, let us embrace his suffering as our own. Let us observe with awe and reverence what Jesus willingly embraced on our behalf.

B. COMMENTARY

1. Betrayal and Blessing (14:1–11)
2. Betrayal and the Lord's Supper (14:12–26)

3. Running Scared (14:27–31)
4. Father . . . Please (14:32–42)
5. The Kiss of Death (14:43–52)
6. The Beginning of the End (14:53–65)
7. I've Never Met the Man (14:66–72)

C. CONCLUSION: THE REJECTED CORNERSTONE

VIII. ISSUES FOR DISCUSSION

1. Have you ever been betrayed by someone whom you trusted? How did you respond? How did you feel? Did you have anyone to give you support or affirmation like Jesus received from the woman in Mark 14:3–9?
2. Jesus talks about being abandoned by his disciples during desperate time. Describe what it would be like to be abandoned by your friends.
3. Have you ever been falsely accused of something? If so, how did you respond? How should a person respond to such accusations?
4. What did Jesus do when faced with the most stressful time of his life? What do you do? What does Jesus teach about the purpose of prayer?

Mark 15

His Pain—Our Gain

Quote

"*W*hen I consider my crosses, tribulations and temptations, I shame myself almost to death, thinking what are they in comparison to the suffering of my blessed Savior Jesus Christ."

Martin Luther

Mark 15

 IN A NUTSHELL

*C*hapter 15 of Mark is a continuation of the mock trials begun in chapter 14. It ends with the beatings and crucifixion of Jesus Christ. We will see in the midst of false accusations, severe beatings, and the cruelest form of punishment that Jesus, our Lord, shows compassion and calmness toward those who mistreat him. In this chapter we will see no words of revenge. Rather, we will see the act that brings reconciliation between God and man—the death of our Lord Jesus Christ.

His Pain—Our Gain

I. INTRODUCTION

USS Pueblo

*O*n January 23, 1968, the USS Pueblo, a U.S. Navy intelligence ship, was hijacked by North Korean patrol boats in international waters off the coast of North Korea. The incident provoked a tense diplomatic and military standoff for eleven months. The eighty-two surviving crew members were taken into captivity. In one particular instance, thirteen of the men were required to sit in a rigid manner around a table for hours. After several hours, the door was flung open, and a North Korean guard brutally beat the man in the first chair with the butt of his rifle. The next day, as each man sat at his assigned place, again the door was thrown open, and the man in the first chair was brutally beaten. On the third day, it happened again to the same man.

Knowing the man could not survive, the next day, another young sailor took his place. When the door was flung open, the guard automatically beat the new victim senseless. For weeks, a new man stepped forward each day to sit in that horrible chair, knowing full well what would happen. At last the guards gave up in exasperation. They were unable to overcome that kind of sacrificial love.

Each of us is the person sitting in the first chair, but instead of getting beaten, we are to die. Knowing this, Jesus traded places with us and took the death blows that were intended for us. No one suffered more than Jesus. Why? Because he loved us. Mark 15 shows us just how much he loved.

II. COMMENTARY

His Pain—Our Gain

MAIN IDEA: *Jesus, the sacrificial servant, completes his mission of salvation for the world by enduring injustice, abuse, crucifixion, and death.*

A Pilate's Dilemma (15:1–15)

SUPPORTING IDEA: *Jesus is falsely accused and condemned to death for high treason against Rome.*

15:1. Power corrupts. Absolute power corrupts absolutely. Instead of the Sanhedrin using its position and power to give Jesus a fair trial, they used corruption and abuse of their power to condemn him. This was not another meeting of the religious leaders but an extension of the meeting they had been having in chapter 14. Their late night meeting was illegal. In order to justify their actions, they needed to hold the meeting in the day time. Also, these leaders were now ready to discuss their strategy on how to approach Pilate, the Roman governor in their area, concerning their charges against Jesus. The Jewish council could not carry out death sentences. Only the Roman government had the authority to execute a person for a crime.

The Jewish council had to convince Pilate that Jesus was guilty of a capital crime against Rome and therefore worthy of death. Also, the Roman government did not consider blasphemy, a religious offense, to be a punishable crime, let alone a capital offense. As a result, the Jewish council accused Jesus of high treason against Rome. This was considered a capital crime. Jesus would not lead a political revolution to overthrow Rome at the urging of the people, but he now faced charges for that very thing.

The Sanhedrin (Jewish council) led Jesus away and **handed him over to Pilate**. Pilate was the Roman governor of Judea. He was appointed by Tiberius Caesar in A.D. 26. Pilate was in charge of the army, collecting the taxes for Rome and keeping the peace. In addition to holding the power of life and death over his subjects, he also appointed the high priests and decided cases of capital punishment.

Pilate was a true politician. He usually made decisions that would increase his stature and favor with Rome. The people's desires and well-being were secondary to him. He was fickle and weak in character. This was evident in Jesus' case. Pilate was especially careful when it came to working with the Jewish people. Charges had been made against him in earlier reports to Rome—that he had offended Jewish customs and could not control difficult situations. Pilate knew that he must deal carefully with Jesus' case.

The official residence of the Roman governor of Judea was at Caesarea on the Mediterranean coast. When the Roman governors came to Jerusalem, they occupied the palace of Herod. This is where Jesus appeared before Pilate. Jesus was led to Herod's palace early in the morning. This marked the beginning of three civil trials that Jesus faced. The Sanhedrin had to convince Pilate that Jesus had committed high treason against Rome and deserved the death penalty. Pilate had the power to condemn Jesus or to reverse the religious council's decision and let him go.

15:2. Mark's account of the trial is the briefest of all the Gospel accounts. Apparently Pilate had already heard the charge against Jesus. This is seen in the first question he asked Jesus: **Are you the king of the Jews?** According to Luke 23:2, the Sanhedrin brought three charges against Jesus. They were: (1) he is "subverting our nation"; (2) he "opposes payment of taxes to Caesar"; and (3) he "claims to be Christ, a king." The third accusation got Pilate's attention.

Jesus' answer to Pilate's question was **it is as you say.** Jesus in effect was saying, "Yes, I am." But the indirectness of Jesus' answer left open the question of "What does that really mean to be the king of the Jews?" John's Gospel gives us some insight. In John 18:36 Jesus said, "My kingship is not of this world; if my kingship were of this world then my servants would fight." Jesus made it clear that he was not a threat to Rome.

15:3–5. The chief priests also seemed to understand that their charge might not stick since Jesus made it clear he was no threat to Rome. So the chief priests hurled all sorts of accusations against Christ. Pilate said, **See how many things they are accusing you of.** Yet, Jesus did not answer. Jesus refused to defend himself. He stood in front of the man who could condemn him and a mob who wanted to kill him. Yet, Jesus was composed and completely at peace. This **amazed** Pilate. Our composure and calmness in the midst of the trials of life give great witness to the keeping power of Christ to those around us. This is one of the marks of a disciple of Jesus.

15:6. According to the Gospel of Luke, Pilate deferred in making a decision and sent Jesus to Herod, the ruler of Galilee (Luke 23:6–12). This was the second civil trial. Herod only mocked Jesus by asking Jesus to entertain him by performing a miracle. Jesus was then sent back to Pilate for the third and final part of the civil trials. Pilate did not believe Jesus was guilty, but he knew he had to deal with a hostile Jewish leadership and their people. He decided that rather than announcing an acquittal he would give the people a choice. It was a Roman custom during the Passover feast to **release a prisoner whom the people requested.**

15:7–8. According to Luke 23:19, there had been an uprising in the city led by an insurrectionist named Barabbas (his first name may have been Jesus). He and his followers had been thrown in prison for insurrection and murder. **Barabbas** may have been a member of the revolutionary group called the "Zealots." These people resented the Romans and their occupation of Palestine. The surname Barabbas literally translated means "son of Abba" or "son of the Father." Barabbas's full name could possibly have been "Jesus, son of the Father." The crowd was to make a choice between two men: the one who sought solutions by force or the one who ruled by love and was ready to sacrifice himself. It seems that the crowd came to Pilate's tribunal for the primary purpose of releasing Barabbas, even though Pilate gave them a choice.

15:9–10. Pilate's question, **Do you want me to release to you the king of the Jews?** implies that the crowd had asked for the release of Jesus. But which one? It is possible that Pilate mistook the crowd's desire to release Jesus Barabbas as a request for releasing Jesus of Nazareth. Pilate was using the phrase **king of the Jews** sarcastically. Pilate knew that the chief priests had not handed Jesus over to him to do him any favors or out of loyalty to Caesar.

He knew they envied Jesus. Jesus was too popular and had too much influence over the people. The chief priests wanted Jesus out of the way.

15:11. Pilate worked hard to undermine the chief priests' desires to put Jesus to death by offering to release Jesus to them instead of Barabbas. But the chief priests would have nothing of this. They were not about to let Jesus slip through their fingers so easily. Also, it was a battle of the wills. Pilate was trying to get his way and the chief priests were trying to get theirs. The chief priests stirred up the crowd to force Pilate to release Barabbas so Jesus would be put to death. They meant to win.

15:12–14. Pilate, realizing he was about to have a mob scene on his hands, but not wanting to condemn Jesus, seemed to be asking for "other options" or suggestions when he said, **What shall I do, then, with the one you call the king of the Jews?** Could he possibly suggest that they should let Jesus go as well as Barabbas? It is clear that Pilate was reluctant to condemn Jesus to death.

Pilate must have been shocked when the crowd gave only one option: **Crucify him!** Pilate seemed bewildered, and he even defended Jesus when he said, **Why? What crime has he committed?** Pilate seemed to be trying to save Jesus from certain death. In his questioning of the crowd, he showed that he did not believe Jesus was guilty of anything. The crowd ignored Pilate's question. Mob psychology had taken over, and they wanted nothing less than to see Jesus crucified.

15:15. Pilate the politician came out at this point. He knew he could not win, and he did not want bad reports going back to Rome about a mob scene in his jurisdiction. His previous record of handling matters related to the Jewish people was not the best. If he botched this situation up, then he might as well kiss his political career good-bye. Also, his wife's message may have made him think more deeply about Jesus than he otherwise would have done (Matt. 27:19) So he released Barabbas and ordered Jesus to be **flogged.**

Flogging, according to Roman custom, did not necessarily precede crucifixion. Perhaps Pilate hoped that if Jesus were flogged and then presented to the people, they might relent of their determination to have him crucified (John 19:1–7). This may have been one last attempt on Pilate's part to have Jesus released.

Flogging was not a light punishment. The Romans first stripped the person and tied his hands to a post above his head. The whip, sometimes called a "cat of nine tails," was made of several pieces of leather with pieces of bone and lead embedded near the ends of the leather strips. Two men, one on each side of the criminal, did the flogging. The Jews limited the number of hits (stripes) a person could receive, usually no more than thirty-nine. The Romans had no limit. Flogging ripped out chunks of flesh and often left the bones of the victim exposed. Some victims did not survive a flogging.

Once again Pilate's desires were thwarted. The crowd wanted Jesus crucified. So Jesus was delivered to the crowd to be put to death. The phrase **handed him over** may be Mark's attempt to identify Jesus with the Suffering Servant of Isaiah 53:6,12, since these words appear in this passage.

B King of the Jews—Right! (15:16–20)

SUPPORTING IDEA: *Jesus endures verbal abuse and physical trauma by the Roman soldiers.*

15:16. Since the events in the previous section were public, the soldiers now took Jesus into the palace or the **Praetorium.** The word *Praetorium* is a Latin word in Greek, designating the Roman governor's official residence in Jerusalem. Pilate had brought these troops with him to Jerusalem from Caesarea. They were not Jewish, and they came from all over the Roman Empire. Mark points out that the whole **company** took part in what happened to Christ.

15:17–18. Did you ever see a cat play with a mouse? The cat will let the mouse go and then catch it again or toss it into the air just for fun before having it for lunch. The mouse is helpless. The troops "played" with Jesus. They mocked him for claiming to be a king. They took a **purple robe,** a symbol of authority, and threw it across his bleeding back. They took **thorns** and wove them into a crown. They pressed the crown upon his scalp, puncturing his head and causing more bleeding. Then they mocked him by saying, **Hail, king of the Jews!**

15:19. The soldiers then beat Jesus by using a **staff,** an object like a broom handle. They **struck** Jesus on the head, driving the crown of thorns even further into his scalp. The soldiers **spit on him** and then fell on their knees in mocking fashion and **paid homage** to Jesus by saying, **Hail, king of the Jews!** Although this is merely speculation, is it possible that the soldiers showed such incredible cruelty to Jesus because he was a Jew? These men had nothing to gain by treating Jesus like this. Racism causes people to do some terrible things to other people. The Jews were certainly despised and hated by the Romans. This outpouring of anger and ridicule could possibly be because they were venting their bigotry and hatred of all Jewish people upon Jesus.

15:20. Finally, finishing their sadistic acts on Jesus, **they took off the purple robe.** Imagine how this would have felt to Jesus. Like removing a bandage by ripping it off tender skin, so removing the robe from the blood-clotted back of Jesus must have caused excruciating pain when they ripped it off of Jesus' back. Then they **put his own clothes on him.** In John's Gospel account, Pilate made one last appeal to the crowd by bringing Jesus before them one more time (John 19:4–5,12–16). Once again, this mob showed no compassion. Then they **led him out to crucify him.**

C Crucify Him (15:21–32)

SUPPORTING IDEA: *Jesus endures crucifixion, so we would not have to face God's punishment for our sin.*

15:21. According to the law, the guilty victim had to carry his cross, or at least the crossbeam, to the place of execution. Jesus was no exception. Jesus started out carrying the cross from Pilate's hall (John 19:16–17), but in his weakened state he was unable to carry it all the way to the execution site. The physical pain and psychological and emotional stress he felt is beyond description.

Since Jesus could no longer carry the crossbeam, **a certain man from Cyrene, Simon, the father of Alexander and Rufus, was passing by on his way in from the country, and they forced him to carry the cross.** Simon may have become a Christian through this experience. In Romans 16:31 greetings are sent to a certain Rufus. It is possible this could be the same man mentioned by Mark. Mark probably mentioned these men because they were well known to the Roman church. Perhaps these "sons" became believers because of what happened to their "father" on the way to the place of crucifixion.

15:22. Executions for the Romans and the Jews were held outside the city of Jerusalem (John 19:20). **Golgotha** is an Aramaic word that means **The Place of the Skull.** The place where Jesus was crucified could have gotten this name because it looked like a skull or there were many skulls there from the previous crucifixions. The location of "The Place of the Skull" is not known with certainty.

15:23. The victims of crucifixion were customarily given a narcotic drink that would help deaden the pain (Prov. 31:6; Matt. 27:33–34). Jesus refused to drink this potion, choosing instead to stay fully conscious and experience the terrible sufferings of the crucifixion.

15:24. Notice Mark's phrase, **And they crucified him.** Mark gives us just the facts. None of the Gospel writers go into great description about the crucifixion. Mark probably felt he did not need to because his Roman readers would understand the gruesome details of this method of execution.

Sometimes the victim of crucifixion would not die for several days. Death was caused by exhaustion and suffocation. If the victim took too long to die, the Romans would break the victim's legs to hasten the suffocation. In John's Gospel the soldiers came to see if they needed to break Jesus' legs to hasten his death, but they found he had already died (John 19:31–33). All of Jesus' clothes, with the possible exception of a loincloth, were removed before he was nailed to the cross. The soldiers **cast lots,** the equivalent of throwing dice, to see who would get Jesus' clothes. This was the fulfillment of the prophesy in Psalm 22:18.

15:25. Mark says that Jesus was crucified the **third hour** or about 9:00 A.M. This differs from John's account (19:14), which says that Christ was crucified about the sixth hour or 12:00 noon. The difference between the two accounts can be attributed to different ways of calculating time. John was probably using the Roman time system that counted the hours from midnight to midnight. The sixth hour would then be 6:00 A.M. Mark was probably following the Jewish custom of counting hours from daybreak or 6:00 A.M. The third hour would then be 9:00 A.M., according to Mark.

Looking at the text closely, it appears that Jesus' trial concluded about 6:00 A.M. (John) and that Jesus was crucified at 9:00 A.M. (Mark). During the intervening time, Jesus was taken from the court of Pilate, mocked by the Roman soldiers, led to Golgotha, and prepared for crucifixion (Lane, *Mark*, p. 567).

15:26. It was customary for the person being executed to wear a message engraved on a board that indicated the crime he had committed. Over Jesus' head was placed this message, **The King of the Jews.** Jesus was being crucified on the charge of high treason, since he claimed to be the king of the Jews.

15:27. Jesus was placed between **two robbers** when he was crucified. These men were probably insurrectionists (15:7), and they may have been involved with Barabbas.

15:28. This verse is not included in the NIV. Other translations tell us that Jesus' hanging between two "thieves" (John 19:18) fulfilled prophecy (Isa. 53:12). Isaiah 53:12 is quoted in this verse for emphasis.

15:29–30. Like hangings in the old west, crucifixion took place in a public location. Many people, out of curiosity, came out to the crucifixion site to watch. In this case, the crucifixion site was by a major thoroughfare that led into the city, since **those who passed by hurled insults at him.** Notice the cruel mocking of the people. They threw the charges against Jesus in his face: **So! You who are going to destroy the temple and build it in three days.** . . . In essence, they were saying that if he could rebuild the temple then he ought to be able to save himself.

15:31–32. Adding insult to injury, **the chief priests and the teachers of the law** also mocked Jesus. These men were the spiritual leaders of the people. Instead of embracing Jesus as their long-awaited Messiah, they condemned him to be crucified. The phrase, **He saved others . . . but he can't save himself,** was meant to be sarcastic and cruel. Jesus did save others. He raised Lazarus from the dead. But in their mockery there was truth. Jesus could not save himself, and save us, at the same time. He chose to save us. Praise God!

The phrase, **Let this Christ, this King of Israel,** is another way of mocking Jesus for his claim to be the Messiah. The religious leaders taunted Jesus and demanded that he demonstrate his power by coming down from the cross so they might **see and believe.** The criminals on each side of Jesus decided to join in on the insults, although according to Luke, one of them changed his mind (Luke 23:39–43).

Ⓓ My God, my God! (15:33–41)

SUPPORTING IDEA: *Jesus fulfills his mission through his death on the cross and separation from his Father.*

15:33. Matthew, Mark, and Luke report this event. The **darkness** lasted for three hours—from the time Jesus was crucified until the moment of his death. It was probably a solar eclipse. This miraculous darkening of the skies expressed the agony and grief of heaven over the death of the Son of God. Also, it is significant that this is happening during the Passover festival. The ninth plague in Egypt was a three-day darkness followed by the last plague, the death of the firstborn (Exod. 10:22–11:9). The darkness at Calvary was an announcement that God's beloved Son, his firstborn, was giving his life for the sins of the world.

15:34. Jesus made seven key statements when he hung on the cross. Mark records just one, **My God, my God, why have you forsaken me?** (see Ps. 22:1). Jesus Christ was feeling the full wrath of God, his Father, against all the sins of mankind—past, present, and future. Jesus cried out in agony as he bore the sins of the world and was separated for the first time from his Father because of this sin. Jesus expressed horror at being separated from God, his Father. Jesus' death on the cross fulfills the saying, "Cursed is everyone who is hung on a tree" (Deut. 21:23; Gal. 3:13). Jesus expressed the incredible pain of abandonment by God. Paul later said, "God made him who had no sin to be sin for us" (2 Cor. 5:21). Yet, in all of this pain and agony Jesus did not renounce his Father but submitted to his will. Hallelujah, what a Savior!

15:35. Some of the bystanders thought Jesus' cry, *"Eloi Eloi,"* was a call for Elijah the prophet. Elijah was not only the forerunner of the Messiah, but he was also regarded as a deliverer of those in trouble. This shows the crowd's ignorance and heartlessness as they taunted Jesus further by saying, **Listen, he's calling Elijah.**

15:36. A person in the crowd ran to fill **a sponge with wine vinegar** and placed it on the end of a stick so Jesus could suck liquid from it.

15:37. After six excruciating hours of torture Jesus uttered **a loud cry** and died. The fact that Jesus uttered a loud cry indicates that he did not die the ordinary death of one who was crucified. The victims of crucifixion usually had no strength left and often suffered complete exhaustion before dying.

His loud cry was a shout of triumph and victory. Jesus willingly became our sacrifice for sin. Like a runner crossing the finish line to win the race, he shouted the victory.

15:38. The **curtain of the temple** separated the Holy Place from the Most Holy Place in the Jewish temple in Jerusalem. This curtain was approximately two to three inches thick, but it was torn **from top to bottom.** Mark's account of this event is significant because human hands did not tear this curtain. It was torn by the hand of God. Only the priests were allowed to go into the Most Holy Place on behalf of the people. The tearing of the curtain indicated that through Jesus' death on the cross all people now had access to God. Jesus was the once-and-for-all sacrifice for our sins (Heb. 10:12–22; John 14:6). Notice also that many priests were converted to Christianity (Acts 6:7). Possibly these were the priests who were in the temple when they saw the supernatural splitting of the curtain.

15:39. Even the way Jesus died transformed those around him. The Roman centurion in command of the detachment of soldiers at the cross witnessed everything Jesus went through. He saw Jesus scourged, mocked, beaten, spit upon, and crucified and then he watched him die. When the Roman centurion saw the way Jesus died, he proclaimed, **Surely this man was the Son of God!** He had never seen anyone die like this before, and he probably thought he had seen it all. He was deeply moved and drawn to Jesus (Luke 23:47). Mark opened his Gospel by saying that Jesus was the "Son of God" (1:1). This is a major theme in Mark's Gospel (1:1,11; 3:11;5:7; 9:7; 14:61–62), and the centurion echoed this theme at Christ's death. Jesus is Lord—even in death.

15:40–41. Women had always been a significant part of Christ's life and ministry. It is not surprising to see them as a significant part of his death. Mark says that many women watched the crucifixion **from a distance.** He identifies three of them: **Mary Magdalene,** another **Mary,** and **Salome.** Mary Magdalene had been healed of demon possession by Jesus. The second Mary is designated as the **mother of James the younger and of Joses.** Her sons were apparently well known in the early church. Finally, Mark mentions Salome and Zebedee's wife, the mother of James and John (cf. Matt. 27:56). These women had been eyewitnesses to the primary events in Jesus' life: his death (vv. 40–41), burial (vv. 47), and resurrection (16:1). These three key women, among others from Galilee, were in Jerusalem to be with him and serve him.

E Death Is Final—But It Is Not the End (15:42–47)

SUPPORTING IDEA: *Jesus receives tender care and respect from his followers at his burial.*

15:42–43. Preparation Day was the day before the beginning of the Sabbath. The Jews recognized two evenings: (1) the one from 3:00 P.M. to 6:00

P.M., known as "early evening," and (2) the time after 6:00 P.M., when the new day began. Mark and Matthew (Matt. 27:57) are talking about early evening. The approximate time would be around 4:00 P.M. Since the new day started at 6:00 P.M., there was not much time to remove Jesus' body from the cross.

This short period of time is probably what gave urgency to Joseph of Arimathea's request for Jesus' body. Usually the bodies of crucifixion victims were left on the cross for the birds or animals to eat or they were taken down and placed in a common grave. Joseph wanted to bury Jesus with dignity and honor. This was a bold move on his part. Joseph was a **prominent member of the Council,** the very same group that orchestrated Jesus' death. For Joseph to expose himself as a follower of Christ could have serious consequences. He had resisted putting Jesus to death (Luke 23:51). Now he was willing to make public his association with Christ.

The normal custom was for a relative or close friend to come and ask for the body. Jesus' mother had been placed in the care of John. She was not there to claim the body. All of the other disciples had fled. Therefore, Joseph asked for the body. We never know who God has standing in the wings to care for us in our most difficult situations. It may be someone whom we least expect.

15:44–45. Pilate was **surprised** to hear that Jesus was already dead (15:44). Once he received confirmation that Jesus was dead, he released the body to Joseph. For Pilate to release the body of a condemned criminal— especially one condemned for high treason—to a non-relative was quite unusual. This shows that Pilate probably did not take the charges against Jesus very seriously.

15:46. Joseph had help getting Jesus' body down from the cross and preparing it for burial. Another member of the Council, Nicodemus (John 19:38–42), was there to help as well. Joseph, also a prominent member of the Sanhedrin, probably had servants who may have helped as well. The body of Christ had to be ceremonially washed and then wrapped in a large quantity of spices to be prepared for burial. Then the body had to be carried to the tomb. The tomb was probably near the execution site. Jesus' body was then placed in the **tomb,** which was **cut out of rock.** A rock about three feet in diameter was rolled against the opening of the tomb. The rock would have required three or four men to roll it into place.

15:47. The two Mary's mentioned earlier (v. 40) made sure they knew where Jesus was buried. They planned to visit the gravesite later. Little did they know that they would be witnesses to the greatest event of all time—the resurrection of Jesus Christ.

MAIN IDEA REVIEW: *Jesus, the sacrificial servant, completes his mission by enduring injustice, abuse, crucifixion, and death.*

III. CONCLUSION

Our Substitute

During the war between Britain and France, men were drafted into the French army by a lottery system. When someone's name was drawn, he had to go off to battle. But there was one exception to this. A person could be exempted if another man was willing to take his place.

On one occasion, the authorities came to a certain man and told him he was among those who had been chosen to serve. He refused to go, saying, "I was shot two years ago." At first they questioned his sanity, but he insisted that was indeed the case. He claimed that the military records would show he had been killed in action. "How can that be?" they questioned. "You are alive now!"

He explained that when his name had come up before, a close friend said to him, "You have a large family, but I am not married and no one is dependent on me. I will take your name and address and go in your place." And that is just what the record showed. This unusual case was referred to Napoleon Bonaparte, who decided that the country had no legal claim on that man. He was free. He had died in the person of another. A substitute had died in his place.

We needed a substitute. We needed someone who could pay our debt—the debt of death (see Rom. 6:23)—and cleanse us so we could be found blameless regarding the Lord's perfect and holy standard.

Our substitute would have to be perfect in every way—totally sinless. He would have to measure up to God's standards in every way while remaining human so he could take our place. He would have to be divine as well as morally perfect man both by nature and by choice. He would have to be God's Son. Jesus was that One.

PRINCIPLES

- Believers can expect ridicule and disrespect from others when it comes to their faith in Jesus Christ.
- Believers can feel secure in the love of God.
- Knowing that Jesus was willing to pay such a heavy price to have a relationship with us gives us the security of knowing he wants only the best for us.
- Following Christ requires sacrifice.
- The Christian's right response to suffering causes unbelievers to take notice of our faith.

APPLICATIONS

- Sarcasm and snide remarks are never appropriate. They can hurt other people. Monitor your speech and resist sarcasm in your remarks.
- Make a list of countries where believers are persecuted. Pray regularly for God's grace to sustain them in their faith.
- Put a nail in your pocket or place it in a prominent place. Let it be a reminder of the price Jesus paid to purchase our salvation. Then thank him for his great gift.

IV. LIFE APPLICATION

A Clean Slate

For years Marjorie had been burdened by poor self-esteem. She saw herself as unlovely, ungainly, untalented, unintelligent, un-everything that makes people feel valuable and worthwhile as human beings. Over the years, her self-hatred grew to desperation. She finally turned to a Christian psychologist for help. He "walked" her back through her memories to a painful incident from her childhood.

Many years earlier, Marjorie had been caught in some minor act of misbehavior in her third-grade class. Her teacher—a harsh, vindictive disciplinarian—called Marjorie forward and stood her before the class. "Children," said the teacher, "I want each of you to come to the blackboard and write a sentence that begins with the word 'Marjorie.' Write anything you dislike about this bad girl."

The next few minutes were a nightmare for Marjorie as, one by one, each child went forward and chalked a hurtful statement about her in letters several inches tall. "Marjorie is ugly," wrote one. "Marjorie is fat," wrote another. "Marjorie is a slob." "Marjorie has no friends." "Marjorie is stupid." Standing before the class, Marjorie wished she could sink through the floor and out of sight. This went on until all twenty-five classmates had filled the blackboard with hate and ugliness.

"Marjorie," said a kind voice. Gradually, Marjorie realized she was no longer back in school. She was in the present, in the psychologist's office, and the kind voice she had heard was his. Tears flooded her face, and she was breathing deep, ragged sobs.

"Marjorie," the psychologist repeated, "I want you to picture the classroom again—but there is a difference this time. There is a twenty-sixth student in the classroom with you, and his name is Jesus. Now, imagine the scene with me: Jesus gets up from his desk and he walks past the teacher, ignoring the chalk she holds out to him. Instead of writing on the blackboard, he is erasing, erasing, erasing. Do you see it, Marjorie? The slate is clean now."

"Yes," she said. "I see it."

"Now Jesus takes up the chalk and begins to write. 'Marjorie is a beautiful child of God.' 'Marjorie is loved unconditionally.' 'Marjorie is forgiven.' 'Marjorie will live forever with me.'"

For the first time in many years, Marjorie began to feel valuable and loved. It was a giant first step along the path away from the crippling pain of mistreatment and toward wholeness (Davis, *Mistreated*, pp. 84–86).

Sometimes the pain from being mistreated in our past can haunt us and leave us feeling bitter and angry. It could be a father who neglected you, a mother who berated you, a teacher who ridiculed you, a spouse who was unfaithful, a friend who betrayed you, an employer who walked all over you. You can get free from these beasts because Jesus came to kill the beasts in your life. Fresh starts are what Jesus is all about. Just read what Jesus did again in Mark 15 to give us a clean slate. Whatever hurts you have experienced in the past, let Jesus wipe the blackboard clean and replace those images with himself. He will set you free-indeed.

V. PRAYER

Thank you, Lord. Thank you, Lord. Thank you, Lord. I just want to thank you, Lord. When I am tempted to say that life is "too hard" or "It's just not worth it," may the Holy Spirit prompt me to look to the cross and remember Jesus. The Bible says, "Greater love has no one than this, that he lay down his life for his friends. You are my friends" (John 15:13–14). Thank you, Jesus, for not only being my friend—but my Lord. Amen.

VI. DEEPER DISCOVERIES

A. Crucifixion (15:21–32)

This method of execution arose among the Medes and the Persians and was passed on to the Greeks and the Romans. The cross consisted of a perpendicular stake with a crossbeam either at the top of the stake or just below the top. The height of the stake was usually little more than the height of a man. A block or a pin was sometimes driven into the stake to serve as a seat for the condemned person, giving partial support to his body. A step for the feet was sometimes fixed to the stake.

Victims of crucifixion did not usually die for two or three days, but this was determined by the presence or absence of the seat and the footrest. A person suspended by his hands lost blood pressure quickly, and the pulse rate was increased. Usually the victim had been severely beaten or flogged before crucifixion took place. Orthostatic collapse through insufficient blood circulating to the brain and the heart would follow shortly. If the victim could ease his body by supporting himself with the seat and footrest, the blood could be returned to some degree of circulation in the upper part of his body.

To fix the hands to the crossbeam, cords or nails were used; sometimes the feet were nailed as well. The nails were about the size of railroad spikes. When it was desired to bring the torture to an end, the victim's legs were broken below the knees with a club. It was then no longer possible for him to ease his weight, and the loss of blood circulation was accentuated. Coronary failure would follow shortly. The victim's offense was usually published by a crier who preceded him to the place of execution. Sometimes his crime was written on a tablet that was carried by the condemned man himself. Or if the victim carried the crossbeam, another person carried the tablet before him. The tablet was fixed to the cross at the time of execution.

B. Centurion (15:39)

Roman centurions were non-commissioned officers who commanded battle groups called "centuries," each made up of at least one hundred men. Akin to sergeants in a modern army, centurions often led Rome's local police forces in occupied territories.

Centurions were responsible for keeping track of individuals who posed a threat to Rome's security. Because Jesus drew thousands of people to hear him, he was perhaps kept under surveillance. At the time of Jesus' earthly ministry, Rome had an estimated five hundred thousand troops in its army. Thousands of Romans soldiers were deployed in two major cities of Palestine—Sebaste in Samaria and Caesarea on the Mediterranean. A military force was also kept in Jerusalem at the Antonia fortress, guarding Herod's temple palace. During Jewish feasts, Rome moved additional troops into the city to keep order.

It was a Gentile Roman centurion and his troops that crucified Jesus and the two men with him. The officer likely had observed Jesus' trial, his final march to the execution, crucifixion, and the response to the crown who mocked Jesus. He had seen the sky turn black at midday, felt the earthquake, and heard Jesus' last words and shout of victory. Probably having little regard for the Hebrew religion, he not only saw a "righteous man" die (Luke 23:47) but in fact declared him to be the very "Son of God" (Mark 15:39; Matt. 27:54).

C. Took down the body, and wrapped it in the linen (15:46)

Often the body was washed (Acts 9:37), anointed with aromatic preparations (Mark 16:1; John 19:39), and wrapped in cloth (Acts 5:6) or bound with burial bandages (John 11:44) usually of linen (Mark 15:46; John 19:40). The face was apparently covered or bound separately with a face cloth (John 11:44).

Henry Latham says, "What is here called 'aloes' was a fragrant wood pounded or reduced to dust, while the myrrh was an aromatic gum, morsels of which were mixed with the powdered wood. It was also the practice, so we gather, to anoint the body with a semi-liquid unguent such as nard. One effect of this would be to cause the powder immediately about the body to adhere to it, but the great bulk of it would remain dry. The hair and head were also anointed with this unguent. When the Lord's body was hurriedly prepared for the tomb, there would not be time for anointing the body or for any elaborate process, because sunset was fast approaching and with it the Sabbath would come. The body would be simply embedded into the powdered spice. It may have been that the women desired to repair this omission as far as they could, and that what they brought on the Sunday morning was nard, or some costly perfume, in order to complete the anointing. John speaks only of myrrh and aloes, but Luke says the women prepared spices and ointments, and in Mark we have they "bought spices so that they might go to anoint Jesus' body" (16:1) (Latham, *Evidence that Demands a Verdict*, p. 214).

D. Then he rolled a stone against the entrance of the tomb (15:46)

In his book *The Resurrection Factor*, Josh McDowell says this about the stone placed at the entrance of the tomb of Jesus: "In the Mark 16:4 portion of the Bezae manuscripts in the Cambridge library in England, a parenthetical statement was found that adds, 'And when he was laid there, he (Joseph) put against the tomb a stone which 20 men could not roll away.' The significance of this is realized when one considers the rules for transcribing manuscripts. It was the custom that if a copier was emphasizing his own interpretation, he would write his thought in the margin and not include it within the text. One might conclude, therefore, that the insert in the text was copied from a text even closer to the time of Christ, perhaps, a first-century manuscript. The phrase, then, could have been recorded by an eyewitness who was impressed with the enormousness of the stone which was rolled against Jesus' sepulcher."

McDowell goes on to say,

> Two Georgia Tech faculty members remembered the comments I had made about the large size of the stone. So, being engineers, they took the type of stone used in the time of Christ and calculated the size needed to roll against a four to five foot doorway. Later, they

wrote me a letter containing all the technical terms, but on the back put their conclusions in simple language. They said a stone of that size would have to have had a minimum weight of 1 1/2 to 2 tons. No wonder Matthew and Mark said the stone was extremely large. One might ask, 'if the stone were that big, how did Joseph move it into position in the first place?' He simply gave it a push and let gravity do the rest. It had been held in place with a wedge as it sat in a groove or trench that sloped down to the front of the tomb. When the wedge was removed, the heavy circular rock just rolled into position" (McDowell, *The Resurrection Factor,* pp. 53–54).

VII. TEACHING OUTLINE

A. INTRODUCTION

1. Lead Story: USS Pueblo
2. Context: The next eight hours are the most horrifying and brutal times Jesus will face in his human existence. He will face ridicule and pain that is beyond comprehension. Even more amazing is that he does so willingly for us. Mark 15 continues the description of the gauntlet Jesus will go through, ultimately leading to his death so we might have life.
3. Transition: As we look at Mark 15, we see God's love in action. Truly, his pain is our gain. Jesus will show that salvation is free but it is not cheap.

B. COMMENTARY

1. Pilate's Dilemma (15:1–15)
2. King of the Jews—Right! (15:16–20)
3. Crucify Him (15:21–32)
4. My God, My God! (15:33–41)
5. Death Is Final—But It Is Not the End (15:42–47)

C. CONCLUSION: OUR SUBSTITUTE

VIII. ISSUES FOR DISCUSSION

1. Describe Pilate. From his handling of Christ's trial, what seemed most important to him and how did this influence his decision-making? What do Pilate's actions teach us about status and power?
2. Why did the soldiers treat Christ so cruelly? What was Jesus' reaction to the abuse he took? What does his response teach us? Are there

times when we should speak up about our abuse? When are those times?

3. Jesus suffered through the darkest time of his life—separation from his father. Describe one of the darkest times of your life. How did you get through it?

4. What did the "tearing of the curtain" in the temple represent? How does that impact us?

5. Even the way Jesus handled death on the cross affected those around him (the centurion's response). Give examples of people you know who have ended their lives well. What impact did this have on others?

Mark 16

❧

He Is Risen . . . He Is Risen Indeed

"All the world's joys come from the

grave of our risen Lord."

Unknown

Mark 16

IN A NUTSHELL

In chapter 16 we see Jesus landing the final victory blow on Satan in the resurrection. The resurrection of Christ is the heart of the gospel, truly, the "good news."

All four Gospels tell the story of the resurrection and, like the crucifixion, describe it as an actual historical event. Jesus was placed in the tomb on Friday but when Sunday came, the tomb was empty. An angelic ambassador proclaimed Christ's rising from the dead to be a fact. Mark 16 finishes the way his Gospel began by declaring that Jesus Christ is the Son of God.

He Is Risen . . . He Is Risen Indeed

I. INTRODUCTION

University of Colorado

*I*t was a crisp fall day and football was in the air—literally. The University of Colorado Buffaloes were playing the University of Michigan Wolverines. Both of these teams were undefeated, and both hoped to stay that way. Michigan had the advantage because the game was being played on their home field before 105,000 fans.

The game was everything diehard football fans hoped for. Every play was crucial, and every tackle was bone jarring. There were lots of big plays. The biggest one seemed to happen during the last two minutes of the game when Michigan scored a touchdown to go ahead of Colorado by four points. When Michigan kicked off and Colorado received the ball, they had only one minute to go eighty yards down the field. They could not just score a three-point field goal; they had to score a touchdown. Time to go. Over. Forget it. But wait.

As one wag said, "The opera ain't over till the fat lady sings." In other words, "It ain't over 'til it's over." Colorado had the ball. They tried two passes and failed. Now they had only six seconds left. Time for the "Hail Mary" pass. The "Hail Mary" play is when all the receivers run toward the end zone and the quarterback heaves the ball with all of his might toward the end zone, hoping one of his guys will catch the ball and score. Everybody in the stadium knew this was coming, especially Michigan's football team. They were ready.

The ball was snapped and the Colorado quarterback dropped back and threw the ball with all his might, approximately sixty yards to the end zone. The Michigan defenders were in the end zone to block the pass and the Colorado receivers were there to try to catch it. The ball came sailing into the end zone—and the unthinkable happened. The ball was tipped by a Michigan defender as a Colorado receiver was falling to the ground. Amazingly, the ball was tipped in such a way that as the Colorado receiver was falling he caught the ball on his way to the ground.

One hundred and five thousand people stared in stunned silence while the Colorado football team, first in shock and then delirium, began to jump and shout. This desperation play won the game. "It ain't over 'til it's over."

This is how we as believers are to live life. We never put a period on a sentence. We put a comma and let God finish it. Just ask a wiry teenager named David, armed with only a sling and a stone, who defeated a giant over nine feet tall by the name of Goliath. Or how about the fleeing Israelites? An Egyptian army was approaching and they had no possible way to escape except through the Red Sea. Against nature and reversing the pull of gravity, the water opened up and allowed Moses and the Hebrews to walk across. Who would have thought it?

Or, how about a place called Golgotha and a sealed tomb? It was found empty three days later. With God, anything is possible. He has a way of bypassing what seems inevitable. Do not be too quick to come to any conclusions. Be open. When the Lord is in something, anything is possible. Just ask a handful of disciples who saw their Lord crucified, only to find he had risen three days later. They ended up turning the world upside down. Who would have thought it? No one but God.

II. COMMENTARY

He Is Risen . . . He Is Risen Indeed

MAIN IDEA: *Jesus, the sacrificial servant, fulfills his gospel mission by rising from the dead, encouraging and empowering his disciples, both then and throughout all generations, to continue preaching the good news of salvation.*

A I Am the Resurrection and the Life (16:1–8)

SUPPORTING IDEA: *Jesus fulfills his gospel mission by rising from the dead.*

16:1. The Sabbath was over around 6:00 P.M. Saturday evening. The same three women who were mentioned at the crucifixion (15:40) wanted **to anoint Jesus' body.** Even though they were adamant followers of Christ, they did not expect to see him alive; hence their desire to anoint his body. This anointing was not for the purpose of embalming the body, since this was not a practice of the Jews. It was more an act of love and devotion. Anointing with spices was necessary to reduce the smell of a decomposing body in such a hot climate as Palestine's.

16:2. The phrase, **just after sunrise, they were on their way to the tomb,** indicates that the women waited until Sunday morning since it would have been too dark right after the Sabbath ended. The Sabbath ended at 6:00 P.M., and it would have been getting dark.

16:3. The question on their mind was, **Who will roll the stone away from the entrance of the tomb?** (cf. 15:46–47). Matthew tells us that guards had been posted and the tomb had been sealed (Matt. 27:62–66). The women would not have known these events had taken place. The stone would have been very difficult to move because of its enormous weight and size (v. 4). The stone would have to be rolled back up the incline or lifted out of the grooved slot it was in before they could enter the tomb.

16:4–5. Upon arriving at the tomb, the women were greeted with a surprise: The stone had been moved back. Mark does not tell us who moved the stone. Yet, we do know that it had to be a supernatural act to remove such a large stone (see chapter 15, "Deeper Discoveries"). The women entered the tomb and were greeted by two angels (see Luke 24:4). Mark focuses on one angel and describes him **as a young man dressed in a white robe sitting on the right side.** The white clothes indicated the dazzling character of their glory (cf. Mark 9:3; Rev. 6:11; 7:9,13) (Lane, 587).

The angels were witnesses of the resurrection of Christ and the behind-the-scenes work Jesus was doing during those three days in the tomb. Even if we do not see God at work, this does not mean he is not working. God is often working on our behalf in ways we cannot fathom. The women were **alarmed.** This was a total surprise to them. It is not every day that a person has a conversation with an angel about someone rising from the dead. This truly would be a frightening experience.

16:6. The angel attempted to calm the women's fears by saying, **Don't be alarmed.** The angel knew they were looking for **Jesus the Nazarene.** He was letting them know that they had not come to the wrong grave by accident. In fact, the one they were seeking—**He has risen! He is not here.** The angel then invited them to see that the tomb was empty. The angel's explanation made it clear that the bodily resurrection of Jesus Christ had taken place. Good news!

16:7. The angel told the women, **go, tell his disciples and Peter.** This shows the great concern Jesus had for his disciples—especially Peter, who had denied him. These men needed reassurance and encouragement during these dark times, especially Peter. Peter needed to know he had been forgiven and restored. John's Gospel describes how Jesus did just that (John 21).

It is also interesting that it is Mark, who received his material from Peter, who puts this phrase in his Gospel. Peter, it seems, wanted us to know that no matter what we have done, God's gracious hand of forgiveness can bring us back. Even in our darkest moments of despair, Jesus is there. Jesus said his disciples would gather in Galilee after his resurrection (14:28). The angel reminded them to go there and meet him. Why Galilee? This is where Jesus would meet with the disciples as well as the larger community of his followers. Here he would give them last-minute instructions before his ascension back to heaven.

16:8. Mark records that the women, **trembling and bewildered . . . went out and fled from the tomb.** Wouldn't you? They needed time to process this experience and collect their thoughts, so **they said nothing.** Also, **they were afraid.** Who would believe them? Jewish law, which was very male dominated, discounted the witness of women. Yet, good news cannot be contained. After they had composed themselves, they did a lot of talking (Matt. 28:8; Luke 24:9).

B Seeing Is Believing (16:9–14)

SUPPORTING IDEA: *Jesus encourages his disciples in the midst of their doubt by appearing to them.*

16:9. This is the fourth time that Mary Magdalene is mentioned in the last two chapters of Mark (15:40,47; 16:1). Mark states that she was the person **out of whom he had driven seven demons.** This indicates the supernatural healing of Christ in Mary's life. It also explains her devotion to him to the very end. John tells us that Mary Magdalene stayed around the tomb after the appearance of the angels to the women (John 20:11–18). She was the first believer to see the risen Christ

16:10–11. The Gospel of John tells us that Mary specifically went to tell Peter and John what she had discovered (John 20:2–10). The other disciples probably overheard Mary's eyewitness account of the good news about Jesus being alive when she told Peter and John. Yet, they refused to believe it.

16:12–13. These verses parallel, in a shortened account, Luke's account of the two believers on the road to Emmaus (Luke 24:13–35). Even though Jesus appeared to these two disciples, they had the same reaction as Mary and the women when relating their experiences. The disciples **did not believe them either.**

16:14. When Jesus did appear, he rebuked the disciples **for their lack of faith and their stubborn refusal to believe.** Jesus wanted them to know that the witnesses of his resurrection could be trusted. The phrase **the Eleven** means the apostles because there were only ten of them together at the time, since Thomas was absent (John 20:19–25). Verse 14 parallels the account in Luke (24:36–44).

C Keep on Keeping On (16:15–20)

SUPPORTING IDEA: *Jesus empowers his disciples by commissioning them to continue preaching the good news.*

16:15–16. This is Mark's version of the Great Commission (Matt. 28:18–20). This commission is for all of us. Jesus made it clear that our message is to **preach the good news** of salvation through Jesus Christ. Our ministry is to take this message throughout the world.

At first glance, verse 16 seems to suggest that in order to be saved a person must be baptized. Yet, the emphasis is on believing. This whole section centers on belief versus unbelief. If a person does not believe, he is condemned, even if he has been baptized (John 3:16–18,36). The early church had an expectation that believers would be baptized in order to confirm the inward work of salvation in their lives. They were baptized not to "be saved" but because they were saved (Acts 2:41; 10:44–48).

16:17–18. Most of the signs listed here took place in the days of the apostles, and they are recorded in the Book of Acts. The closest thing to taking up **snakes** was Paul's experience on Malta (Acts 28:3–6). But other than that, there is no biblical record of people purposely picking up **snakes**. Also, the drinking of **poison** is not recorded in Scripture either. There is no doubt that God has performed many wonders that are not recorded in Scripture. The context seems to be referring to the apostles. In order to establish the credibility of their message, they needed to be able to perform miracles. Yet, as we continue to read in the New Testament, miracles became less prominent and living out the principles of the faith became more important.

Just a word of caution. The person who takes up snakes to prove his or her faith is yielding to the temptation Satan presented to Jesus on the pinnacle of the temple in Matthew 4:5–7. Satan said, in effect, "Cast yourself down and see if God will take care of you." Satan wants us to "show off" our faith and force God to perform unnecessary miracles. Warren Wiersbe puts it well: " Jesus refused to tempt God, and we should follow his example. Yes, God cares for his children when, in his will, they are in dangerous places; but he is not obligated to care for us when we foolishly get out of his will. We are called to live by faith, not by chance, and to trust God, not tempt him" (Wiersbe, p. 155).

16:19–20. The ascension of Jesus had been predicted by Jesus himself (14:7), and it was witnessed by the apostles (Acts 1:9). Jesus sitting at God's **right hand** was a matter of faith, but this was firmly believed and preached in the early church (cf. Acts 2:33–35; 7:56). Jesus' ascension marked the completion of his earthly ministry and the beginning of his heavenly ministry. Jesus is now in heaven as our High Priest and Advocate. Christ is literally praying on our behalf (Heb. 7–10; 1 John 2:1–3).

The description of Jesus at **the right hand of God** implies one who has honor and authority (Ps. 110:1; 1 Pet. 3:22). Also, one of Jesus' heavenly ministries is to enable us to do his will (Heb. 13:20–21). Even in heaven, Jesus is still serving his people. Just as Jesus served us, it is now our responsibility to serve the world by preaching everywhere the good news of our risen Savior, Jesus Christ.

MAIN IDEA REVIEW: *Jesus, the sacrificial servant, fulfills his gospel mission by rising from the dead and encouraging and empowering his people to continue preaching the good news of salvation.*

III. CONCLUSION

Bringing Life Out of Death

In Tewin church yard, a short distance from King's Cross Station in England, stands a great four-trunked tree growing out of a grave. This has given rise to much speculation among the residents of that region. The grave from which it grows is that of Lady Anne Grimston. Is the tree a monument to a woman's disbelief or did it happen to grow there by chance? Lady Anne Grimston did not believe in life after death. When she lay dying in her palatial home, she said to a friend, "I shall live again as surely as a tree shall grow from my body."

She was buried in a marble tomb. The grave was marked by a large marble slab and surrounded by an iron railing. Years later the marble slab slipped. Then it cracked, and through the crack a small tree grew.

The tree continued to grow, slowly tilting the stone and breaking the marble masonry until today it has surrounded the tomb with its roots and torn the railing out of the ground. The tree at Lady Anne Grimston's grave is one of the largest in England. Is it possible that God decided to take her challenge? One thing is certain. This story graphically illustrates God's ability to bring life out of death. He showed us even more poignantly by raising his son, Jesus Christ, from the dead. Mark 16 shows that we serve a living Savior.

PRINCIPLES

- The announcement by the angel about Christ's resurrection teaches us that God is always at work on our behalf, whether or not we see anything happening.
- God has the power to "roll away" the stones that block us from living life fully.
- Unbelief and hardness of heart keeps God from working through the believer's life.
- God is disappointed when we fail to believe him.
- The resurrection of Jesus teaches the believer that in the darkest circumstances there is always hope.
- Every believer is responsible for telling the "good news" of Jesus Christ.

APPLICATIONS

- Identify the "stones" that keep you from breaking free and experiencing the fullness of the Christian life.

- Commit each obstacle to God and ask him to help you "move" the stones from your life.
- Memorize key verses about Christ's resurrection from the dead. Let these be reminders to you that God can bring hope in seemingly hopeless situations.
- Write down the names of three or four people and pray for the opportunity to share the "Good News" of Jesus Christ with them.
- Pray about the possibility of going on a mission trip to impact another culture for Jesus Christ.

IV. LIFE APPLICATION

Every Day Is Christmas

Christmas is a great time of the year—great food, beautiful carols, egg nog, parties, and decorating the Christmas tree. Then there is Christmas Eve when Santa Claus comes and delivers gifts to children. One little boy was told by his parents that Santa liked cookies and milk because they gave him energy to deliver presents to children around the world. So, before he went to bed, he put out some cookies and milk on a table by the Christmas tree for Santa Claus.

The little boy woke up at the crack of dawn and rushed downstairs. He squealed with delight at the presents under the tree, which had been barren the night before. And then, to his utter amazement, there was an empty glass and cookie crumbs. The presents, the empty glass, and the cookie crumbs were evidence to a little boy that Santa had been to his house, even though he had not seen him. Eventually, little boys grow up and learn the truth about Santa. But the mystery, delight, and amazement when one is small is priceless.

For the believer in Jesus, every day is Christmas. The tree, in this case the cross, was barren, but Jesus Christ, God's only Son, put himself on that tree for us. He became wretched so we could be righteous. He became filth so we could be free. He came down so we could go up. Our lives were as barren as that tree, but he decorated us with the gift of his salvation.

By rising from the dead and entering our lives, Jesus gave us some wonderful gifts—gifts like peace with God as well as the peace of God; the comfort and encouragement of the Holy Spirit; a worldwide family of believers who will be there when our own families cannot or will not; a future and a hope—an eternal destiny. All we have to do is be like little children and believe. It is a mystery, but it is true. It is amazing, but it is true. It is priceless, and it is forever. He is Lord—he is risen—and he is coming back—for real.

Celebrate Christ every day. Thank him that every day is a "fresh start." "For his compassions never fail. They are new every morning; great is thy faithfulness" (Lam. 3:22–23). Rejoice that you serve a God of the second, third, and fourth chance. And remember, "The one who is in you is greater than the one who is in the world" (1 John 4:4).

V. PRAYER

Lord, I affirm and sing to you that "You are Lord, You are Lord, You have risen from the dead and You are Lord. Every knee shall bow, every tongue confess that Jesus Christ is Lord." May I never see my salvation as ancient history but current events, remembering that what Jesus did then makes life worth living now. Help me to live life with the hope and in the power of your resurrection. Amen.

VI. DEEPER DISCOVERIES

A. The ending of Mark (16:9–20)

There is much debate about whether the last twelve verses of Mark's Gospel are part of the original text. Scholars have discovered that there are actually four possible endings to the Gospel of Mark. Which one of these endings represents the original text of Mark is key for interpretation, inspiration, and application of these verses in our lives. Carl Laney, in his book, *Answers to Tough Questions,* gives four possibilities for the ending of Mark. Following is a summary of Laney's insights:

1. *There is a manuscript called the Codex Washingtonianus.* In the fourth century A.D. the traditional ending of Mark was circulated in an expanded form (beginning after v. 14). This particular text is preserved by Jerome and the Codex Washingtonianus.

2. *Only two verses after Mark 16:8.* An abbreviated ending of Mark is attested by four Greek manuscripts from the seventh, eighth, and ninth centuries. It reads: "And they promptly reported all these instructions to Peter and his companions. And after that, Jesus himself sent out through them from east to west the sacred and imperishable proclamation of eternal salvation."

3. *The last twelve verses absent.* The last twelve verses of Mark are absent from the two oldest complete manuscripts of the Greek New Testament— Codex Vaticanus and Codex Sinaiticus. Eusebius, the father of church history, and Jerome, biblical scholar and translator of the Latin Bible, wrote that the passage in question was absent from almost all Greek manuscripts known to them. It is argued that the last twelve verses of Mark differ in style and vocabulary from Mark 16:1–8. The connection between Mark 16:8 and 16:9

is awkward. It seems in Mark 16:9 that Mary Magdalene is introduced to the audience all over again when she has already been introduced earlier in the text. Most of those who take this position believe that the last page of Mark's manuscript was lost and the last twelve verses were added by someone who wanted to supply a more appropriate conclusion than the women being afraid after leaving the tomb.

4. *The traditional ending.* The traditional ending, which is the last twelve verses, found in the King James Version and other translations of the Greek manuscript called Textus Receptus, is supported by a vast number of Greek manuscripts and two early witnesses—Irenaeus (A.D. 202) and the Diatessaron (second century A.D.). In his review of W. R. Farmer's *The Last Twelve Verses of Mark,* Hodges warns, "The reviewer recommends that all teachers and students of the Greek text read this volume carefully before they make any public utterance which could cast doubt on the validity of an ending to Mark which is found in the overwhelming majority of the surviving Greek manuscripts and which is attested by supporting evidence earlier than any manuscript which omits it" (Z. C. Hodges, *Bibliotheca Sacra,* June 1976, p. 178).

B. Whoever believes and is baptized will be saved (16:16)

This phrase seems to indicate that a person must be baptized in order to be saved. This is where context is so important. The very next phrase is the key: "But whoever does not believe will be condemned." The emphasis is on belief and unbelief. The only basis for condemnation is the refusal to believe. There is no condemnation for the failure to be baptized. The conclusion is clear—that the only basis for salvation is belief in Christ, not belief and baptism. Please do not get the impression that baptism is not important. Believers are baptized to show their identification with Jesus Christ and his church (Acts 8:36–38; 16:31–33).

C. And these signs will accompany those who believe (16:17–18)

These verses seems to indicate that all believers will be able to perform certain spectacular miracles, such as casting out demons, picking up serpents, and drinking deadly poisons. In fact, some believers feel they are commanded to do these things because it is in the Bible and it proves their faith.

Once again, context is important when understanding God's Word. The issue is not whether believers could do these miracles. The greater questions are "why and when" and "do we need to have these signs follow us to prove our faith?"

Jesus promised that certain signs and miracles would characterize the age of the apostles. Paul referred to these miracles as the "things that mark an apostle" (2 Cor. 12:12). Miracles did indeed follow the proclamation of the gospel from Jerusalem to Samaria and Judea and throughout the Roman Empire (Acts 1:8). God used these miracles to introduce the church and to authenticate the message and messengers of that new era.

Is it possible that the promise of immunity to snakebites and poison was given in the context of persecution and the traveling conditions during the early spread of the gospel and the apostolic age? It is possible that Jesus was referring to situations where persecutors would force believers to do certain life-threatening things. The first two clauses, according to Greek grammar, could be translated, "If they are compelled to pick up snakes, and if they are compelled to drink deadly poison, it shall not harm them." The use of "if" makes this conditional and not mandatory.

There is no question that God can do whatever he wants, when he wants, and however he wants. There is no question that God can perform miracles today. Yet, we find that even in the Bible miracles were not the norm but were the exception. The purpose of miracles was to authenticate God's message. Even in the life of Jesus we see fewer miracles at the end of his earthly ministry, except for one—the resurrection.

Carl Laney says, "A thorough study of the apostolic miracles indicates that they fulfilled their function in the apostolic era and ceased around A.D. 70. This is evidenced by the decline in miracles following Pentecost, with none being recorded in the last decade of the apostolic age. The early church fathers Chrysotom and Augustine confirm the fact that there was an absence of miracles after the apostolic age" (Laney, *Answers to Tough Questions, pp.* 217–218).

Miracles are possible today, but there is no biblical basis for us to expect them or command them. The true miracle is the ability to live out the Christian life. This can only be done through the indwelling resurrection power of Jesus Christ. When people observe us living a Christlike life in today's world, they see the miracle of redemption and salvation through Jesus Christ in our lives.

VII. TEACHING OUTLINE

1. Lead Story: University of Colorado
2. Context: At this point in the lives of the disciples, all seemed hopeless. Their Lord had been crucified and buried in a tomb. It was over. Not! As one wag said, "It ain't over 'til the fat lady sings." In other words, "When God is in something, anything is possible. Gloom turns into glee because Jesus has risen from the dead."

3. Transition: What emotions do you feel when you are surprised by someone? Now magnify this about ten times. This is how the women at the tomb and disciples must have felt. You would want to believe that Jesus had risen from the dead but you dared not believe lest you be disappointed again. Let us look at the roller coaster emotionally and psychologically as they deal with the fact that their Lord is alive.

B. COMMENTARY
1. I Am the Resurrection (16:1–8).
2. Seeing Is Believing (16:9–14).
3. Keep On Keeping On (16:15–20)

C. CONCLUSION: BRINGING LIFE OUT OF DEATH

VIII. ISSUES FOR DISCUSSION

1. Describe how the women felt when they found the stone removed, the tomb empty, and an angel sitting there. Why would they be afraid?
2. What stones does God need to move in your life to make you free?
3. Why would the disciples not believe that Jesus had risen? Why did Jesus rebuke them for their unbelief? How does God feel about unbelief? How does this apply to us?
4. The resurrection is the heart of the gospel. What does it mean to you? What does it mean for your future?

Glossary

advent—Christ's coming through the virgin birth to minister and provide salvation; his advent will also occur in the clouds for final judgment

apostles—Men chosen by Jesus as his official messengers; this term refers generally to his twelve disciples

atonement—God's way of overcoming sin through Christ's obedience and death to restore believers to a right relationship with God

church—The community of those who believe in and follow Jesus Christ; used to designate a congregation, a denomination, or all Christians

consecration—Setting apart for God's use

creation—God's bringing the world and everything in it into existence from nothing

crucifixion—A form of execution by affixing a victim to a cross to die; Jesus' death on the cross for sinners

deacon—An office in the church that involves ministry and service

disciple—A follower and learner of Jesus Christ

end of the ages—A reference to the death of Christ as the decisive event of world history and the event which begins the final age of time

evil—Anyone or anything that opposes the plan of God

faith—Belief in and personal commitment to Jesus Christ for eternal salvation

fasting—Going without food as a sign of repentance, grief, or devotion to God; often connected with devotion to prayer

Gentiles—People who are not part of God's chosen family at birth and thus can be considered "pagans"

gospel—The good news of the redeeming work of God through the life, death, and resurrection of Jesus Christ

Gospels—The four New Testament accounts of the life of Jesus Christ; Matthew, Mark, and Luke are called synoptic gospels because they relate many of the same events and teachings of Jesus; John is the fourth Gospel and tends to be more theological in nature, telling events and teachings not in the synoptics

Herodians—An aristocratic Jewish group who favored the policies of Herod Antipas and thus supported the Roman government

high priest—The chief religious official for Israel and Judaism appointed as the only person allowed to enter the Holy of Holies and offer sacrifice on the Day of Atonement

holy—God's distinguishing characteristic that separates him from all creation; the moral ideal for Christians as they seek to reflect the character of God as known in Christ Jesus

incarnation—The act of the divine Son Jesus becoming human and enduring all the experiences which tempt us and cause us to suffer, thus qualifying him to be the agent of God's saving plan for humanity

interpretation—The human effort to understand the Bible with the guidance of the Holy Spirit and to apply its meaning to contemporary life

Jerusalem—Capital city of Israel in the Old Testament; religious center of Judaism in the New Testament; also name of the heavenly city John describes in Revelation (New Jerusalem)

judgment—God's work at the end time involving condemnation for unbelievers and assignment of rewards for believers

kingdom of God—God's sovereign rule in the universe and in the hearts of Christians

Glossary

Law—God's instruction to his people about how to love him and others; when used with the definite article "the," *law* may refer to the Old Testament as a whole but usually to the Pentateuch (Genesis through Deuteronomy)

laying on of hands—Setting apart or consecrating a person to God's service through placing hands on the head of the person being dedicated

martyr—A person who bears witness to Jesus Christ and consequently suffers or dies rather than deny Christ

Messiah—the coming king promised by the prophets; Jesus Christ who fulfilled the prophetic promises; Christ represents the Greek translation of the Hebrew word "messiah"

minister—the loving service of Christians to each other and to those outside the church in the name of Jesus

miracle—An act of God beyond human understanding that inspires wonder, displays God's greatness, and leads people to recognize God at work in the world

parable—A short story taken from everyday life to make a spiritual point; Jesus' favorite form of teaching

passion—The suffering of Christ during his time of trial and death on the cross

Passover—The Jewish feast celebrating the Exodus from Egypt (Exod. 12); celebrated by Jesus and his disciples at the Last Supper

ransom—Payment offered to secure someone else's release

redemption—The act of releasing a captive by the payment of a price; Jesus' death provided our redemption from sin's power and penalty (Heb. 9:12)

repentance—A change of heart and mind resulting in a turning from sin to God that allows conversion and is expressed through faith

righteousness—The quality or condition of being in right relationship with God; living out the relationship with God in right relationships with other persons

Sabbath—The seventh day of the week corresponding to the seventh day of creation when people in the Old Testament were called on to rest from work and reflect on God

sacrifice—According to Mosaic Law, an offering to God in repentance for sin or as an expression of thanksgiving; Christ as the ultimate sacrifice for sin

Sadducees—A religious group which formed during the period between the Testaments when the Maccabees ruled Judah

salvation—Deliverance from trouble or evil; the process by which God redeems his creation, completed through the life, death, and resurrection of his Son Jesus Christ

sanctification—The process in salvation by which God conforms the believer's life and character to the life and character of Jesus Christ through the Holy Spirit

Satan—The personalized evil one who leads forces opposed to God and tempts people

scribe—A Jewish teacher of the law who studied and copied Scripture

Scripture—The Bible, the divinely-inspired record of God's revelation of himself and the authoritative source for Christian doctrine and teaching

sin—Actions by which humans rebel against God, miss his purpose for their life, and surrender to the power of evil rather than to God

Son of Man—The title Jesus most frequently used for himself that emphasized both his divinity as the prophesied One in the Old Testament and his identification with people

temptation—The pull toward sin which all humans experience; it comes from Satan, not God

transfiguration—Jesus' appearance in full glory to Peter, James, and John

Trinity—God's revelation of himself as Father, Son, and Holy Spirit unified as one in the Godhead and yet distinct in person and function

unpardonable sin—Persistence in refusing to accept Christ as Lord and Savior which prevents one from receiving God's forgiveness; blasphemy that reflects such a condition

Word of God—The Bible, God's inspired written revelation; God's message in oral form revealed through prophetic or angelic speakers; Jesus Christ, God's eternal Word in human flesh

Yahweh—The Hebrew personal name of God revealed to Moses; this name came to be thought of as too holy to pronounce by Jews; often translated LORD or Jehovah

Bibliography

Barclay, William. *The Gospel of Mark*. Daily Study Bible. Philadelphia: The Westminster Press, 1975.

Barbieri, Louis. *Mark*. Chicago: Moody Press, 1995.

Brooks, James A. *Mark*. New American Commentary. Nashville: Broadman Press, 1991.

Cole, Robert Alan. *The Gospel According to Mark*. Tyndale New Testament Commentaries. Grand Rapids: Eerdmans, 1961.

Cranfield, C. E. B. *The Gospel According to St. Mark*. Cambridge: Cambridge University Press, 1963.

Earle, Ralph. *The Gospel According to Mark*. Evangelical Commentary on the Bible. Grand Rapids: Zondervan, 1957.

Elwell, Walter A. *Evangelical Dictionary of Theology*. Grand Rapids: Baker Book House, 1984.

Guelich, Robert A. *Mark*. Word Biblical Commentary. Dallas: Word Books, 1989.

Hendriksen, William. *Exposition of the Gospel According to Mark*. New Testament Commentary. Grand Rapids: Baker, 1975.

Hiebert, D. Edmond. *Mark: A Portrait of the Servant*. Chicago: Moody Press, 1974.

Lane, William L. *The Gospel According to Mark*. New International Commentary on the New Testament. Grand Rapids: Eerdmans, 1974.

Powell, Ivor. *Mark's Superb Gospel*. Grand Rapids: Kregel Publishing Co., 1985.

Taylor, Vincent. *The Gospel According to St. Mark*. London: Macmillan, 1963.